Rome in Africa

Mosaic in the Bardo Museum, Tunis

Rome in Africa

Susan Raven

Evans Brothers Limited London

Published by Evans Brothers Limited
Montague House, Russell Square,
London, W.C.1.

First published 1969
© Susan Raven 1969

Set in 11 on 12 point Baskerville and printed in
Great Britain by William Clowes & Sons Ltd.,
London and Beccles.

237 44357 0   PR 2059

Excudent alii spirantii spirantia mollius aera,
Credo equidem, vivos ducent de marmore voltus,
Orabant causas melius, caelique meatus
Describent radio, et surgentia sidera dicent:
Tu regere imperio populos, Romane, memento;
Hae tibi erunt artes, pacisque inponere morem,
Parcere subiectis, et debellare superbos.

Virgil, Aeneid VI, l. 847-53

Many of the photographs in this book were taken by the author, but for permission to reproduce the remainder the publishers are grateful to the following:

Marcel Bovis for pages 4, 48, 74, 76, 112, 122, 123 and 125; British Museum for page 157; Compagnie Aerienne de Photographie for pages 57 and 60; *Enchanted Morocco* by F. Garrique (B. Arthaud, Paris) for page 77; *Fossatum Africae* by J. Baradez (Paris) for pages 50 and 51; French Air Force (Armée de l'Air) for pages 58 and 59; Professor W. H. C. Frend for pages 138 and 160; Jean-Dominique Lajoux for page xvi; *Life and Death of Carthage* by Gilbert and Colette Picard (Sidgwick and Jackson, London) for pages 12, 18, 19, 20 and 21; Mansell Collection for pages 5, 35, 38, 102, 144; John Saumarez-Smith for page 92; *Some Authentic Acts of Early Martyrs* by E. C. Owen (Oxford University Press) for page 120; Khaled Abdul Wahab for pages 31, 64, 71, 73, 92 and 129; Roger Wood for pages 8, 13, 15, 41, 88, 89, 91, 93, 96, 98, 99, 109, 111, 121 and the colour section.

Pull out map Edgar Holloway
Drawings Dennis Ranston

Mosaic from Sousse, Tunisia

Contents

Acknowledgements   viii

Preface   ix

Chronology   xii

1 Between the desert and the sea   1

2 The rise and fall of Carthage   9

3 New masters for Africa   35

4 The conquest of a country   49

5 Granary of the Empire   63

6 The six hundred cities   79

7 Careers open to talent   99

8 The new religion   113

9 A church divided   131

10 The greatest African   145

11 The Vandal interregnum   153

12 Africa returns to the east   165

Selected bibliography   183

Index   185

Acknowledgements

I received much kindness and hospitality in North Africa during the autumn of 1965, for which I shall always be grateful. In particular I should like to thank Mr Cecil Hourani, then Director of the Centre Culturel International at Hammamet, Monsieur Mohammad Bellamine, Governor of Kasserine, and his wife, and, in Algiers, Mr Simon Dawbarn, at that time Counsellor at the British Embassy, and his wife Shelby. I am also grateful to Monsieur Moncef Ounaies for rescuing my car from the Tunis customs, and to a number of total strangers who on various occasions mended its five punctures, twice patched up its electrical system on the open road, and once pushed it over several hundred yards of mud when I imprudently embarked on a detour.

My thanks are due, too, to the Director and his staff for allowing me to use the library of the Institut National d'Archéologie et d'Arts in Tunis, and to the Directors of the Musée National du Bardo in Tunis, the Musée Stéphane Gsell in Algiers, the Archaeological Museum at Tripoli, and the museums at Cherchel, Timgad, Sousse and Sfax for allowing me to take photographs of exhibits on display.

Unfortunately, though I brought back with me a large number of photographs, fewer than I hoped have proved fit to print. I am therefore extremely lucky that Mr Roger Wood has allowed me to include a number of his, particularly those in colour.

Another most valuable source has been a documentary film on the Seigneur Julius mosaic made by Monsieur Khaled Abdul Wahab, of El Djem; Monsieur Wahab gave me two or three hundred frames from his film of this and of other mosaics in the Bardo Museum which might otherwise have ended up on the cutting room floor. I am also grateful to Professor W. H. C. Frend of Glasgow University for a couple of black and white photographs of exceptional interest.

I am indebted to Professor Frend on another score, for he was kind enough to read this book in manuscript. He has done his best to preserve me from error, and if he has not succeeded the fault is not his. Finally, I should like to thank my publishers, and in particular Mr Michael Gabb and Miss Jacqueline Miller, for their patience.

Susan Raven, London, 1969

Preface

North Africa is wonderfully rich in Roman remains. There is nothing as monumentally impressive, perhaps, as the temples at Baalbek in the Lebanon, or as well preserved as the Pantheon in Rome; nothing as historic as the Forum of the Caesars, or as haunting as the ruins of Pompeii. But the sight of Timgad in Algeria, its acres of half-demolished buildings and flagged streets stretching for what seems like miles on the edge of a baked plain, or Djemila, perched on its tilted spur among hills now wrinkled with erosion, is unforgettable. The great amphitheatre which still stands at El Djem in Tunisia is almost as big as the Colosseum in Rome—and, towering as it does over the one-storey Arab dwellings clustering round it, almost more overwhelming. In Libya, Leptis Magna and Sabratha survive, at least in part, to bear witness to the one-time prosperity and grandeur of the great seaports of Roman Tripolitania. And there are many smaller cities which were, like them (and unlike Carthage and most of the cities of the coast), never overlaid by overbuilding and which have therefore been comparatively simple to excavate: Mactar, Dougga and Thuburbo Maius in Tunisia, for example, or Khémissa and Tipasa in Algeria.

None of the cities of North Africa is more than a ghost town. Monuments have survived, but not—with rare exceptions—shops and houses, except for walls a few feet high. Even the monuments, when the Romans departed, eventually fell into disuse and decay, and most were pillaged and used as quarries by succeeding generations. This was to be expected of the cities of the coast, from which transport was easy: indeed, in the middle ages boatloads of the columns of Roman Carthage found their way to Spain and Italy, as well as to mosques all over North Africa, and in later centuries columns from Leptis Magna were supplied, through the agency of enterprising European consuls, for the palace of Versailles, for the church of St Germain des Prés, and even for George III's improvements at Virginia Water in Surrey. The cities of the interior scarcely fared any better; by and large they were less rich to begin with, and they bore the brunt of the invasion of the Hillalian Arabs in the eleventh century—a disaster which finally destroyed the last vestiges of the Roman inheritance and made of North Africa a land almost wholly given over to the nomadic life, as it had been in prehistoric times.

A good deal remained, however, to amaze the French when they invaded Algeria in 1830. But the nation which, under Napoleon, had founded Egyptology and whose scholars were later to pursue the study of archaeology, both in North Africa and elsewhere, with unsurpassed brilliance, was in the early years of its rule responsible for nearly as much damage as its predecessors. At Philippeville (ancient Rusicade), the army commander ordered the destruction of the Roman theatre and amphitheatre, the forum, a basilica, a temple and a water tower. At Tipasa the most accessible ruins were removed in 1847 to build a cholera hospital. Two huge temples were pulled down at Constantine, and the Roman bridge over the Rummel was allowed to fall down. Just south of Bône (now Annaba) a beautiful hump-backed bridge was pulled down and replaced. At Lambèse, Roman remains were used to build a penitentiary over a large part of the former garrison of the Third Augustan Legion, the best preserved army camp of the Roman world.

Within the last half-century, too, the conquering armies of Europe have much to answer for, quite apart from the damage to be expected during fighting. The Italians, after taking over Libya, used stone from Leptis Magna to build military forts. They also used to collect Roman milestones from the surrounding desert to embellish their barracks at Mizda, and, since no record was kept of where their trophies had been found, archaeologists trying to work out the network of Roman roads in Tripolitania have been deprived of valuable evidence. During the Second World War, British and American soldiers sheltering in the underground houses at Bulla Regia lit cooking fires against the walls, and mutilated mosaics.

The study of Roman North Africa does, however, owe something to the military. Already in the 1840s the French army was undertaking scientific expeditions of exploration, and the names of Capitaine X and Lieutenant Y virtually monopolise the early reports and maps of Roman hydraulic works. In 1851, French officers and their prisoners were embarking on the excavation of Lambèse, and it soon became fashionable for young French officers to spend their leave and their spare time investigating Roman remains. (In the First World War, German prisoners were set to work excavating at Volubilis.) Fifty or sixty years later, the French and Italian air forces were taking the aerial photographs which have unlocked some of the secrets of Roman exploitation.

By the end of the nineteenth century French archaeologists—and pre-eminently Stéphane Gsell, whose eight-volume *Histoire Ancienne de l'Afrique du Nord* was to appear between 1913 and 1929—were laying bare both outline and details of the pre-Islamic past of north-west Africa, and the great civilian work of rehabilitating as much as could be uncovered or restored had begun. It was work to which other nationalities—the Italians, the British, the Americans and the modern inhabitants—subsequently contributed.

The finest, most important or extensive remains have by now, one must suppose, been rescued—Leptis Magna from the sand dunes of Libya, the *tophet* at Carthage from the encroaching suburban gardens—or at least identified; but much, clearly, remains underground. There are frequent uncoverings of a minor sort: cisterns or Christian tombs are exposed when a new road is cut through a hillside, or mosaics are revealed under the sand when a modern theatre auditorium is carved out of the seashore. There must be uncounted statues and artefacts also awaiting discovery, and perhaps some stone-strewn acres where once a city of the Tunisian plateau flourished will yield an excavation as interesting as neighbouring Mactar. But there will not be another Capitol like that at Sbeïtla, or an aqueduct like that near Cherchel. Even so, much survives.

* * *

The charm of the ancient sites of north-west Africa is their unselfconscious informality, the unpretentiousness of their setting and display. At least until a year or two ago, although the boys seemed to spring out of the cracks in the paving with coins for sale or guide-book information, there was a refreshing absence of the paraphernalia of tourism which can make visits to some of the major classical sites of the Mediterranean world a doubtful pleasure.

There is a healthy, sometimes too healthy, lack of reverence. The furrows run right up to the crumbling walls of ancient Lambaesis, in and among the ruins wherever soil has settled. Uncounted Corinthian capitals are used as stands for flowers or garden seats in every self-respecting hotel or private house in Carthage and Tunis. At Tébessa, a Roman house which was once, perhaps, a governor's residence, is part of a row of shops. At Mactar, the old amphitheatre where wild beasts tore their victims to death houses in the remnants of its galleries the *gourbis* of the poor; near Tunis the vast pillars of an aqueduct offer shelter for lean-to huts huddled into a hamlet. The great bridge over the Medjerda at Chemtou, where the much-prized henna red Numidian marble used to be hewn from the quarries of ancient Simitthu, lies in ruins and has never been replaced; one must cross the river by a watersplash. A fine Roman bridge near Béja, which once carried the traffic from Carthage to Bulla Regia and the west, now carries men and donkeys from one ploughed field to another; of the highway which it served there is no sign. It is all a long way from the harsh, rich, orderly world in which these Roman monuments were originally constructed, and in which the men who created them were born and lived and died.

Main street at Tipasa, Algeria

Chronology

c. 1000 B.C.	Phoenicians from eastern Mediterranean acquire trading concession in Spain and found ports of call in Sicily, North Africa and elsewhere in the western Mediterranean.
c. 814 B.C.	Carthage founded by Phoenicians fleeing from Tyre with Princess Dido.
6th century B.C.	Arrival of Greek colonists in the western Mediterranean; gradually Carthage becomes leader and protector of Phoenician colonies in the west.
mid 6th century B.C.	Carthage sends an army to Sicily to help Phoenician colonies there against Greek cities; beginning of intermittent warfare.
510 B.C.	Carthage expels Greek colony from Tripolitania.
509 B.C.	Foundation of Roman republic.
480 B.C.	Carthaginian fleet and mercenary army defeated by Greeks at battle of Himera; Carthaginians withdraw from Sicily.
Early or mid 5th century B.C.	Rome becomes leading city of central Italy. Voyage of Hanno down the West African coast; voyage of Himilco up the Atlantic coast of Spain.
5th century B.C.	Carthage conquers and colonises her African hinterland.
409 B.C.	Carthage sends an army to Sicily to fight the Greeks once more; beginning of a century of warfare in Sicily.
4th century B.C.	Numidian and Moorish kingdoms begin to form beyond Carthaginian frontiers; Central Italy under direct control of Rome.
310 B.C.	Cape Bon, near Carthage, invaded by army under Agathocles of Syracuse. Carthaginians sacrifice 500 children to Baal Hammon.
307 B.C.	Defeat of Agathocles' expedition.
3rd century B.C.	Rome controls almost all the Italian peninsula south of the River Po.
264 B.C.– 241 B.C.	First Punic War with Rome, fought mostly in Sicily and at sea – though a Roman army under Regulus invades Africa at Clupea (Kelibia, Cape Bon) in 256 B.C., only to be defeated the following year.
241 B.C.	Carthaginian fleet destroyed at the battle of the Aegates Islands; Carthage sues for peace, and leaves Sicily.
240–237 B.C.	The Mercenary War: the revolt of Carthage's army – finally defeated by Hamilcar Barca.
237 B.C.	Hamilcar – accompanied by son-in-law Hasdrubal and son Hannibal – leaves to conquer new Carthaginian empire in Spain; after 16 years, Carthaginians control whole of southern Spain.
218–202 B.C.	Second Punic War.
218 B.C.	Hannibal's crossing of the Alps.
216 B.C.	Rome defeated at the Battle of Cannae; followed by long war of attrition in southern Italy.
209–206 B.C.	Conquest of Carthaginians in Spain by Roman army under Scipio.
204 B.C.	Scipio invades Africa.
202 B.C.	Scipio defeats Hannibal at the battle of Zama.
Early 2nd century B.C.	Rise of the Numidian kingdoms; King Masinissa (d. 148 B.C.) begins to encroach on Carthaginian territory.
149–146 B.C.	Third Punic War, and the final destruction of Punic Carthage by Scipio Aemilianus. Africa Proconsularis founded; rest of Africa divided between native kings.

123–122 B.C.	Abortive attempt of Gracchi brothers to send colonists to Carthage; beginning of Africa's exploitation by Roman capitalists – the era of the great wheat farms.
112–105 B.C.	Jugurthine War. Masinissa's bastard grandson Jugurtha defies the Romans, and is eventually betrayed by King Bocchus of Mauretania. The Romans take over the Tripolitanian ports. Veterans of the Roman army given land in Africa.
First half of 1st century B.C.	Intermittent civil wars in the last years of the Roman Republic. Warfare spreads to Africa in the 80s and again in 49 B.C.
46 B.C.	Caesar conquers his rivals, the followers of the dead Pompey, and their ally King Juba of Numidia, at the battle of Thapsus. Juba's young son, another Juba, is taken off to Rome. The territory of the province is trebled to include Numidia. Africa Proconsularis divided into Africa Vetus and Africa Nova; the historian Sallust is appointed Africa Nova's first governor. Caesar founds a number of veterans' colonies.
44 B.C.	Murder of Caesar, which leads to further struggles for leadership at Rome, and confused fighting in Africa.
36 B.C.	Octavius becomes uncontested master of Africa; the Romanisation of Africa begins.
33 B.C.	Death of King Bocchus of Mauretania; Mauretania taken over by Roman administrators, and Roman colonies founded there.
31 B.C.	Battle of Actium: Octavius defeats Mark Antony. Octavius becomes Augustus Caesar.
29 B.C.	Official refounding of Carthage. Augustus Caesar founds many veterans' colonies in Africa.
25 B.C.	Augustus gives Mauretania to Juba II as a client kingdom.
Late first century B.C.	Constant frontier risings until A.D. 6.
19 B.C.	Cornelius Balbus occupies Garama (Germa), capital of the Garamantes.
A.D. 14	Third Augustan Legion begins construction of Ammaedara-Tacapae road.
A.D. 17–24	Revolt of Tacfarinas.
A.D. 23	Death of Juba II; accession of his son Ptolemy.
A.D. 40	Murder of Ptolemy by Caligula; rising of the Moors under Aedemon leads to annexation of Mauretania to Roman Empire.
A.D. 42	Suetonius Paulinus crosses Mt Atlas and penetrates Western Sahara.
Mid 1st–mid 3rd century A.D.	Era of greatest prosperity for Roman Africa.
End of 1st century A.D.	Journeys into the central Sahara of Septimius Flaccus and Julius Maternus
2nd century	The century of consolidation; spread of the olive tree and the road network; Africans begin to have influence in Rome.
A.D. 117	Lusius Quietus, a Moor, appointed to the Senate.
A.D. c. 125	Birth of Apuleius at Madauros.
A.D. 143	Marcus Cornelius Fronto of Cirta, former tutor to Marcus Aurelius, becomes consul.
A.D. 155	Birth of Tertullian.
A.D. c. 170	Apuleius writes *The Golden Ass*.
A.D. 180	First known Christian martyrs of Africa executed.
A.D. 189	Victor I becomes the first African Pope.
A.D. 193	Septimius Severus from Leptis Magna becomes the first African Emperor.
A.D. 197	Publication of Tertullian's *Apologia*.
A.D. 202	Martyrdom of St Perpetua and her companions at Carthage.
A.D. 211	Death of Septimius Severus; accession of his son Caracalla.
A.D. 217	Murder of Caracalla; Macrinus, a Moor, becomes Emperor.
A.D. 218	Deposition of Macrinus; accession of Elagabalus.
A.D. 222	Murder of Elagabalus; accession of Severus Alexander.
A.D. 235	Murder of Severus Alexander – and end of the Severan dynasty.
A.D. 238	Proclamation as Emperor of Gordian I, proconsul of Africa, with his son Gordian II. Death of Gordian II in battle, and suicide of Gordian I. Accession of Gordian III, and disbanding of Third Augustan Legion. Garrison withdrawn from desert outpost of Castellum Dimmidi established by Septimius Severus 40 years earlier.
A.D. c. 240	Death of Tertullian.

Mid-3rd century	Cities of the province of Africa become poorer; but olive-tree country in the south continues to flourish.
A.D. 248	St Cyprian becomes bishop of Carthage.
A.D. 250–1	Decian Persecution of Christians.
A.D. 253	Serious insurrection on southern frontier; re-formation of Third Augustan Legion.
A.D. 256	Renewal of persecution under Valerian.
A.D. 258	Martyrdom of St Cyprian near Carthage.
A.D. 259	Martyrdom of Sts Marian and James at Cirta.
A.D. 284	Accession of Diocletian.
late 280s on	Tribal insurrections; co-Emperor Maximian comes in person to suppress it in A.D. 298; puts defences of province in order again. Meanwhile Diocletian reorganizes Empire. The Romans withdraw from Volubilis – the province is shrinking. Spread of Christianity to Numidian countryside. Beginning of building of country houses for the rich.
A.D. 303–5	Persecution of Diocletian.
A.D. 311	Constantine becomes co-Emperor.
A.D. 312	Donatist schism begins.
A.D. 313	Edict of Milan: Christianity becomes official religion of the Roman Empire.
A.D. 314	Council of Arles.
4th century	Increasing strength of Donatism; age of church-building; appearance of the cirumcelliones in 340s.
A.D. 354	Birth of St Augustine at Thagaste.
A.D. 355	Death of Donatus in exile.
A.D. 363–4	Devastation of city lands of Leptis Magna by Austuriani tribe.
A.D. 372	Revolt of Firmus in the Kabylie mountains, with support from the Donatists.
A.D. 375	Firmus defeated by the *comes* Theodosius.
A.D. 386	Conversion to Christianity of St Augustine.
A.D. 395	Augustine becomes bishop of Hippo.
A.D. 397	St Augustine writes his *Confessions*.
A.D. 397	Revolt of Firmus's brother Gildo, with support of the Donatists.
A.D. 405	Donatism at last declared a heresy by an Edict of Unity.
A.D. 406	The barbarians breach the Rhine frontier.
A.D. 409	The Vandals reach Spain.
A.D. 410	Alaric the Goth captures and loots Rome for three days.
A.D. 411	Council of Carthage: Augustine finally discredits the Donatists.
A.D. 413–427	St Augustine works on *The City of God*.
A.D. 416	Visigoths make an abortive attempt to invade Africa.
A.D. 429	Invasion of Africa by the Vandals, who are Arian Christians.
A.D. 430	Death of St Augustine during the siege of Hippo.
A.D. 439	Vandals seize Carthage.
A.D. 455	Gaiseric, king of the Vandals, loots Rome.
A.D. 468	Vandals defeat imperial fleet.
A.D. 477	Death of Gaiseric.
A.D. 490s	*Tablettes Albertini* written.
A.D. 533	Re-conquest of Africa for the eastern Empire by Count Belisarius; restoration of Catholic supremacy; Solomon undertakes the conquest of the barbarians and the re-organization of the frontier defences.
A.D. 543	Massacre at Leptis of elders of Louata tribe by Sergius, duke of Tripolitania and nephew of Solomon; general insurrection of the tribes. Death of Solomon in battle near Theveste. Period for Africa of civil war.
A.D. 544	Beginning of Three Chapters controversy.
A.D. 546	John Troglita appointed *comes Africae*; after two years' fighting, peace for 15 years.
A.D. 563	New governor murders main barbarian ally of the Byzantines. New uprising – warfare intermittent until end of century. Growing strength of the Pope.
A.D. *c.* 570	Birth of Muhammad.
Late 6th or early 7th c.	Apparent success of Christianity in the oases of the Sahara.
A.D. 595	Heraclius, leading general of the Emperor Maurice, becomes exarch of Carthage.

A.D. 602	Emperor Maurice murdered by Phocas. Heraclius leads opposition to the usurper; sends his son to avenge the Emperor.
A.D. 610	Heraclius the younger becomes Emperor in Constantinople.
A.D. 632	Death of Muhammad at Medina.
A.D. 641	Death of Emperor Heraclius. By now Palestine and Syria are ruled by Arabs.
A.D. 641–2	Arabs occupy Egypt.
A.D. 642	Arabs occupy Cyrenaica.
A.D. 643	Arabs beseige Tripoli, lay waste Sabratha, and invade eastern Fezzan.
A.D. 646	Exarch Gregory declares himself Emperor, although he remains in Africa. Moves his capital to Sufetula.
A.D. 647	Arabs invade Maghreb; Gregory dies when defeated outside Sufetula.
650s/660s	Series of Arab raids.
A.D. 669	Campaign of Okba, who seizes Tripolitania and Byzacena. Foundation of Arab city of Kairouan in Tunisia.
A.D. 683	Okba's expedition to the Atlantic; is defeated near Thabudeos on his return by Koseila, a berber chieftain. Arabs retreat from Maghreb.
A.D. 695	Invasion of Hassan who captures Carthage; but Arabs are defeated by the Kahena, Queen of the Aures.
A.D. 697	Carthage recaptured by Byzantines; Hassan retreats to Cyrenaica.
A.D. 698	Carthage conquered by Arabs for good.
A.D. c. 700	Final defeat of the Kahena.
A.D. 708	Septem (Ceuta), Byzantium's last outpost in Africa, falls to the Arabs. The conquest of Spain follows, and by 711 the Arabs are threatening the heart of Gaul.

Temple of Septimius Severus, Djemila

1 Between the desert and the sea

Evidence that giraffes once lived in the heart of the Sahara desert: prehistoric rock painting in the Tassili n'Ajjer

The history of north-west Africa is largely the history of foreigners. Its civilizations have been imposed from outside, and usually conquered from outside. Yet they have endured with considerable vigour. The Arabs and their descendants, for instance, dominated North Africa from the seventh to the eleventh century A.D.; their religion and language survives to this day. The Phoenicians arrived at the beginning of the first millenium B.C. and remained its most powerful inhabitants until the second century B.C. Their maritime empire under the Carthaginians lasted nearly four centuries – longer than that of Athens to the east, and far longer than the land empire of Alexander the Great. Their influence – like that of the Arabs after them – survived for centuries afterwards, even when their power had been completely destroyed, and Carthage itself obliterated by the Romans.

The achievement of the Romans, in their turn, was even more remarkable. They ruled north-west Africa for more than five hundred years, and the country which they had almost inadvertently conquered became, under the Antonine Emperors of the second century A.D., their most profitable province and the one which demonstrated most strikingly their gift for government. Though its natural resources were greatly inferior to those of Gaul, for instance, and though the Romans occupied less than one hundred and forty thousand square miles, Africa contributed far more to the agricultural wealth of the Roman Empire. Its cities numbered nearly six hundred to Gaul's sixty, and one of them, Leptis Magna, provided an imperial dynasty, that of the Severi. It was the birthplace of Terence and Apuleius, of Tertullian and St Augustine, and its passionate inhabitants adopted Christianity with an exuberance equalled only by the enthusiasm with which they adopted its heresies and, later, welcomed Islam. It was in some ways the most romanized of all Rome's provinces, and in its turn it influenced the destiny of the Empire.

The social and political forms of Rome outlasted the extraordinary interregnum of the Vandals, who set sail with wives and children from their base in Spain and seized Africa in A.D. 429; they lingered on, weakened but still recognizable, when the Byzantines reconquered Africa a century later for the eastern Empire. Roman methods of farming and irrigation even survived the invasion of the camel-borne Arabs in the seventh century. It was only with the second wave of invasions, in the eleventh century, that Roman influence finally vanished – as completely as if it had never been. North Africa became once more part of Africa and the east. Her brilliant Mediterranean past was forgotten. The lessons of Punic and Roman agriculture were ignored. Aqueducts which sprang a leak were not repaired, harbours silted up. Most of the twelve thousand miles of Roman road sank either under a tide of sand blown in from the desert or soil washed down from the mountains; cities fell under the hammer of the quarrier or were engulfed by the dunes. The all-devouring goat supplanted the ox, the camel and the horse; and in the towns of the coast the merchant made way for the pirate, whose predatory activities warded off the European until the nineteenth century.

In the eighteenth century, less was known about the northern half of Africa than had been known in the days of the Romans (the Carthaginians had explored the coast of West Africa in the fifth century B.C.; it was two thousand years before the Portuguese followed in their wake). Maps were non-existent or worthless. The most accurate was still that of Ptolemy, who lived in the second century and whose map of the world, in a twelfth-century Byzantine copy, was the only one known to survive from antiquity. European knowledge of the interior depended still on Herodotus and Pliny. There were one or two explorers in the seventeenth and eighteenth centuries, but it was only in the nineteenth that the northern Mediterranean seriously re-discovered the southern. Napoleon's 1798 campaign in Egypt led directly to the discovery of the temples of the Nile and the beginnings of Egyptology, and the French annexation of Algeria in 1830 (an interregnum which has fared hardly better than that of the Vandals) at last revealed to the modern world the wealth of Roman remains in North Africa. Of all Rome's provinces, Africa is richest, at least in quantity, in the monuments of her might. She built to last, and neither the Arabs nor the encroaching desert were able to extinguish entirely the marks of her rule.

Most of North Africa is desert. It forms the western end of the vast belt of virtually rainless land which stretches diagonally across Arabia, Syria and Jordan, Turkestan and north of the Himalayas to the Gobi desert in northern China. On either side of the Tropic of Cancer, crossing from Rio de Oro on the Atlantic to the Red Sea three thousand miles to the east, lie the Saharan, Libyan and Nubian deserts – nearly four million square miles of sand, gravel, bare rock and mountain ranges. They cut off the equatorial forest of the Congo and the Niger from the Mediterranean coast as effectively as an ocean. Rain is not unknown; without it there would be no oases. But it is nowhere more than five inches a year, and only its irregularity can be relied on. One oasis has recorded a drought lasting twelve years and, although torrential rain occasionally falls for as much as two or three days together in mountainous regions of the central Sahara, there are huge tracts where rain never falls at all.

Such rainfall as there is mostly evaporates under the African sun; but enough finds its way underground to supply a certain number of oases – some large, like Ghadames, Germa, Kufra or Tamanrasset, which all support palm groves and other crops; others hardly more than wells. Oases may be close together or as many as one hundred and fifty or two hundred miles apart. The water is often brackish, but its existence has meant that the North African desert belt has never been entirely uninhabited. In historic times there have always been nomadic tribes moving from oasis to oasis and feeding their animals on such long-rooted scrub as somehow survives years of drought, or the plant life that springs up on the most barren land after a sudden shower of rain. Even in its driest period there have been caravan routes between the Mediterranean and the Niger, bringing gold, ivory or slaves from Central

Africa; and it was across the worst desert of all, the Libyan, that the Arabs came to conquer Roman North Africa.

Quite distinct from the rest of sub-tropical North Africa are four areas which can support a settled population because they have a regular supply of water: Egypt, to which the Nile brings the rainfall of the highlands of Ethiopia and Uganda; Cyrenaica, six hundred miles across the desert from the Nile delta, on the Libyan coast; the tiny coastal belt of Tripolitania, a further eight hundred miles to the west; and finally, separated from Tripolitania by a comparatively brief stretch of desert, the whole region of north-west Africa the Arabs call the Maghreb. The Maghreb corresponds roughly to the Atlas mountains and their coastal plain. This is a region some two or three hundred miles deep from the Mediterranean to the southern foothills on the edge of the Sahara, which stretches one thousand four hundred miles from the Atlantic to the Gulf of Gabès opposite Sicily. It comprises Morocco (Mauretania to the ancient world), northern Algeria (eastern Mauretania and Numidia) and Tunisia. The Maghreb's source of water is not, as in Egypt, a river, but rain, brought in on the west winds of winter from the Atlantic and falling on the flanks of its mountain ranges. Like the Maghreb, Tripolitania and Cyrenaica have mountains to attract rainfall, though their highest peaks, only some two to three thousand feet high, do not compare with Mount Atlas's fifteen thousand, and they are both in fact a good deal drier. But they are all part of the general geological structure of the Mediterranean basin. They have the same steep-sided mountains of porous limestone that ring the north Mediterranean coast from the Pyrenees through the Alpes Maritimes and the Dolomites to Greece and Asia Minor; they share the same tendency to earthquakes; and they enjoy the same general climatic conditions – rain in winter, drought in summer. Indeed the Maghreb, which has some rain in spring and autumn as well, is wetter than parts of Spain.

As well as sharing the typical climate, north-west Africa has had for thousands of years a plant life which is also more Mediterranean than African. The mountains are still partly, and were once wholly, covered in forests of conifers, and evergreens such as holm oak and wild olive; and like other Mediterranean lands the country took readily to the vine, the olive and the fig and, in the most fertile regions, to cereals when they were introduced in historical times. But the fauna is nearly all of African origin. The poisonous snakes of Tripolitania and Tunisia are not found in Europe; the scorpions are tropical varieties. The so-called Barbary sheep, which is neither sheep nor goat, is an African species. Ostrich, gnu, several varieties of antelope and gazelle were once or still are found in north-west Africa, and one Roman mosaic in the Bardo museum in Tunis shows a hartebeest.

As late as the first century A.D., and probably later, elephants inhabited the Maghreb, and few of the wild beasts – panthers and leopards, lions and bears – which Africa shipped to Rome for the games and circuses came from the Niger basin: almost all were captured north of the Sahara.

These animals migrated to the Mediterranean coast from Central Africa at a period when the North African interior was much wetter than it has been for the last three thousand years. Our own era is possibly the driest phase, in an alternation of wet and dry, that it has ever known. There was once much more rainfall, rivers, and even vast lakes. There is still an enormous water table under the eastern desert, laid down hundreds of thousands of years ago, which supplies the oases in low-level depressions like Siwa and Kufra. In the western desert, it seems likely that the Niger, which runs north-east from the mountains of French Guinea to Timbuctoo, where it turns sharply to the south-east and flows out into the Bight of Benin, as recently as five thousand years ago continued north from Timbuctoo into the vast flats of the El Juf depression. There it evaporated from a shifting series of marshes and shallow lakes some sixty thousand square miles in extent. A watercourse from Timbuctoo has been traced far to the north

of the present Niger bend, and fossil remains of fish, hippopotamus, reed-rat and a variety of mollusc have been found. There are also signs of past habitation of giraffe and elephant, which suggests that what is now desert was once open steppe. The whole western Sahara is seamed with dried-up watercourses, too long and too well defined to be accounted for by the run-off from rainfall as intermittent as it is today; the most famous runs from the Hoggar massif to the Touggourt Depression, and possibly as far as the Chott Melrhir just south of the Aurès mountains in northern Algeria – a distance of some seven hundred miles. As far north as Biskra a Central African mud-fish has been found, and in the Hoggar there have been reports of Central African crocodiles whose ancestors can have established themselves there only in a much wetter period.

These species must have crossed what is now the Sahara tens of thousands rather than thousands of years ago; elephants, for instance, probably arrived early rather than late, for the North African variety is believed to have shown distinct signs of dwarfing in Roman times, a change which must have evolved over a long period. But wet periods made possible not only the spread of animals but also large-scale migrations of peoples. North-west Africa's prehistoric inhabitants, like the animals, came overland. They did not, however, come from Central Africa. The earliest inhabitants, in the ninth millenium B.C., were a Mediterranean stock probably originating in the Levant; and the great migrations of the fifth millenium were of a Hamitic people who also penetrated from the east, across Egypt. They spread all over northern Africa, and, as the central area gradually grew drier, they settled more thickly in the Maghreb and, at the same time, drove the Negroes of the 'desert' further and further south. There was a small admixture of Negro blood, but no Negro people ever settled in the Maghreb.

The descendants of this migration were the tribesmen with whom the Phoenicians came in contact, the people whom the Greeks called Libyan and the Romans called Berbers or Moors. This is the stock from which the modern North Africans and the white tribes of the desert are descended—for neither Carthaginians nor Romans, Vandals nor Arabs invaded in sufficient numbers greatly to alter the ethnic inheritance.

These early North Africans were hunters and pastoralists, and they have left records of themselves and their environment in countless rock engravings. The southern foothills of the Atlas range are rich in engravings of the extinct giant buffalo, elephant and panther; the sides of desiccated watercourses in the Libyan Fezzan show domestic cattle and hunting scenes as well as giraffe, elephant, sheep, rhinoceros and hippopotamus. The engravings cannot be dated with any certainty, but they reveal a past age when the large mammals of Central Africa were a commonplace sight in regions which now support only the occasional hyena or wild boar, and bear witness to the survival of many of them, though by then cut off from the land of their origin, in the Africa known to the ancient world.

With the gradual drying up of the desert the tribes which had settled in the mountains of north-west Africa were, like the animals, virtually isolated. They remained at a Stone Age level of development, hunting wild animals, raising indigenous cattle and the newly introduced domestic horse, or settling to a simple form of agriculture in the more fertile parts of Tunisia, when the Minoans, the Greeks and the Phoenicians were taking to the sea, to commerce, and to conquest.

* * *

The mariners of the eastern Mediterranean had penetrated into the western Mediterranean long before the Phoenicians settled on the coasts of North Africa and Spain. The Minoans, who were trading by sea with Egypt at least four thousand years before Christ, must have obtained the block of liparite found by Sir Arthur Evans in the palace of King Minos at Knossos from the Aeolian islands north of Sicily; they may even have sailed beyond the Straits of Gibraltar (the pillars of Hercules of Greek legend) in the second millenium B.C. The

Elephant in North Africa: bas-relief on the El Kantara bridge at Constantine

Old Testament ships of Tarshish were Phoenician ships sailing to Tartessus, on the Atlantic coast of Spain, around 1000 B.C. Although it is not possible to chart any coherent route for the voyages of Odysseus, the Odyssey shows that by 800 B.C., when Homer lived, the Greeks also had accurate knowledge of the countries of the west: the lotus plant, for instance, does grow on the coast of Tripoli, and the land of the Lotophagi has been confidently identified with the island of Djerba, in the Gulf of Gabès.

From the end of the ninth century B.C. onwards the North African coast was colonized first by the Phoenicians and then by the Greeks. That is fact. The details, however, are largely lost in legend. The western Phoenicians left no written records, but a third century B.C. Sicilian Greek, Timaeus, who very probably derived his information direct from Carthaginian sources, recorded that Carthage was founded in 814 B.C. by the Phoenician Princess Elissa, or Dido, who fled from Tyre when her husband was murdered by her brother, King Pygmalion. The date is convincing (though Virgil, writing after the destruction of Carthage, ante-dated the legend by some centuries to the time of the Trojan War, so that Dido could welcome Aeneas, the founder of Rome, on his way to Italy after the sack of Troy); the princess's great-aunt Jezebel had married

King Ahab of Israel some forty or fifty years earlier. But Dido, if she existed at all, was simply following the example of others of her countrymen: Utica, a few miles along the coast to the north-west, and Gades (Cadiz) in Spain were already Phoenician settlements.

As for the Greeks, they were reputed, according to Herodotus, to have founded fishing colonies in Cyrenaica at the prompting of the Delphic oracle. But it was at a time, a century or so after the Phoenicians, when the Greeks too were colonizing all round the western Mediterranean – part of a general movement dictated first by the desire for trade, and later by pressure of population at home. Delphic oracle notwithstanding, the founding of Cyrene in 630 B.C. fitted naturally into this pattern.

The Phoenicians, however, were the people who first opened up a regular trade route to the far west and monopolized the coast of north-west Africa. It was not the land itself which drew them. Apart from the beds of murex, the shellfish from which the Phoenicians extracted their celebrated purple dye and which was to be found in quantity in the Gulf of Gabès, Africa held few attractions – rather the reverse, in the shape of dangerous wild animals and potentially hostile tribes. Its metals – iron, zinc and lead – were un-

Seventh century B.C. Assyrian bas-relief from Nineveh of a ship thought to be Phoenician, now in the British Museum

suspected by the new invaders. In any case, access to the interior was always difficult: what rivers there are run off the mountains in torrents after the winter rains, down steep ravines, and nearly all dry up in summer like most other Mediterranean rivers. The mountain ranges lie parallel to the coast, with few valleys reaching back into the interior, and although they afforded some protection against sudden raids by the indigenous tribes, they also cut off the coastal settlements, not only from their hinterland but from each other. Even the possibilities of anchorage were poor. Ancient ships being made of wood were better beached than anchored or tied up at a jetty all night, since constant immersion soon fouled the hulls, but shelving beaches were few, and such natural harbours as had been eroded in the rocky limestone cliffs were exposed, if not to the west wind, then to the north. 'No other part of the earth,' reported Pliny in his *Natural History*, 'has fewer bays or inlets in its coast.'

But North Africa lay along one of the two sea routes to Spain, where the ships of Tarshish bartered for silver and tin with the Tartessians, at prices extremely favourable to themselves. The developing civilizations of the eastern Mediterranean were hungry for metals, and it was on this trade that the prosperity of the Phoenicians was based. They needed watering places for their ships, for even with a following wind the small vessels of the ancient world (they rarely exceeded two hundred and fifty tons burthen) could sail only thirty odd miles a day. The two thousand mile journey from Tyre to Tartessus can hardly have taken less than nine or ten weeks. The Phoenicians, therefore, soon established a chain of settlements, to serve not only as victualling points but also as refuges from the sudden storms typical of the Mediterranean, occasionally as winter quarters (for November to March was a close season for sailing), and later as bases from which to protect their sea routes from the encroaching Greeks. With Utica in Tunisia and then Motya in western Sicily, two of their earliest foundations which were more than 'landfalls', they commanded the straits of Sicily. They soon added Carthage, Malta, and Nora in Sardinia.

Unlike those of the Greeks, which were from the start independent city states, the early Phoenician settlements were not intended even then to be much more than rest and repair stations or places of temporary exile from troubles at home in Phoenicia. They were established on off-shore islands like Motya and Utica (now, because of silting, a full fifteen miles inland), on peninsulas like Carthage, or on coasts virtually inaccessible from inland like Hippo Diarrhytus (Bizerta): all sites which could be defended by a small population. They remained under the direct suzerainty of the Phoenician kings; even Carthage, long after all genuine dependence had disappeared, continued to pay some tribute to her mother city of Tyre. Yet the name of Carthage, Kart Hadasht to the Phoenicians (Carthago was the Roman corruption), meant 'new capital' as well as 'new town'. It may well have been planned from the first as a possible alternative capital in the west, for at this time Tyre itself was being seriously harried by the Assyrians. The Phoenicians who came west during the next couple of centuries were as much refugees as colonists, exactly as Dido herself had been. Phoenicia never had population to spare as the Greeks had; it was only after the conquest of Tyre by Nebuchadnezzar in the sixth century that settlements like Mogador on the Atlantic, Tipasa in Algeria and Hadrumetum in eastern Tunisia became fair-sized towns, and that Carthage itself became the leading Phoenician city of the west.

But throughout the history of Carthage, shortage of manpower put a brake on both her colonial and her military activities; it meant that, ultimately, she was no match for Rome. It also made her achievements the more remarkable.

*　　*　　*

The early Phoenicians made themselves masters of the sea clinging to the rim of the Mediterranean; the rise of Carthage was to have a transforming effect on the hinterland

6

of Africa. The Roman province cannot be understood without some knowledge of its pre-Roman past. Carthage was to be destroyed utterly; but she was the greatest city of the western Mediterranean for several hundred years, and she left behind her not only a legend that has haunted the European imagination ever since but customs, language and habits of mind which interacted with those of her African neighbours. The Phoenicians colonized a Stone Age, the Romans a Liby-Phoenician Maghreb. The non-Punic inhabitants were, by then, already as much Mediterranean as African.

Almost nothing is known of the early development of Carthage, except what can be deduced from archaeological evidence. Though her inhabitants' ancestors in Phoenicia invented the alphabet, by an irony of fate only the most fragmentary written records of the Carthaginians of any period have survived. When Carthage was destroyed, her libraries were given to the kingdoms of Numidia; their contents vanished as the Punic language gradually fell into disuse in the later centuries of Roman rule and the scrolls could no longer be understood. Even for the centuries when her power and prosperity were greatest, therefore, the history of Carthage that has come down to us was written by her Greek or Roman enemies. Any historian of the ancient world is working with painfully incomplete information, with fragmentary data that have escaped destruction more or less by accident; some names, some incidents, and those not always the most important, are far better documented than others. In the case of Carthage, the accidents of time have been compounded with bias.

In the sixth century, the spread of Greek colonies in the western Mediterranean was rapidly catching up with that of the Phoenicians. The newcomers showed every sign of seizing control of the sea from their rivals and – worse – were prizing away a significant share of the Spanish metal industry. They may even have been diverting direct through Gaul some of the north European tin which had until then been brought by ship to Tartessus by the sea-going inhabitants of the Atlantic seaboard. Finally the Greek city states in Sicily tried to push the Phoenician settlements out of the island.

Until this point Carthage is scarcely mentioned in the surviving records. But now she emerges as leader and protector of the Phoenicians of the west. She was already the largest of the Phoenician colonies, and had begun to found daughter colonies (Ibiza was the first); and when Tyre fell to Nebuchadnezzar in 574 B.C. she became at last the 'new capital' of the west. But she depended for her security on her command of the straits of Sicily; a wholly Greek Sicily was therefore unthinkable. She put a standing army into the island and looked round for allies.

The struggle went on for a hundred years, and not only in Sicily. In alliance with the Etruscans, with whom she had long had trading relations and who were at that time the most powerful people in the Italian peninsula, Carthage drove the Greeks out of Corsica. In 510 B.C., with Persian backing, she expelled a Greek colony from Tripolitania, on her doorstep. She probably also managed to restore her monopoly of the Spanish metal trade, and with it her maritime supremacy. But Etruria was in decline, and the Persians were decisively defeated by the Athenians in the naval battle of Salamis in 480 B.C.; in the same year, the Carthaginians had to sue for peace in Sicily, when they lost an army and, more disastrously, most of their fleet at Himera. They withdrew from the island, and their fellow-Phoenicians were left to manage as best they could.

The Carthaginians were not cut off from the source of their wealth in the west, and they were still able to buy foodstuffs from Sicily; but the rise of Athens made the eastern Mediterranean a Greek lake. This deprived the Carthaginians of a ready outlet for their wares in the east, and immobilized most of their gold, silver and tin in their own treasuries. During the rest of the fifth century they had to learn, quite literally, to cultivate their own back garden. This they did so successfully that, in the words of the Greek historian Dio Chrysostom, they turned 'from Tyrians into Africans'.

2   The rise and fall of Carthage

Punic mask in the Bardo Museum, Tunis

The Lake of Tunis forms a vast land-locked harbour, protected on the seaward side by two arms which meet so closely that there is barely room for ships to enter the man-made deep-water channel which cuts across the seven miles of shallow water to Tunis. Alongside this channel a dyke carries a road and a little local railway out from Tunis towards the sea. On the far side of the lake, where they reach the harbour bar, they turn along the northern arm of land. Three miles further on, road and railway reach Carthage.

It is impossible to visualize one of the great cities of the ancient world in the string of suburban railway stations and the rows of seaside villas which have inherited that legendary name. There are few traces of the Carthage which became, under the Romans,

second only to Rome itself. The Romans built streets and aqueducts, baths and houses, a theatre and an amphitheatre; the Christians built basilicas, as they built them in dozens of cities all over North Africa; but in Carthage little remains. Streets and the foundations of houses have been uncovered, but the only private building standing is a reconstruction, put up to house statues, pottery, coins and mosaics dug up during the excavations. The amphitheatre, originally almost the size of the Colosseum, now hardly rises above ground level; it has been hideously restored with concrete. The theatre, also restored, though more tactfully, is nowhere near as well-preserved as the comparatively modest theatre at Kasserine (Cillium), for instance, where the stones are as sharp-edged

Roman theatre overlooking the oued Derb at Kasserine (ancient Cillium), near Sbeïtla, Tunisia

as if they were cut yesterday; and the Odeon, the only one built in Africa, is hardly more than a site. The Baths of Antoninus, which once rivalled the Baths of Caracalla at Rome for magnificence, have long since been robbed of their marble facings; the upper storeys have vanished, and though the vast brick and rubble piers suggest their former immensity it is still hard to imagine that the four-ton Corinthian capital now lying on the ground was once one of eight, each on a grey granite column six feet in diameter, in the main hall on the first floor. Down on the shore, the rubble cores of outlying pillars are battered by the sea; half the pebbles on the beach are the smoothed remains of Roman brick or concrete. The best statues and mosaics have long since been removed to museums, to the Louvre or to the Bardo in Tunis; weeds push their way through the everyday paved floors that have been left behind. The great cisterns which stored water for Roman Carthage are now outdoor cellars for the hamlet of La Malga, used as rubbish tips and hen-runs and stables; the aqueduct which supplied them with the waters of Zaghouan, fifty miles away, is here almost crumbled away. An occasional misshapen lump of rubble betrays its route through the fields towards Tunis. Without

Fallen Corinthian capital, its column long since vanished, in the ruins of the Baths of Antoninus at Carthage

Remains of cisterns in the hamlet of La Malga which stored water for Roman Carthage

its once-impregnable fortifications, Carthage was too vulnerable, too accessible by land and sea. Throughout the centuries of the Arab occupation its buildings served as quarries for its new conquerors. The ruins of Roman Carthage were plundered to build mosques and palaces all over North Africa and Spain. There are dozens of Corinthian columns in the prayer room of the Great Mosque of Tunis, their capitals now painted red and green, and the Alhambra at Granada was largely built of stone from Carthage. The Arabs even exported marble columns to the Christian world, some of which may be seen in the cathedral at Pisa; there was enough and more to spare. But there is not much left at Carthage.

Of Punic Carthage, even less remains: so little, that until this century its site had not been established by modern scholars with any certainty. Rival theories disputed the claims of half a dozen places along the ten miles of coast north of the Lake of Tunis. Several ancient writers describe its topography in considerable detail but, since the Romans razed the Punic city to the ground in 146 B.C., and during the next two thousand years parts of the coastline silted up and identifying landmarks disappeared, judgement between these rival theories had to await the development of archaeology. In the last eighty years, however, a quantity of Punic tombs and foundations of houses have been excavated round the hill dominated by the ugly cathedral erected by the French in honour of St Louis XII, who died in Tunis in 1270 on his way to the Crusades. This hill is now accepted as the Byrsa, or citadel, of Punic Carthage. Half a mile to the south, on the coast towards Tunis, the mysterious Le Kram lagoons have been identified with the rectangular and circular ports which are described in ancient texts. They are bordered now, not with warehouses and docks, but

with three or four dozen pleasant suburban villas; residents beach their dinghies on the artificial mound that reaches towards the centre of the circular lagoon, where the Carthaginian admiral's headquarters used to stand.

Nearby, inland, excavation has uncovered the sinister precinct of the Punic goddess Tanit, with thousands of urns containing the remains of little children burnt alive as offerings in the hideous ceremony described with such verve by Flaubert in *Salammbô*: horrible proof that the infant sacrifice for which the other peoples of the ancient world so detested the Phoenicians was practised right down to the last days of Carthaginian independence. No ghosts walk: the sanctuary has been tamed into a sunken garden, with pelargoniums planted beside the neatly ranged votive tablets under the cypress trees. Like the rest of Carthage, it has been suburbanized.

One of the Le Kram lagoons: the ancient Carthaginian circular port, seen from the channel linking it to the rectangular port. Beyond the rising ground is the cathedral of St. Louis XII

For the first three or four hundred years of the city's existence, the Carthaginians occupied barely twenty square miles round their Byrsa. Dido herself, it was said, had paid a sum to the Libyan tribe of the Maxitani for as much land as would be covered by an ox-hide (Greek *byrsa*); then, by cutting the ox-hide into narrow strips and laying them end to end in a vast semi-circle, had secured not only a beaching point for her party but also the hill. In succeeding centuries, the suburbs, with their cemeteries and market gardens and summer villas of the rich, had crept outwards round the citadel; for the land on the fringes the Carthaginians continued to pay tribute in rent to the Libyans, except for a brief period when their power was at its height in the sixth century. The isthmus they lived on, between the Lake of Tunis and the Sebkhet er Riana, a bay (now land-locked, then open to the sea) some three miles north-west of the Byrsa, was enough for a city which can hardly have numbered a hundred thousand souls, a merchant people who had no thought of earning their living except by the sea and commerce.

Not, that is, until their defeat at the hands of the Greeks in 480 B.C. Now they had lost control of half their sea routes, and with them half their livelihood. Protected by cliffs towards the open sea, a bay and a lake on either side, Carthage was admirably placed for defence, but it was a tiny, and an insecure, base for a trading power to which commerce was vital. Carthage responded to the challenge.

Priest preparing to sacrifice a child: part of a fourth-century B.C. *stele found in the precinct of Tanit, Carthage, and now in the Bardo Museum*

*　　*　　*

Throughout the fifth century, at a time when Greek civilization both in Greece and in Sicily was entering its golden age, brilliant, prosperous and powerful, and when Rome was taking over the leadership of Italy from Carthage's old allies the Etruscans, the Carthaginians turned in on themselves. It was a time of revolution and reform. A brutal and inflexible oligarchy set about the task of restoring the city's fortunes with energy and ruthlessness. Austerity was the order of the day, for rich and poor alike, and there was a strong reaction against all foreign, especially Greek, influence, which had become strong during the Sicilian wars. The poverty of all fifth century graves in Carthage, compared with those of the seventh and sixth centuries B.C., is notable. The power of the priesthood, reinforced by refugees from Tyre, became a stranglehold. The genius of the Carthaginians was concentrated in the elaboration of their hideous rituals, and in the creation of their national character: superstitious, Philistine, harsh, conservative, and by turns obsequious and obstinate, and yet, *in extremis*, capable both as a people and as individuals of great courage and nobility.

But the most important factor in the regeneration of Carthage was the conquest of her Tunisian hinterland. Until the fifth century, food had been imported from Carthaginian allies in Sicily and Sardinia, or bought from Libyan cultivators. They were cut off now from their main overseas sources of food, and in any case no longer had a fleet to transport what they needed. The Libyans, therefore, had to be taught to make the most of their potentially fertile corner of Africa.

Almost nothing is known of how the Carthaginians did it, but there is no doubt that the development of agriculture in Tunisia was the great achievement of the century and a half following the defeat at Himera. The only Carthaginian work which is known to have been translated into Latin was a treatise on agriculture by one Mago, who was recognized as a considerable expert by the ancient world. Both original and translation have been lost, but Mago was constantly quoted by later Latin authors. He probably lived in the third century B.C., at the time of Hannibal, but he clearly drew on a considerable body of experience: his immediate predecessors had put their talents and the traditions of their Middle Eastern ancestors to work to some effect. Cape Bon, on the other side of the Lake of Tunis, must have been one of the first areas to be colonized, and by the end of the fourth century B.C. Diodorus Siculus was describing it in these words:

'It was divided into market gardens and orchards of all sorts of fruit trees, with many streams of water flowing in channels irrigating every part. There were country houses everywhere, lavishly built and covered with stucco, which testified to the wealth of their owners. The barns were filled with all that was needed to maintain a luxurious standard of living, as the inhabitants had been able to store up an abundance of everything in a long period of peace. Part of the land was planted with vines, part with olives and other productive trees. Beyond these, cattle and sheep were pastured on the plains, and there were meadows filled with grazing horses. Such were the signs of the prosperity of these

Terracotta mask, probably of the Carthaginian goddess Tanit, dating from the fifth or sixth century B.C., now in the Bardo Museum

regions where leading Carthaginians had their estates.'

The Carthaginian merchant plutocracy had turned themselves into gentlemen farmers. They also showed what could be done in north-west Africa by methodical exploitation. Before the final destruction of Carthage by Rome, records Plutarch, 'it is said that Cato shook out the folds of his toga and contrived to drop some Libyan figs on the floor of the Senate house, and when the senators admired their size and beauty he remarked that the country which produced them was only three days sail from Rome', hoping to

13

inspire his fellow senators with greed for – and also perhaps fear of – the wealth of Carthage. It was not virgin soil which the Romans later turned into a granary.

The Carthaginians farmed directly only northern and eastern Tunisia, where the land flattens out between the foothills of the Algerian mountains and the Gulf of Gabès. This was clay and marl country, moderately well watered, and they concentrated on the kind of produce best suited to it. They bred poultry and domestic animals on scientific principles. They introduced olives – essential in ancient times not only for cooking but for lighting and bathing (though the poet Juvenal complained in the second century A.D. that African oil smelt disgusting) – either grafting them on to the native wild mastic or planting new trees. Mago directed that they should be planted seventy-five feet apart; that is how they are grown in the olive groves of eastern Tunisia today. Vines were grown, and date palms (the symbol of Carthage), and fruit trees: not citrus fruits, which were introduced only in Arab times, but almonds, figs and pomegranates, which the Romans called *mala punica*. They raised bees for honey, which was the ancient world's only form of sugar, and Punic wax, used not only in industry but for medicinal purposes,

Votive tablets dedicated to Baal Hammon and Tanit, or their thinly disguised Roman successors Saturn and Caelestis, assembled in the gardens of the Antonine Baths at Carthage

Aerial view of the olive groves near El Djem

was later much sought after by discriminating Romans.

Most of the native African farmers and pastoralists in the most fertile parts of Tunisia must have been dispossessed, either driven west into the mountains or south to the drier steppe-lands, or impressed into serfdom to work the new estates. It is possible that some Libyan small holdings remained more or less independent alongside their new masters, in Cape Bon for instance; and the upper valleys of the Bagradas and the Miliana, and the high plateaux of central Tunisia, which were more suited to the growing of cereals (which the Carthaginians seem not to have cultivated themselves), were left in the hands of Libyan farmers. But the Carthaginians, like the Romans after them, appear to have forbidden them to grow anything other than cereals, in order to keep up the value of their own mixed-farming produce. They also exacted a tithe of the crop to feed the city of Carthage – a tithe which at times was raised to a quarter or even a third.

They were not popular with their new subjects. The dispossessed hovered outside Carthaginian territory, casting hungry eyes on the fertile land they had been driven out of, ready to stir up disaffection among those of their kinsmen who had been left behind in servitude.

The Carthaginians, who were short of manpower, had always depended to a large

15

extent on their African subjects and neighbours for the mercenaries of which their armies were composed. They recruited their soldiers all round the western Mediterranean, but the core of their fighting strength consisted of their Libyan infantry, who stood up to hot weather better than Greeks or Romans, and the famous Numidian cavalry for which they recruited tribesmen from the mountains further west (the only battle Hannibal lost was the one in which he was not supported by Numidian cavalry). It was a serious source of weakness that these subjects and neighbours, professionally trained for war as many of them were, were so readily provoked or tempted to turn on the Carthaginians. Once Carthage had turned herself into a landed power, she found she had to be ready to defend herself as much against Africa as against Greeks and Romans. The discord between conqueror and conquered was complicated in this case by the fundamental incompatibility of the nomad and the settled farmer. It was a problem the Romans were to inherit.

For the moment, however, Carthage could feed herself without having to import. But her ambitions remained those of a maritime trading nation. During the fifth century, she also tightened her hold on the whole north-west African littoral, from the Gulf of Syrte to the Atlantic. Daughter colonies properly settled the trading posts of Tripolitania at Oea (Tripoli), Sabratha and Leptis Magna to keep firm control of the mysterious but evidently profitable Saharan caravan trade – in gold perhaps, in precious stones (especially carbuncles) certainly, and probably in negro slaves – which was conducted by the powerful tribe of the Garamantes. Here, too, the Carthaginians introduced agriculture, in particular the growing of olive trees. In the east, their territory stretched to the border of the powerful Greek city of Cyrene in Cyrenaica – a border settled, it was said, by two Carthaginian brothers who ran from Leptis to meet envoys who had left Cyrene at the same time, and then, when accused by the Greeks of cheating, volunteered to be buried alive in defence of their victory. Arae Philaenorum was so-called after their supposed burial mounds.

In the west, it was an age of great expeditions. In the first half of the fifth century B.C. the admiral Hanno, the first individual Carthaginian of whom a record survives and one of the great explorers of antiquity, sailed down the west coast of Africa with the intention of founding trading posts nearer the source of the Senegalese gold trade. He may have reached the Bight of Benin, but the expedition was not repeated and nothing is known of the fate of any colonies he may have founded. It was cheaper, both in money and manpower, to let others bring the goods. At the same time, another Carthaginian, Himilco, was exploring the sources of the Tartessian tin trade along the Atlantic coast of Gaul; he may have crossed to Britain and Ireland. Again, if he had Carthaginian successors, nothing is known of them. Madeira and the Canary Islands were also known to the Phoenicians by this time, but here, too, no permanent posts were established, and visits were probably extremely rare: there was no good commercial reason for them.

By the end of the fifth century Carthage had become the overlord of the other Phoenician settlements along the Algerian and Moroccan coasts. She proved hardly more popular with them than with the native Africans, for in return for her offer to defend them she greatly restricted their right to trade. There was much grumbling, and one or other of them, in despair at the harshness of her rule, was constantly defecting to her enemies. This, too, contributed to Carthage's eventual downfall. Where Hannibal, in Italy, could never persuade Rome's allies to desert her, the Romans had little difficulty in Africa in persuading Phoenician cities to turn against Carthage.

Carthage's land empire, though scarcely a tenth the size of the later Roman province, was now as large as it was ever to be. The voyages of Hanno had restored the metal trade to its former lucrative level. It was thanks to him, Dio Chrysostom claimed only a little extravagantly, that the Carthaginians 'lived in Africa rather than Phoenicia, became very wealthy, acquired many markets, ports and ships, and ruled on land and sea.'

*　　*　　*

The Carthaginians celebrated their revived prosperity by returning to the attack in Sicily, where the warring tyrants of the rival Greek city states, besides threatening the remaining Phoenician settlements, offered plenty of tempting opportunities for meddling. But the war which broke out in 409 B.C. went on with scarcely a break for over a century, and led directly to the first great war with Rome. During that time the armies of Carthage managed to sack, on one occasion or another, all the Greek cities of Sicily except Syracuse: the ruins of Selinunte and Agrigento bear eloquent witness to this day to the ferocity of the fighting. The war was marked on both sides by unspeakable atrocities. A Carthaginian general tortured and sacrificed three thousand prisoners of war in revenge for the death of his grandfather at Himera seventy years before; the Greeks massacred the entire civilian population of Motya. Neither side ever succeeded in conquering the whole island. The war was vastly complicated for the Greeks by the internecine rivalries of the various city tyrants: Greek fought Greek in alliance with the Carthaginians. The Carthaginians were severely hampered by desertions and revolts in their armies and by risings at home among the African population (who on one occasion seized the town of Tunis). Twice Syracuse was saved from capture only by an outbreak of disease in the ranks of the Carthaginian army. Twice Carthage had to sue for peace, twice she was obliged to pay a heavy indemnity. Yet she still did not give up, and not only because control of the far side of the straits of Sicily had for centuries been the cornerstone of her foreign policy.

For this savage warfare paid off. It was, for Carthage, a source of revenue; almost an arm of trade. The loot sent back to Carthage from captured Greek cities more than compensated for military and naval expenses, and even for the indemnities that were demanded. Further, the war was fought on foreign soil, and with mercenary troops. It was not Carthaginian farms and cities that were razed to the ground, nor Carthaginian crops that were laid waste, nor – on the whole – Carthaginian families who lost sons and brothers. Although the generals were always Carthaginian citizens (rather than the *condottieri* to whom the Greeks tended to entrust their fortunes), and although it was a point of pride among the nobility to volunteer, their *corps d'élite* was a tiny minority beside the hired mercenaries: cavalry from Numidia, slingers from the Balearic Islands, javelin throwers from Spain, Libyans, Celts, Ligurians, even Greeks and Italians.

But this immunity did not last. Between 310 and 307 B.C., Carthage itself was threatened. Agathocles, the reigning tyrant of Syracuse, unable to raise the siege of his city, boldly set sail for Africa with fourteen thousand men to make a counter-attack. He landed on Cape Bon, burnt his boats behind him because he could not spare the men to guard them, and for three years lived off the countryside – at one point, with help from the Greeks of Cyrenaica, capturing both Utica and Hippo Diarrhytus (Bizerta), where he was able to build shipyards and then ships to re-establish his communications with Sicily. For the rulers of Carthage, the pillage of their estates was a novel experience. Yet they did not attempt to treat with Agathocles by yielding in Sicily; they were not open to blackmail. Instead, two hundred children from the leading families were sacrificed to Baal Hammon – children known to have been improperly saved on previous occasions by the substitution of slave children. Agathocles was seen as the instrument of the cheated god's revenge. Three hundred more children were voluntarily sacrificed by other parents who were suspected of similar impiety.

The fearful holocaust was shortly rewarded by the departure of Agathocles (who spent the last years of his life planning to re-invade Africa). Temporarily, though she was obliged to return to her old boundaries in Sicily and to pay an indemnity, Carthage had been spared. Yet an example had been set, a lesson learned. Africa was not im-

First century A.D. *terracotta statuette of Baal Hammon from Cap Bon, now in the Bardo Museum, Tunis*

which Semitic peoples, with their distrust of the graven image, were notably deficient. Greek luxury objects reappear in the graves of the period, and Greek plumbing was installed in rich men's houses. At Kerkouann on Cape Bon, where the only known Carthaginian township not later overlaid by Roman building has been uncovered, one can see the smart bathroom floors of the period: a pink or blue cement inlaid with chips of white marble, which the Romans called *pavimenta punica*. They were paid for not only in Senegalese gold and Sicilian loot, but perhaps also in the wheat Carthage was now able to export. The Greek goddesses Demeter and Persephone became a cult at Carthage – to expiate, it is thought, the destruction of their sanctuary outside Syracuse (an act to which the superstitious Carthaginians had attributed a subsequent reversal of fortune) and because harvest goddesses might answer the prayers of a people now dependent on their own farmlands. Dionysius was also worshipped at Carthage; and Hellenistic religion, perhaps because it offered a more cheerful after-life than their own, became so popular that the Greek funeral custom of incineration replaced burial. The Carthaginians, though loyal to the end to their own relentless gods, were like magpies in their adoption of other people's. As extra security, they had early imported various Egyptian gods and goddesses.

pregnable and, moreover, she was worth having: it was through the eyes of Agathocles' troops that Diodorus Siculus was describing the countryside of Cape Bon in the passage quoted earlier. Where they had led, others could follow. For Carthage, it was the most serious consequence of the hundred years' war in Sicily.

The other main result of the war was that she was drawn back into the mainstream of Mediterranean civilization. Greek prisoners of war in Sicily were shipped back as slaves to Carthage, where they re-introduced Greek skills in the plastic arts – a field in

Copper razor in the Hellenistic style of the third century B.C., *now in the museum at Carthage*

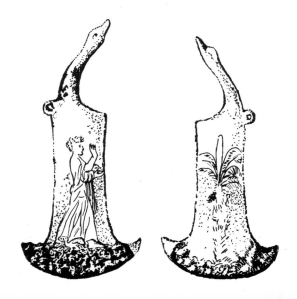

Tanit in the guise of an Egyptian lion goddess: a terracotta statue of the first century A.D. *found at Thinissut, Cape Bon peninsula*

ficial, even among the rich. Education was either severely practical, or in the hands of the priesthood: boys who learnt Greek mostly learnt it because they were going to be merchants in their fathers' businesses. It is possible that girls, who did not need vocational training of this kind, were actually better educated than their brothers. Although some Carthaginians did go to Greece to study, and one of them later became head of the Academy at Athens, there is no sign in Carthage of the humanism of the Greek world. The elaborate religious ceremonies were the only public festivities: theatres were unknown. The dulcimer and the zither were frequently represented on sacred statues, and music was played at religious ceremonies or to accompany ritual dances, but in general the arts were neglected. This nation of merchants took a great interest in clothes and hair, in cleanliness and, like the modern Arab, in perfume and jewellery, in food and creature comforts; but none in their bodies. Their textiles, their pastry-cooks and their confectionery were famous, but there were no games in Carthage, no athletes, and their gods, like those of all Oriental peoples and unlike those of the Greeks, were always represented clothed. Although the women adopted female Greek costume (its elegance spoilt, however, by over-abundant jewellery), the men remained faithful to the beards, the skullcaps and the long-sleeved robes of their

Egyptian amulets are one of the commonest finds from the Punic period, and in the third century B.C. the influence of Hellenistic Egypt remained strong.

Shifting alliances in Sicily also led to some intermarriage between Greeks and Carthaginians: the mother of Hannibal was a Greek. Both Hannibal and his father, the general Hamilcar, modelled their strategy on that of Alexander the Great. The use of elephants in war was also adopted from the Greeks; so was the minting of money.

Yet the Hellenization of Carthage, though in some ways real enough, remained super-

Bronze Hellenistic-style jug manufactured at Carthage and now in the Bardo

Statue of a worshipper wearing Punic dress: from Utica (third century B.C.*)*

ancestors, which were less appropriate to physical exercise than to impressing others with the wearers' dignity. They tended to overweight and self-importance. 'The Carthaginians,' wrote Plutarch in the second century A.D. but quoting an earlier opinion, 'are a hard and gloomy people, submissive to their rulers and harsh to their subjects . . . they keep obstinately to their decisions, are austere, and care little for amusement or the graces of life.' This judgement might be modified if their literature had survived, and if we knew more about their domestic life; they were, for instance, exceptionally for that time, monogamous. It serves to show, however, 'how alien they always seemed to the Greeks and Romans.

The half-century that followed the failure of Agathocles' expedition was an extremely prosperous period in the history of Carthage. She resumed trading relations with the eastern Mediterranean. She was growing enough wheat to export; her textiles were much in demand; and a falling-off in the supply of Spanish tin (due possibly to insurrections among Iberian tribes) now mattered less than in the days when her only other exports were the indifferent pottery and metal artefacts which, though they satisfied her barbarian customers, were despised by those who could choose the marvellous ceramics and *objets d'art* manufactured by the Greeks.

If Carthage herself was now, to a certain extent, open to outside influences, she was also – rich, powerful and landed as she was – beginning to have a significant effect on her immediate neighbours. Her African mercenaries returned home to their tribes with at least a smattering of civilization, and a taste for more. Their chieftains sought to emulate in their own territories the successes of Punic agriculture, borrowing Punic experts to help them, and to embellish their own settlements with some of the symbols of city wealth. Turning their pastoral tribesmen into settled farmers, they soon realized, made possible an increase in the productivity of the land, and also added to their power: farmers were easier to control – and to tax – than shepherds. It added to their prestige, too. Where Dido had refused to marry a Libyan chieftain, preferring to throw herself on a funeral pyre, now the daughters of Carthage were given away in marriage to African princelings. Africans gave Carthaginian names to their children and adopted both Carthaginian gods and, in part, the Punic language. In turn, the Carthaginians adopted African fertility gods – necessary to them, like Demeter and Persephone, now that they were farmers themselves – and certain African funeral customs. It was a trend which operated like a kind of crystallizing process during the final century and a half of Carthage's existence. More than Hanno in the fifth century B.C., it was the Libyans in the third who finally turned Tyrians into Africans and, in turn, became the upholders of neo-Punic language and traditions for centuries under the Romans.

The earliest of the barbarian kingdoms to emerge was, however, the one furthest from Carthage. The Moors of Mauretania had formed themselves into a tribal federation by the fourth century B.C. Though they had probably not then turned from their nomadic pastoral life to a settled agriculture, they were growing wheat by the time the Romans colonized their country. In the third century B.C., northern Algeria was shared between two powerful Numidian, or nomadic, tribes. The kingdom of the Masaesyli stretched from Siga, where Moorish rule began, nearly a thousand miles to the east to Cape Bougaroun, north of Constantine. It was loosely based on two widely-separated 'capitals', Siga and Cirta (Constantine). The kingdom of the Massyli further east was more modest in extent, but bordered Punic territory. Nothing is known of the intertribal warfare by which they must have established their supremacy over other tribes. Both were to play a leading part in the downfall and destruction of Carthage, before they themselves fell victim to the Romans. Further south, the Saharan foothills, from the Atlantic to southern Tunisia, were inhabited by the Gaetules, who remained, not least because their territory was much less amenable to cultivation, comparatively untouched by Mediterranean influences. They

Statue of Demeter (reconstructed) found in a rural sanctuary near Korba (ancient Curubis) in the Cape Bon peninsula

controlled the west Saharan caravan trade down to the Niger river. To the east, in the hinterland of Tripolitania, were the Garamantes, who occupied the oases of the Fezzan and controlled the eastern routes across the desert. Their horse-drawn chariots, probably adopted from the Greeks of Cyrenaica, are mentioned by Herodotus in the fifth century B.C., and are represented in rock engravings in the dry wadi valleys of the central Sahara. There were other desert tribes, such as the Nasamones; but altogether they can have numbered only some tens of thousands, or a modest six-figure number at most, since their dry country could not have supported more. Yet they were to be a constant anxiety to the Romans, especially as the army pushed the frontier further and further south.

By the middle of the fifth century B.C., when Carthage had temporarily withdrawn from Mediterranean life, Rome had become the leading city of central Italy. In the fourth, when Carthage was once more at war in Sicily, the other towns of central Italy yielded to Rome the right to control their foreign policy and call on them for military help, in return for protection against the Gauls to the north or other enemies and for the right to Roman citizenship if they chose to live in Rome – and in some cases if they did not. Liberal treatment of defeated neighbours was something quite new in Mediterranean history; the Romans were to be rewarded for it. The rest of Italy soon joined their confederacy, and by the third century the Romans controlled almost the whole of the Italian peninsula south of the Po valley, including all but one of the Greek city states of southern Italy. This was to give them a commanding advantage in manpower during the Punic wars. Not that their armies were conspicuously well led: rather the reverse, since their political constitution gave military command to two elected leaders for a year at a time only. This preserved them from tyranny, but too often proved a recipe for incompetent generalship; or, if by good fortune the assembly elected as one of its chief magistrates a man who had both military experience and a talent for command,

his successes were liable to be undone either by his fellow consul or by their successors when their year in office was up. The Romans did not destroy the Punic empire until they entrusted command to a general who was a match for Hannibal – and allowed that general to remain in command until Hannibal had been defeated.

According to Polybius, the earliest record of dealings between Rome and Carthage was a treaty which must have been signed in 510 or 509 B.C. The Romans were at that time under the protection of Carthage's allies, the Etruscans, and the treaty merely defined their respective fields of interest: the Romans were to have limited rights to trade in African and Sardinian ports, and Carthage recognized Rome's territorial rights in Latium (central Italy). It was a treaty neither side would be tempted to break. In 348 B.C., another treaty was signed; Carthage still recognized Rome's rights in central Italy, but Rome was now allowed to trade only in Sicily and in Carthage itself. The balance of power remained with Carthage; but the terms implied that she was conscious of Rome's growing strength, and that their respective spheres of interest might collide. Forty years later, Rome was agreeing not to interfere in Sicily, in return for Carthage not interfering in Italy. In 278 B.C., they came to their last agreement: this time it was a modified alliance against the Greek King Pyrrhus of Epirus, who had come west to carve out a new kingdom for himself at the expense first of Rome and then of Carthage.

Fourteen years later, Rome and Carthage were fighting for Sicily.

The causes of the First Punic War seem trivial, almost accidental. A group of Italian colonists in Sicily, technically Roman citizens, appealed to the Romans for help against the Greeks of Syracuse. They had also appealed to the Carthaginians. The Romans were afraid that the Carthaginians would use this local quarrel as an excuse to defeat Syracuse and make Sicily at last a Carthaginian island (though she had never managed to do this before, and was not likely to now); the Carthaginians were afraid the Romans would make it a pretext to drive them out of Sicily. The local quarrel was soon forgotten in the war which broke out in 264 B.C., and which lasted, with intervals for recuperation, more than twenty years. It was Rome's first military venture outside Italy.

The Romans soon realized that they would never conquer the Carthaginians in Sicily without defeating them at sea. Their own maritime strength hitherto had amounted to fewer than fifty ships manned by Greek or Italian allies, yet they refused to be intimidated by the reputation of the Carthaginian navy for invincibility, and in spite of horrifying reverses never gave up their aim of destroying the enemy's sea power.

Their first fleet of a hundred quinqueremes, begun in 261 B.C., was sensibly modelled on a Carthaginian ship which had been wrecked on the Italian coast, and was manned by rowers trained on dry land. The Romans also armed each ship with a boarding device known as a 'crow', which could be swung outwards and attached by spikes to enemy ships and was intended to turn a sea battle into a 'land' battle. Their optimism was fortified by a couple of unexpected successes during the next couple of years, which did much for their morale and dissipated the legend of unconquerable Carthage, though it did not shake the Carthaginian hold on Sicily. The Romans began building another, larger, fleet in 257 B.C. and set sail for Africa the following year. But the fate of Agathocles half a century before was repeated. The first Roman invasion of Africa came to an ignominious end, in spite of initial successes: seventeen thousand of their twenty-thousand strong army under Regulus were killed or captured in 255 B.C. by the Spartan Xanthippus, to whom the Carthaginians had in desperation appealed for help. It was immediately followed by a disaster at sea. The Roman fleet, returning to Sicily from Africa with the remnants of Regulus's army and with a large number of captured Carthaginian ships, some two hundred and sixty-four ships in all, was hit by a southerly gale. Two hundred and fifty-six ships were driven on to the rocks of Sicily and destroyed, with a loss of life, including rowers and soldiers,

which probably approached one hundred thousand men. Polybius considered that it was the greatest disaster ever to have happened at sea. Yet the Romans were not deterred: they built another fleet, and when one hundred and fifty ships were destroyed in another storm, they prepared to replace them once more. And their policy was justified: sea power was to win the war, in spite of the successes of the Carthaginian general Hamilcar Barca (father of Hannibal) in Sicily some years later. For the Roman losses lulled their enemies into a false sense of security, and the Carthaginians laid up their own war fleet.

Throughout, the Carthaginians reckoned without Roman resolve, that blind determination to win no matter what the cost. (A census of 247 B.C. suggests that the war had already cost them seventeen in every hundred of their adult males – a higher loss than that of Germany in the First World War – and it is likely that their allies had suffered similarly.) Short of money and manpower though they were, in 243 B.C. the Romans built another two hundred quinqueremes on a more recent Carthaginian model, and found they had the sea to themselves. It was eight months before Carthage got a fleet to sea again. Her rowers were out of practice, and the battle of the Aegates Islands was at last a decisive victory for Rome. Carthage sued for peace. She had to give up Sicily, the Aegates Islands and Lipara, and pay an indemnity of 3200 talents spread over ten years.

There now occurred one of the most horrifying episodes in the entire history of Carthage. Hamilcar's mercenaries had been sent back from Sicily to Carthage, where they were to be paid what was owing to them. But the rulers of Carthage, thinking of the losses they had sustained and the enormous indemnity they would have to pay, hoped to avoid paying them as much as had been promised. The mercenaries were sent with their families to Sicca (Le Kef), a hundred miles off, with a gold coin apiece, to await the balance. The money did not arrive, and the mercenaries tired of waiting. They left Sicca, and returned to threaten Carthage

Coin portrait of Hamilcar Barca

from the neighbourhood of Tunis. The Carthaginians, terrified, now paid the money – too late. The mercenaries, who were of several nationalities, had tasted opportunity, and stepped up their demands. These were not met, and a slave, Spendius, and a Libyan called Matho stirred up a mutiny not only among the mercenaries (and opponents of their plan were stoned to death) but among the Libyan peasantry, who, profoundly oppressed by the heavy taxes levied during the war, willingly swelled their ranks by twenty thousand men. Meanwhile the Carthaginians raised a citizen army and recruited fresh mercenaries.

What followed was the fearsome 'truceless war' described by Polybius, otherwise known as the Mercenary War, which provided Flaubert with the subject of his novel *Salammbô*. Dreadful crimes were committed by both sides. Carthaginians captured by the mercenaries had their hands and parts cut off and legs broken before being flung into ditches and buried alive. Hamilcar had his prisoners trampled to death by elephants. At one point the starving mercenaries were reduced to eating their prisoners and slaves; at another, Hamilcar crucified a peace party of ten men, among them Spendius. The war lasted more than three years. It ended, though only after the Numidian tribe of the Massyli had joined the Carthaginians, in the

virtual annihilation of the mercenaries.

During the crisis, Rome sympathetically returned to Carthage her unransomed prisoners and forbade the Italians to help the rebels; but at the end of the Mercenary War she took advantage of Carthage's weakness to seize Sardinia and 'demand a further 1200 talents, which Carthage was in no position to refuse. This was one action in Rome's history that even her most patriotic apologists could not justify as 'self-defence' – even Livy admitted that it was adding insult to injury. It certainly made impossible a genuine peace between Rome and Carthage. The vengeful hatred it inspired in the hearts of the Carthaginians had not a little to do with the support they gave a generation later to the Barcid family in their long-laid plans to destroy Rome.

*   *   *

Sicily had been the guiding principle of Carthage's foreign policy for three hundred years. For Sicily she had embarked on wars, first against the Greeks and then against the Romans, which were among the bloodiest known to the ancient world. Where the Greeks had failed, the upstart Romans had succeeded. Sicily was lost for ever. (It was the first Roman province outside Italy.)

Its loss did not ruin Carthage. But she now had to look for new sources of money and manpower to raise the indemnity and to restore her fortunes. She turned to Spain, rightly believing that the iron, silver and copper mines of the interior had by no means been exhausted. In 237 B.C. Hamilcar Barca left Carthage to conquer a new empire, taking with him his son-in-law Hasdrubal and his nine-year-old son Hannibal, who, according to Livy, 'begged, with all the childish arts he could muster, to be allowed to accompany him; whereupon Hamilcar, who was preparing to offer sacrifice for a successful outcome, led the boy to the altar and made him solemnly swear, with his hand upon the sacred victim, that as soon as he was old enough he would be the enemy of the Roman people'.

In the next sixteen years, the whole of southern Spain fell into the hands of Hamilcar, and, after his death, those of his son-in-law, either by military conquest or by diplomatic alliances. Hasdrubal, indeed, after his first wife's death, married an Iberian woman, as Hannibal himself did later. The Barcids modelled themselves on Alexander the Great, who a century earlier had conquered the whole of the Persian Empire in ten years with a comparatively small but loyal army. They never tried to break the link with Carthage, but the regime they established in Spain did resemble, at least superficially, a Hellenistic kingdom. The coins they minted show them wearing the royal wreath, and the capital Hasdrubal founded on the site of modern Cartagena was named Qart Hadasht – 'new capital' – like Carthage before it, and perhaps with the same end in view, that it should be the cornerstone of a new Phoenician Empire. But, like the Hellenistic kingdoms, the conquest did not strike roots; the Romans had no difficulty later, using the same opportunist methods, in seducing the Iberian tribes from the Carthaginian cause.

Meanwhile, New Carthage provided a base, and Spain provided the manpower and the wealth, for the extraordinary enterprise which the young Hannibal, now twenty-eight, undertook in the year 218 B.C., three years after he had taken command on the death of his brother-in-law.

Bas-relief of Roman warship, in the Vatican Museum, Rome

Coin portrait of Hasdrubal, son-in-law of Hamilcar Barca

Terracotta of war elephant, found at Pompeii

This was the famous crossing of the Alps in order to invade Italy. It took the Romans almost completely by surprise, and astonished the whole of the ancient world; it remains astonishing today. There were no proper paths; guides proved incompetent; local tribes, hoping for loot, harried Hannibal's army as it struggled through steep ravines, and caused severe casualties; rock barred the way, and had to be cracked apart by picks after being heated by bonfires and made friable with sour wine; men and animals slid down ice-bound slopes, or fell off precipices; for a fortnight, in late September, animals and men together, most of them used to a warmer climate, were above the snowline. The crossing cost Hannibal half his troops by death or desertion, many of his horses and almost all his celebrated elephants. Yet he remained in Italy for the next seventeen years, and never lost a battle.

That autumn, he defeated a Roman army led by the consul Publius Cornelius Scipio in one of his most audacious battles. The following spring, in spite of losing the sight of one eye from a chill caught while crossing the marshes of the middle Arno, he annihilated another Roman army of twenty-five thousand in an ambush on the shores of Lake Trasimene. For a year, while Rome recovered from the shock of being faced with a general of genius, Quintus Fabius Maximus was able to employ his famous 'Fabian tactics' and never gave Hannibal the opportunity of battle; but the consuls who succeeded him, one a great deal less prudent and the other less firm-minded, attacked Hannibal at Cannae in the August of 216 B.C. This was Rome's greatest military disaster. Polybius put the Roman losses at seventy thousand, Livy at fifty thousand; they were certainly thirty-five thousand, the bulk of their army. Hannibal's casualties were fewer than six thousand. It was no wonder that the cry of *Hannibal ad portas* – which the Romans expected on the morrow – became for centuries the catchphrase with which Roman mothers alarmed their children.

No one has put the situation which faced the Romans when the first news of the disaster reached the capital more clearly than

Livy: 'Never, without an enemy actually within the gates, had there been such terror and confusion in the city . . . Rome left without a force in the field, without a commander, without a single soldier, Apulia and Samnium in Hannibal's hands, and now nearly the whole of Italy overrun. No other nation in the world could have suffered so tremendous a series of disasters, and not been overwhelmed . . . Nobody doubted that Hannibal, now that the armies were destroyed, would attack Rome . . . the streets were loud with the wailing and weeping of women, and nothing yet being clearly known, living and dead alike were being mourned in nearly every house in the city.'

The Carthaginians had brought the war home with a vengeance. Yet the Romans did not ask Hannibal for peace terms. Livy's pride was justified: they really were like 'no other nation in the world'. They even, it was said, gave a sympathetic welcome to the surviving consul after his escape from the field of battle. No energy was wasted on recrimination. They had some extra edge of pride, tenacity and that disbelief in final defeat which had enabled them to win the First Punic War a generation before. This was the spirit which was to conquer the known world. It was given a voice by a survivor of Cannae, the young son of the Scipio whose army had been defeated two years earlier: 'I swear, with all the passion of my heart, that I shall never desert our country, or permit any other citizen of Rome to leave her in the lurch.' This younger Scipio was destined to conquer Hannibal fourteen years later. Cannae was a great battle, not a decisive one. What changed the history of the ancient world was Rome's refusal to surrender.

Two Vestal Virgins who were discovered to have broken their vows of chastity were, of course, condemned to death, and the populace demanded that two Gauls and two Greeks should be buried alive; human sacrifice was not unknown outside Carthage in times of stress. This offering to the gods was rewarded, so it seemed, just as the sacrifice of five hundred Carthaginian children had been a century before; Hannibal did not, or

Coin portrait of Hannibal Barca

Breastplate, of Campanian workmanship, which belonged to one of Hannibal's soldiers. It was found buried at K'sar-es-Souf, Tunisia

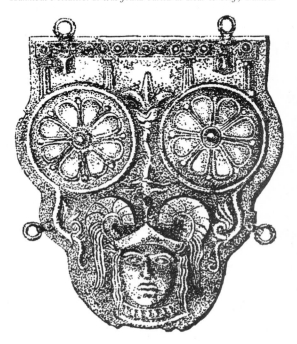

could not, follow up his victory.

For he had not, in spite of his lenient treatment of their captured soldiers, persuaded any of the allied cities of central Italy to give him more than the most trivial help in his fight against Rome. There had been no rising of the Italians against their masters. Although in Sicily the Syracusans revolted, the Romans eventually re-took the city after a long and arduous siege (the defence was directed by the great Archimedes, whose machines of war proved a serious obstacle to the attackers; Archimedes was killed by a Roman soldier when the victors sacked the city), and defeated a Carthaginian fleet at the same time. Nor, without a fleet, was Hannibal able to make the most of a personal alliance he had formed with Philip of Macedon. His army was simply too small to follow up his dazzling victories. Living from hand to mouth in southern Italy as best he could during the years that followed, he and his army were bound to be increasingly dependent on reinforcements. They never came, either from his base in Spain or from Carthage. Carthage had no fleet; Spain was having serious troubles of its own. The Roman army which, right at the beginning of the war, had been sent to cut Hannibal's lines of communication, had gone on to Spain and, in spite of initial reverses, had eventually seized Cartagena. Hannibal's brother, another Hasdrubal, whom he had left in charge, was pinned down; Carthaginian troops which had been intended for Hannibal had to be diverted to help him. In vain: when Hasdrubal at last followed his brother to Italy in 207 B.C., nine years after Cannae, it was because the Romans, now under the command of young Scipio, virtually pushed him out of Spain. Hasdrubal and his troops had no more luck in Italy. Cannae was revenged by the Romans at the battle of the River Metaurus: Hasdrubal was killed, and his head, so it was said, was sent to Hannibal. It was the first and last time in more than ten years that the latter saw the brother for whose help he had waited so long.

Hannibal now had no prospect of defeating Rome. The most he could hope for was a decent peace. This was thwarted by Scipio, who followed up the advantage he had at last secured in Spain by finally driving out the remaining Carthaginians in the year after the battle of the River Metaurus. That done, he was free to return to Rome to urge that he should be allowed to attack, not Hannibal, but Carthage itself. However enfeebled, Hannibal's magical gifts could not be discounted: he had pulled off too many incredible victories out of the most unpromising situations. The tough, single-minded Roman recognized that to strike straight at Carthage would cut off any further help for him at source and would also draw him out of Italy. Better to risk defeat at Hannibal's hands in Africa than dangerously near Rome. But Scipio did not expect defeat. He had already come to an arrangement, if not an alliance, with Syphax of the Masaesyli, king of the most powerful of the African kingdoms at that time, which controlled western Numidia. The Roman Senate agreed to his plan.

The position of Carthage was now extremely vulnerable. At last, too late, she made two attempts to get help to Hannibal. Both failed, and their failure left her even more exposed. But it happened that Hasdrubal (not one of the Barcid family), the general who had been in command latterly in Spain and was now in charge of the defence of Carthage, had a daughter, Sophonisba, and the ageing Syphax was persuaded to desert the Roman cause – for love. According to Livy, Syphax fell passionately in love with Sophonisba. He was given her hand in marriage, and was quite won over to the cause of his new in-laws.

Carthage was not out of danger, but Scipio had lost his major ally. He had to make do with the problematical support of Masinissa of the Massyli (the other major kingdom of Numidia), son of the king who had been Carthage's ally at the time of the Mercenary War half a century before. The tortuous succession arrangements which operated in the African kingdoms had led to such confusion on the death of this king that Syphax had been able to steal the territory of the Massyli, in eastern Numidia, and the young Masinissa was little better than an outlaw, constantly on the run from Syphax's troops. But it was this unpromising ally who – in spite of a dramatic temporary defection – helped Rome defeat Carthage.

Hasdrubal, who knew Masinissa's quality of old, recognized that he 'was a man of far loftier spirit and far greater ability than had ever been seen in anyone of his nation'. He might yet offer a serious threat to Carthage. The Carthaginian general urged his new son-in-law to destroy him if he possibly could. Masinissa and his tiny band of followers were therefore hounded by Syphax and, it was thought, exterminated. But three survived, among them Masinissa. His reappearance among his own people, after he had been given up for dead, created such an upsurge of loyalty that large numbers flocked to his standard; and, although Syphax conquered him in battle, he was able to retreat to southern Tunisia, to await the arrival of the Rome invasion and his chance to avenge himself on Syphax.

Scipio landed on Cape Farina in 204 B.C., and set up his headquarters near Utica (ever Carthage's rival, and willing enough to be Rome's ally when prompted by Roman troops on the doorstep). In the first year Scipio had little more success than the Greek Agathocles and the Roman Regulus before him. However, under cover of peace negotiations he was able to discover the disposition of the Carthaginian and Numidian camps and succeeded in setting fire to them, killing a large number of the opposing armies. Soon after, he scored a victory over Hasdrubal himself, and seized Tunis. He also captured Syphax. Masinissa, seeing his opportunity, invaded the territory of his old enemy and captured Cirta, Syphax's capital. On the threshold of the royal palace the Numidian conqueror was met by Sophonisba, who 'was in the full flower of her youthful beauty; as she clung to Masinissa's knees or clasped his hand, begging him to promise never to give her up to a Roman, her words grew little by little more like the blandishments of a lover than the supplication of a captive, and at this the conqueror's heart not only melted into pity but – with the characteristic inflammability of the Numi-

dian race – was itself vanquished and led into captive love.' So went the legend recounted by Livy; and Masinissa married her that very day.

Scipio was understandably alarmed on hearing the news. He had lost one ally to Sophonisba; now he had lost the other – just as he was beginning to be useful. The captive Syphax added fuel to the flames, by declaring that it was some comfort to him that Sophonisba had now 'transferred her corrupting influence to the house and home of his bitterest enemy'. Scipio sent word at once to Masinissa, pointing out that his bride belonged, as the wife of Syphax, to the Roman people, and must be given up. Masinissa, after much groaning and sighing, yielded to the thinly veiled threat; but, remembering his promise to her that she should not fall into the hands of the Romans, he sent her a cup of poison. She drank it, saying to the slave who brought it: 'I accept this bridal gift – a gift not unwelcome if my husband has been unable to offer a greater one to his wife.' Livy adds that she showed no sign of perturbation. Thus, it was said, died Hasdrubal's daughter.

Her bridegroom was welcomed back into the Roman fold, and rewarded with the title of king and a Roman triumph; the first foreigner to be so honoured. His reign was to be long and glorious.

*　　*　　*

With Syphax defeated and Masinissa once more an ally of Rome, the Carthaginian leaders sued for peace. But negotiations broke down when a Roman fleet bringing food to Scipio's army was shipwrecked near Carthage and the citizens, famished after a year cut off from their farmlands, salvaged what they could for themselves. News had also reached Carthage that Hannibal had disembarked at Leptis Minor (Lemta), and with it came new hope. Hannibal was resting his army and raising reinforcements among the African tribes.

The final confrontation was not long delayed. The armies of Hannibal and Scipio met near Zama in central Tunisia. The two generals were reputed to have met before the battle; and indeed, how curious they must have been to see each other, the elder who had been uncrowned king of Spain and seen his kingdom wrested from him by the younger, the younger who remembered the shame of Cannae. But if, as Livy suggests, Hannibal proposed peace terms, Scipio refused them. The battle took place in October 202 B.C. Masinissa was there to support Scipio; but Syphax's son Vermina, with the remnants of his father's army, arrived too late to help Hannibal. It was Hannibal's first defeat in the field, and Scipio's final revenge. It ended the Second Punic War.

Carthage was not yet destroyed: that fate was half a century distant. But she gave up all her foreign territories, and her African land was limited by a trench which Scipio had dug from Thabraca (Tabarka) to Thaenae (near Sfax); beyond, Masinissa was left the ruler of the whole of Numidia. She gave up all her war loot, all the riches she had brought back from Sicily, and had to pay a crippling indemnity of ten thousand talents. She gave up all her warships bar ten triremes, and all her elephants – so deadly an instrument of war did these tanks of the ancient world seem to the Roman legionaries, though their effectiveness was mostly

Ruins of Kerkouann, on the east coast of Cape Bon—the only Phoenician town so far discovered in Africa which was not subsequently built over

limited to inspiring terror (and they tended to be almost as dangerous to their own side as to the enemy).

She still had her greatest son; after a lifetime's absence from his native city, Hannibal by the strength of his personality pushed through financial and agricultural reforms which enabled the Carthaginians to pay off the indemnity within a few years; and she took up once more her old maritime trade. But Carthage was not allowed to wage war, even in self-defence.

Of this fact, Masinissa took full advantage. When Carthage protested to Rome about his annexations the Senate chose not to intervene. For reasons that remain obscure, Hannibal fled into exile in 195 B.C., and spent the remaining dozen years of his life as a soldier of fortune in the pay of Rome's enemies in Asia Minor; had he remained, it is doubtful whether even his genius could have forestalled the ambition of Masinissa to create, out of North Africa, a genuinely African kingdom.

Hitherto, the African kingdoms had been temporary tribal coalitions; Masinissa did not wish to be a tribal chieftain, but a true king, with settled subjects, with a proper army and a fleet financed by taxes rather than by irregular and erratic tribal contributions of men and money.

The Punic example had inspired some agricultural advance in Numidia and there was already a number of towns and villages; but before Masinissa's reign most of the inhabitants remained faithful to their old way of life. 'This was the greatest and most remarkable thing he did', wrote Polybius. 'Before him, the whole of Numidia was useless, and thought to be by its very nature incapable of cultivation. He was the first, he alone, to show that she could yield everything, as much as any other country, for he put to the fullest use enormous areas.' These were mostly in the east of Numidia, but the king himself farmed large estates – so many, according to Diodorus Siculus, that he was able to leave each of his sons, and there were around fifty of them, a property of more than two thousand acres. The new farmers were not settled in outlying farms –

Elephant in North Africa: detail of Roman mosaic in the Bardo Museum, Tunis

the 'unreformed' nomads were too much of a risk for that – but were grouped in townships. Punic administration was borrowed for these new towns, and the worship of the Greek harvest goddesses was introduced, as it had been to Carthage when the Carthaginians took to agriculture two hundred years earlier. Masinissa built himself a new palace at his capital, Cirta, struck his own coinage, and gave his huge family a Greek education. He intended Africa to become part of the Hellenistic world.

Coin portrait of Masinissa

Yet the richest farmlands still belonged to Carthage. Masinissa had his eye on them: was he an ally of Rome for nothing? He seized first one piece of Carthaginian territory, then another; and was encouraged in this rape on his old enemy because the Romans turned a deaf ear to the complaints of Carthage. Masinissa announced that Africa belonged to the Africans.

Rome was content, for the moment, to allow Masinissa to harass Carthage on her behalf: though the graves of the period with their impoverished funeral furnishings show that her previous wealth had vanished, she was building new fortunes. Her merchants were once more familiar in the ports of the east (one of them figures in a comedy of Plautus), she was able to volunteer to build a fleet for her conquerors for their war against Antioch (the offer was refused), and when the elder Cato visited Africa in 153 B.C. he was struck by the threat which the prosperity of Carthaginian agriculture posed to the sadly declining fortunes of his fellow landowners in Italy.

In 174 B.C. Masinissa annexed part of the coast of the Gulf of Syrte, and in 154 B.C. the fertile region around Souk El Khemis. This last was too much; Carthage, illicitly, prepared to defend herself, and sought allies in Mauretania and Libya. Masinissa, now eighty-eight, led the Numidians to victory in 150 B.C.; he hoped to secure Carthage, which he must have looked on as a suitable crown for his life's work.

Rome was by this time alive to the possible dangers of his ambitions: a new and prosperous kingdom, based on Carthage, on the other side of the straits of Sicily. Carthage's action provided her with the perfect excuse to forestall him without actually fighting a friend of fifty years' standing. She would destroy Carthage and annex her territory as a Roman province. Yet fear of Masinissa, whose kingdom was still poor and backward, was certainly not the uppermost motive. Carthage had been the most feared enemy for so long that the Third Punic War was undertaken in a spirit of very real hate, with all the force of ancestral tradition behind it.

The story of Carthage's three-year struggle for survival is one of the most haunting and horrifying in history. It was marked on the Roman side by unsurpassed duplicity and cruelty, and on that of Carthage by all the contradictions of the Punic character: folly and humiliating self-abasement, heroism and self-sacrifice.

The Carthaginians realized they could not hope to win when four legions were landed at Utica in 149 B.C.; the peace party, ready to accede to Roman demands, executed those who counselled resistance, and gave up to the Romans all their armaments, their ships, and three hundred noble children as hostages, even before they knew what the Roman terms would be. These were cruelly, impossibly severe: Carthage was to be abandoned, and its inhabitants, dependent on maritime trade as they were, left free only to rebuild twelve miles from the sea.

It was too much, and Carthage, in her extremity, sold herself dear. 'They no longer fought for their interests,' in the words of the French historian Charles-André Julien, 'but for an idea'. They restocked their arsenals: every day, hundreds of swords and lances were manufactured. The women sacrificed their hair to make ropes for the catapults, for which thousands of large stone bullets were fashioned, some scratched with letters and symbols: great piles of them can be seen today in the garden of the Lavigerie Museum at Carthage and in the Antonine Baths down by the shore. For three years the Carthaginians resisted behind their enormous ramparts, half starving but with no further thought of yielding to anything except death. The city was finally conquered by assault in 146 B.C. by the Roman commander, Scipio Aemilianus, adopted grandson of the Scipio who had defeated Carthage in 202 B.C.; even then, when the Romans had breached the defence, the carnage went on for six days and six nights. The second-century A.D. historian Appian has left an unforgettable account, based on a lost chapter of Polybius, who actually witnessed the siege:

'Three streets leading from the market place to the citadel were lined on both sides with six-storey houses, from which the Romans were pelted. They seized the first houses and used them as a base for attacking the next. From their roofs they made bridges of planks and beams to cross over to the next. While one battle was in progress on the roofs, another was fought, against all comers, in the street below. Everywhere there was groaning and wailing and shouting and agony of every description. Some were killed out of hand, some flung down alive from the roofs to the pavement, and of these some were caught on upright spears or sabres or swords. Fires . . . spread devastation far and wide . . . Those told to remove the debris with axes, crowbars and boathooks and smooth a way for the infantry shoved the dead and those still living into holes in the ground, using their axes and crowbars and shoving and turning them with their tools like blocks of wood or stone. Human beings filled up the gullies. Some were thrown in head down, and their legs protruding from the ground writhed for a considerable while. Some fell feet down and their heads were above the surface. Their faces and skulls were trampled by the galloping horses, not through the riders' design but because of haste.

'Nor had the sweepers done their deed of design: there was the tension of battle, the expectation of quick victory, the excitement of the soldiery, the shouts of the criers and blasts of the trumpets, the commands of officers to advance or retire – all of which created a kind of madness and an indifference to what their eyes saw. Six days were spent on this effort . . .'

House by house, street by street, the city was taken. The wife of the Carthaginian commander sent a message to Scipio, begging that her two children might be spared; the request was granted. But when she saw her husband finally give himself up to the Romans she turned on him for not fighting to the death, and threw herself with her children into the flames of the dying city: a true compatriot of Dido and Sophonisba.

Even at that moment, Scipio saw the poignancy of the city's fate, and thought of Rome: Polybius noticed him weeping and heard him quoting Homer's lines, 'One day Holy Troy will perish also, and Priam, and the people of Priam . . .'

The few survivors were sold into slavery; the ground was formally cursed and sprinkled with salt; the first Roman governor took up residence at Utica.

Ammunition of a war of long ago: stone catapult balls used during the siege of Carthage in 146 B.C., now piled in the gardens of the Antonine Baths

3   New masters for Africa

Street at Djemila (ancient Cuicul), Algeria

The fertility of North Africa had certainly not been lost on Cato, brandishing figs in the Roman Senate as he reiterated 'Delenda est Carthago', nor on his hearers; but the new masters of Africa did not at once set about exploiting their conquest. For a hundred years, their policy was dictated by defence. They were resolved that no power should again arise on the far side of the straits of Sicily which could threaten either their hold on Sicily or their sea routes across the Mediterranean. Not that their acquisition of Africa can exactly be regarded as an accident: during the next century they established their rule round the whole of the Mediterranean basin, and the coasts of Carthage and the Berber kingdoms could scarcely have escaped the common fate for long. But the Romans persuaded themselves, even in the time of Augustus when the whole of the civilized western world, and much beyond, was patrolled by their legions, that their Empire was won simply to safeguard their own position. 'According to Livy,' said Gibbon of the great historian of the Augustan age, 'Rome conquered the world in self-defence.' It was a self-deception which was shared by many of his contemporaries, and explains, at least in part, why Rome was so slow to take advantage of the province which was to become perhaps the most valuable as a source of food, and at the least cost in men and money.

But there was another reason. The Republic was not equipped, and never adapted itself, to run an empire. It was as if 'Marylebone Borough Council suddenly found itself presented with Ireland, France, and half Spain,' in J. C. Stobart's apt simile. Rome had acquired Sicily after the First Punic War, Corsica and Sardinia after Carthage's Mercenary War, Spain after the Second Punic War, Africa after the Third, and Macedonia in the same year, 146 B.C. – five provinces in the space of a century, and the Romans still had no coherent provincial administration. Senators were sent out to govern for one year; they had absolute authority, military, executive and judicial, and there was no bureaucracy either to help them or to keep a check on them, just a

Ruins of Kbor Klib, near Mactar, a vast monumental altar built to celebrate the safety of the nearby city of Zama during Caesar's African campaign in 46 B.C.

virtually private staff who gathered the taxes which Rome had decreed more or less as she thought fit. The traditional honesty of the Roman aristocracy which had so amazed Polybius when he first went to Rome soon deserted its representatives abroad, surrounded by the temptations offered by rich provincial cities; speculation and the worst forms of usury and tax-farming were to become so commonplace that even a man of Cicero's probity did not hesitate to line his pockets with a fortune. The provinces did not regret the death of the Republic. It was left to the Empire with its colonial service to restore to the Romans some pride in doing their best for their subject peoples, rather than merely for themselves.

Carthage having been sacked, Africa was not ripe for this kind of wholesale exploitation. A watching brief limited to peace-keeping and the exaction of war tribute was the extent of official Roman policy. The territory enclosed by the ditch which the earlier Scipio had had dug after Hannibal's defeat, from Thabraca on the north coast south-east to the Gulf of Gabès, was surveyed and divided to simplify the calculation of the burden of tax. It was rented either in small parcels to those inhabitants who had not sided with the Carthaginians, or to Roman *censores* who farmed it out themselves; or the land was sold in larger lots to rich men in Italy – the beginning of the vast *latifundia* which were later to arouse the cupidity of Nero. There was room enough for extortion and repression, but only of a comparatively minor sort. Elsewhere, the Romans left the provincials to manage their own lives. Although towns and villages which had been loyal to Carthage were sacked and their occupants sold into slavery, the remainder, even in Carthaginian territory, continued to govern themselves in the Punic manner. Even the official language was Punic (many Numidians now learnt it for the first time). Enterprising Italian traders came to settle in the coastal towns and at Cirta; a few impoverished Italian farmers immigrated under their own steam; and a quarter of a century after the sack of Carthage the Gracchi brothers tried to settle several thousand Italians in holdings in northern Tunisia as part of their agricultural reforms. But there was no serious official colonization of the new province by the Romans, and the native kingdoms were left to themselves.

This proved a mistake. Carthage as a military threat may have been destroyed for ever, but the Africans could be counted on to quarrel among themselves, largely because the problem of the succession to African thrones, which was not based on primogeniture but on the eldest-of-the-family principle or a division between brothers, was never resolved. The Romans found themselves dragged against their will into dynastic squabbles. Worse, during the civil wars of the last decades of the Republic, rival candidates to the throne of Numidia took opposite sides in the struggle for power in Rome. This was their undoing. It was one thing to make trouble for each other, quite another to interfere in the internal affairs of Rome itself, to side with one Roman general against another. From that moment, even nominal independence was doomed.

Masinissa, who had died during the siege of Carthage, had been succeeded as king of Numidia by his son Micipsa; he, like his father, was a loyal ally of Rome and a competent ruler. But the succession problem which had bedevilled Masinissa's own rise to power was masked, not ended; Micipsa's

two brothers had died, leaving him sole heir. One of those brothers, however, had left a bastard son, Jugurtha, who was older than Micipsa's two sons. Jugurtha was a young man worthy of his grandfather, outstandingly handsome and brave, a great huntsman and soldier, and very popular with his uncle's subjects. According to Sallust, whose *Jugurthine War* is the principal source for the dramatic feud which was to follow, Micipsa realized that his nephew would be a dangerous rival to his own sons and for this reason sent him as commander of Numidian troops to fight for the Romans against the rebellious Iberian tribes, hoping that he would be killed. The plan, if such it was, failed. Jugurtha distinguished himself during the campaign, made many friends among the young Roman noblemen who were fighting alongside him, and returned to Numidia more popular than ever with his troops, and with an enthusiastic letter of recommendation to Micipsa from the Roman commander, Scipio. Micipsa took the hint: he made Jugurtha joint heir with his two sons, Hiempsal and Adherbal.

It was disastrous. When Micipsa died in 118 B.C., the cousins were unable to keep up the pretence. Micipsa's sons were jealous, and Jugurtha, believing himself the better man, was impetuous and greedy. Murdering Hiempsal and defeating Adherbal in battle, he seized the throne for himself and set about bribing his friends in the Roman Senate to turn a blind eye to his action.

The Romans were in some difficulty. Jugurtha was clearly in the wrong, and it was difficult to resist the appeals of Adherbal, who had fled to Rome to canvass for the support he deserved. They could hardly ignore the situation, since Numidia was a client kingdom; but they delayed. Jugurtha visited Rome to distribute more bribes, to encourage further delay. When, eventually, they decreed that half Numidia should go to Adherbal, they did not back up the decision with force. Jugurtha was soon showing further contempt for the imperial power, and the cousins were once more at war. Still the Romans showed no signs of intervening.

In 112 B.C., however, Jugurtha brought

them down on his head. He committed the error, while sacking Cirta as a punishment for sheltering Adherbal, of killing indiscriminately all the adult male inhabitants, a large number of whom were Italian settlers. The Romans felt obliged to avenge this atrocity. The war which then broke out, during the latter stages of which the generals Marius and Sulla made their names, lasted for six years, and ended only when Jugurtha's father-in-law, King Bocchus of Mauretania, was induced to betray him and deliver him in chains to Sulla. Jugurtha died in prison in Rome, but he left behind him the legendary reputation of a heroic defender of Africa against Rome, as his grandfather Masinissa had been the symbol of the struggle against Carthage. He was not the last.

Still the Romans did not learn that they had scotched the snake, not killed it. The Republic contented itself with taking over the Tripolitanian ports which were the outlets for the trans-Saharan trade; it made no move to annex the heartland of Numidia, which was given to a feeble-minded half-brother of Jugurtha called Gauda, from whom, for the moment, they must have felt they had nothing to fear. Their new ally, Bocchus of Mauretania, was rewarded for his treachery to his son-in-law by the western part of Numidia. Some of Marius's veterans, following what was beginning to be standard Roman practice in Italy with retired soldiers, were given land at the end of their army service on the border between the province of Africa and Numidia. But even though it was becoming clear that the Berber princes could not be relied on to rule their client kingdoms in peace or without involving Rome in tiresome and expensive punitive expeditions, the Republic made no attempt to extend its authority.

The next wars on African soil stemmed directly from the civil wars in Italy. The two sons of Gauda who shared the throne of Numidia after his death were delighted to make an excuse of the rivalry between Marius and Sulla in order to advance their own cause at the expense of the other; Hiempsal took the part of Sulla, Hierbas that of Marius. When Marius was defeated,

and with him Hierbas, who was put to death in 81 B.C. by Sulla's troops under their commander Pompey, Hiempsal was left as sole ruler of Numidia. Once more the succession problem had been resolved by force. But the wheel of fortune turned: thirty-five years later Hiempsal and his son Juba I chose the wrong side during the civil war of the Triumvirate. When the Three Men, Caesar, Pompey and Crassus, had divided the Roman provinces between them, Pompey received Africa; not unnaturally, when war broke out between Caesar and Pompey, the Numidian king sided with Pompey, who was not only governor of Africa but had rid him, long ago, of his brother Hierbas. After Pompey's death at Pharsalus, the Pompeian party continued to hold Africa and wage war against Caesar from there. It was not then by any means a foregone conclusion that Caesar would become the master of the Roman world.

It was no more certain when Caesar finally landed in Africa to do battle with his adversaries; his troops were fewer, and his principal ally was an Italian soldier of fortune called Sittius who had fled to Mauretania after a spectacular bankruptcy. Although he could also count on the two kings of Mauretania, well to the west, the Pompeian strength was more than fifty thousand, not counting Juba I's large forces, to his thirty-three thousand. But in 46 B.C. Caesar defeated the Pompeian army at Thapsus, on the coast a few miles north of Mahdia. It was one of the decisive battles of the ancient world. Caesar lost fifty men; his enemies lost ten thousand.

At almost the same moment, Sittius annihilated Juba's army, which was guarding Numidia, and both his kingdom and Pompey's province fell to Caesar. The leading Pompeians committed suicide; for Juba, too, there was only one way out, and he engaged in a fight to the death with a Roman legionary. A slave dispatched the survivor; no one knows which it was. Juba's young son was taken to Rome in Caesar's train to be shown off in his triumph.

*　　*　　*

Coin portrait of Juba I

Statue of a Roman legionary, now in the British Museum

It was Julius Caesar who at last extended direct Roman rule well beyond Scipio's *fossa regia,* which had for a hundred years marked the boundary of the province. At one stroke, the territory of the province was trebled to include most of Numidia. The old *Africa* was now called *Africa Vetus* to distinguish it from *Africa Nova,* as the new annexation was called. The historian Sallust was appointed Africa Nova's first governor; his governorship gave him the opportunity to gather material for *The Jugurthine War* but was principally remarkable for the rapacity with which he made the most of his other opportunities, a rapacity which shocked even his contemporaries, accustomed though they were to the nabob behaviour of Roman proconsuls out to make their fortunes from the luckless inhabitants of conquered provinces. But at least Caesar, if he was unable to introduce the Africans to the happier aspects of Roman rule, had learned the lesson of his campaign in Africa: that from the Roman point of view, and in some ways from their own, the Berber kingdoms were better abolished. True, King Bocchus of Mauretania was rewarded for his support in the Thapsus campaign by the western part of Numidia; but his independence can have been that only in name, since for eight years after his death in 33 B.C. his kingdom was ruled by Roman prefects, and then handed over by Augustus, apparently without arousing any protest from the inhabitants, to Juba II, the Romanized son of Juba I. Numidia itself, as a separate political entity, soon vanished for ever.

Caesar was also responsible for the first major Roman settlements in Africa. Sittius was installed with his veterans on the western frontier of Africa Nova in a client kingdom based on Cirta, which formed a useful buffer state between the Roman territory and Mauretania and, when Sittius died, could be readily absorbed into the province. Caesar also settled in Africa others of his veterans and – following the example of the Gracchi brothers – some of the dispossessed Italian peasants who were by now creating serious population problems in Rome itself. Thysdrus (El Djem), Hippo Diarrhytus (Bizerta), and three or four places in the Cape Bon peninsula were among the townships which probably received Julian colonies during Caesar's brief reign.

His principal project, however, was the re-founding of Carthage, which Caius Gracchus had first suggested eighty years earlier. Before he could make it a reality he was murdered, and although freelance settlers did install themselves on land just outside the city some years after Caesar's death, it was fifteen years before Augustus Caesar, in 29 B.C., officially refounded on the site of the Punic capital a city which, under the Empire, was to become once again a great metropolis of the Mediterranean world.

The struggle for the control of the Roman world which followed the murder of Caesar in 44 B.C. led, again, to a period of confused fighting in Africa. The two provinces passed from Octavius, to Mark Antony, to Lepidus; Africa Vetus fought Africa Nova; and it was only in 36 B.C. that Octavius, Caesar's great-nephew and soon to become Augustus Caesar, became their uncontested master.

The great war lasted until Octavius defeated Mark Antony and Cleopatra at Actium five years later.

Huge armies had been involved in the wars, and Augustus, once he had triumphed over his rivals, was faced with the problem of reducing the number of soldiers and disbanding the rest. In his *Res Gestae*, a summary of his achievements which he composed late in life to be inscribed on his tomb (copies of which have been found in Asia Minor), he claims that during his reign he either sent back to their own towns or settled in colonies more than three hundred thousand men. Some of those veterans, like those of Caesar, were settled in Africa: inland from Carthage, at places like Sicca Veneria (Le Kef), Thuburbo Maius – still, today, one of the most impressive Roman sites in Tunisia – and Uthina (Oudna); and also, a new departure, far to the west in Mauretania. There were half a dozen Augustan colonies on the coast between Igilgili (Djidjelli) and Cartennas (Ténès) and another three inland to help bolster up the authority of the

Portico at Thuburbo Maius, near Pont du Fahs in Tunisia—a city originally settled by veterans of the armies of the Emperor Augustus

new man whom Augustus now put in to rule Mauretania. The Romanization of Africa was about to begin in earnest.

Augustus gave Mauretania in 25 B.C. to Juba II of Numidia, then twenty-six or twenty-seven years old. Julius Caesar, cheated of the chance of displaying the elder Juba in his triumph, had taken his young son to Rome in his stead, and when Caesar was murdered the prince was brought up in the household of Caesar's adopted son Octavius. Like other sons of the Roman nobility of the day, he was given an education more Greek than Latin. He proved a willing pupil. He grew up with a passion for the arts, for literature, and for science, and wrote books himself – all in Greek – on the history of Rome, on Arabia, on the Assyrians, on African geography, on painting, on the

Statue of Augustus in the courtyard of the museum at Cherchel (Caesarea)

theatre, even on a medicinal herb. All these books are lost; their contents are known only through what was repeated or plagiarized by other writers; the king seems, for all his encyclopaedic knowledge, to have been more credulous than critical. Yet in one sphere at least he was exceptional: he had a genuine and discriminating appreciation of art, and especially of Greek sculpture.

Juba married Cleopatra Selene, the daughter of Mark Antony and Cleopatra. She, too, had been taken to Rome after the defeat and death of her parents and brought up in Augustus's household (by his sister Octavia, Mark Antony's generous and forgiving widow). Together these two children of Rome's enemies created at Iol Caesarea (Cherchel), King Bocchus's old capital which Juba renamed in honour of Augustus, what must have seemed to them, in their exile from all they had known in their youth, an oasis of cosmopolitan civilization. A temple, a palace, a theatre were built in classical style, celebrated actors imported, a fine library founded, statues commissioned from Greek ateliers. It is to this royal art patron, wholly African by blood, that the museums of Algiers and Cherchel owe the finest works of Greco-Roman art found in Africa. He also founded a second capital far to the west, at Volubilis in modern Morocco; here, too, many of the beautiful bronzes in the museum are almost certainly a testimony to his taste. Some even think that the splendid cargo of Greek bronzes and statues found in 1907 in a Roman galley sunk two thousand years before off Mahdia, on the eastern coast of Tunisia, and now in the Bardo Museum in Tunis, was on its way not to Rome but to Caesarea.

Although his tastes were Greek and his lineage African, Juba's loyalty was to Rome and to his protector Augustus. It never wavered during his fifty-year reign. From that point of view at least, the Emperor had chosen his agent of civilization with his customary prudence. Juba's kingdom was, however, enormous, mountainous, and extremely vulnerable to attack from nomads who did not relish subservience to Rome as much as he did. If Augustus had hopes that Juba would be able to suppress risings with his own troops without calling on the help of Roman legionaries, they were not fulfilled. If there was trouble, Rome had to go to the rescue.

For the most important factor in the Romanization of Africa was not one client king or a few thousand Italian settlers. The client king and his heir were soon to vanish, and the handful of cities founded by foreigners in the first century or so of the Roman occupation was rapidly outnumbered by the extraordinary flowering of cities both large and small which sprang up all over north-west Africa. By the turn of the second century, at the height of the province's prosperity, there were nearly six hundred.

The Greek city states had declined not least because, both at home in Greece and abroad in Magna Graecia, they had been unable to avoid fighting each other. Roman rule was a mixed blessing, but the *pax Romana* was not an idle phrase. It was Rome's great gift to the decaying Hellenistic world. She acted as foster mother to the old cities of the east and the new cities of the west, so that they lived comparatively peacefully side by side. And although there were slave revolts, although the last decades of the Republic had brought savage wars between rival Roman generals and their armies all round the Mediterranean, and although all too often legion was to fight against legion to secure the imperial throne for their own candidates (the Berbers were not the only people who failed to solve the succession problem), by and large for four hundred years warfare was confined to the frontiers of the Empire.

Arch of Caracalla of early third century A.D. *at Volubilis, Morocco*

The remarkable prosperity of the lands bordering the Mediterranean was made possible by peace; and peace was made possible by the Roman legions under the command of the Roman Emperor.

* * *

In 27 B.C., Augustus had divided government of the Empire between himself and the Senate. The 'frontier' provinces, where fighting was still going on and which needed legions for their defence, he kept under his control, while the pacified provinces, which needed soldiers only for civilian policing purposes or as a token guard for the proconsul who governed in the name of the Roman people, went to the Senate. To this rule, however, Africa was an exception. Although it was a frontier province and needed a legion to defend it, Augustus ceded it to the Senate. This may have been a diplomatic concession. Already, in the twenty years since Caesar's murder, and in spite of frequent fighting, its cornlands were supplying in tribute two thirds of the wheat which the population of Rome required, while Tripolitania, from which Caesar had exacted an annual *stipendium* of three million pounds of olive oil for taking the Pompeian side during the Thapsus campaign, was clearly a source of wealth as well – quite apart from the trans-Saharan luxury trade which reached the ports of Leptis Magna, Oea (Tripoli) and Sabratha from the unknown lands beyond the desert. Together, Tripolitania, Africa Proconsularis (roughly, Tunisia) and the eastern part of Numidia which Caesar had annexed were a valuable property: too valuable, perhaps, for a tactful Emperor to lay his hands on it. So it was the proconsul, the representative of the Senate, now in residence in the newly-founded Carthage, who was commander-in-chief of the Third Augustan Legion which the Emperor seconded to the province.

The Third Augustan Legion's first garrison in Africa was at Ammaedara (Haïdra) in the high plateau country some hundred and fifty miles south-west of Carthage. This was a strategic position from which it could

Part of the great quay at Leptis Magna. The harbour, to the left, is now silted up

defend the fertile river valleys, which drain into the Gulf of Tunis, from the raids of the nomad tribes of the Aurès mountains to the south-west. It was recruited at this time largely from Rome's western provinces, in particular from Gaul (the soldiers of General Bugeaud who conquered Algeria in 1830 were not the first Gallic troops to set foot there); it was Augustus's policy to guard the provinces with legions raised in other parts of the Empire, so that the soldiers were not tempted by ties of kinship to make common cause with refractory natives. This policy was to change; but for the moment the Third Augustan Legion was a body of some five or six thousand foreigners. But they were Latin-speaking and Roman-trained and even when, a century or so later, they raised legionaries in Africa itself, those recruits all had to learn the Latin language and Roman discipline, and were trained in Roman skills of all kinds.

For four hundred years the Third Augustan was the only Roman legion permanently garrisoned in North Africa. Although it was assisted by auxiliary units recruited on the spot, its effective strength was only about thirteen thousand men. The defence of Mauretania, which was economically least valuable to the Romans, was left to two other army corps, which comprised some thirteen thousand auxiliaries. Together they were responsible for the keeping of internal peace and for defence from outside attack. A frontier some fifteen hundred miles long, which stretched from the Atlantic to the Libyan desert, was held, if sometimes with difficulty, by fewer than thirty thousand men, of whom less than a quarter were trained to the most rigorous Roman standards. In times of crisis, reinforcements were drafted in from other parts of the Empire, from Pannonia, for instance, or Spain, as we know from inscriptions and gravestones; but it was the Third Augustan Legion which bore the brunt.

It was kept busy. Although Masinissa and his predecessors and successors had founded townships and had settled some of their tribesmen as farmers, many of the Berbers still followed the traditional life of the nomad,

Remains of an oil press at Timgad

inside the province as well as on the fringes, even in the long settled parts of Tunisia. They mostly kept themselves to themselves in the hills or forests, unless in summer they hired themselves out to the farmers of the plains as casual labour at harvest-time; they seem to have worked out a peaceable *modus vivendi* between them, and they were in any case too few to be a serious threat. As time went on, most of them were absorbed into the farming community. Further west in Numidia, where the mountains were higher and the settled farmers fewer, there were whole ranges which the Romans never attempted to colonize, to which certain tribes retreated to lead their own lives; yet even here, Roman influence eventually penetrated to a considerable extent.

At the southern limit of Roman territory in the east, however, the new order disrupted the old pattern of transhumation. This is the practice whereby grazing animals are moved every spring and autumn between their winter and summer grazing grounds, which are sometimes hundred of miles apart. The tribesmen of the Saharan foothills wintered with their flocks in the warmer south, and in spring, when the fierce sun had burnt off the sparse winter grass and shrubs and the oueds had run dry, would retreat to the wetter, cooler, more fertile steppes further north, returning to their southern pastures every autumn. This need for vast areas of land explains the extraordinary territorial size of the primitive Numidian kingdoms. Now they had to watch the new invaders extending their control, and with it ploughed fields, towards and even beyond the southern limit of the area which enjoyed an annual rainfall of at least twelve inches or more, the limit at which corn could be grown and where, not unnaturally, the grass too grew greener. The nomads were being driven away from their summer grazing grounds; in their eyes, their country was being stolen from them, and with it their livelihood. They did not yield either easily.

In 21 B.C., within a year or two of the Legion's arrival, the proconsul of Africa was awarded a triumph for a military campaign about which nothing is known except that it must have been fierce enough to deserve a triumph; and the following year the new proconsul, L. Cornelius Balbus, was faced with a rising along the whole southern frontier, from Mauretania to Tripolitania. Although Balbus conquered the Garamantes of Tripolitania and, in a notable expedition into the desert four hundred miles south of Sabratha, seized the oases of Garama (Germa) and Cydamae (Ghadames), the Roman victory was not permanent, for a further campaign had to be sent against the Garamantes a few years later; and in Mauretania fighting was endemic for a quarter of a century, until the western tribes were defeated – again, only for the moment – in A.D. 6.

In A.D. 17 the most serious of the African frontier wars broke out. This was the revolt of the Musulamii under Tacfarinas. In A.D. 14, the last year of Augustus's reign, the Third Augustan Legion had constructed their first military road in Africa, which ran north-west from the port of Tacapae (Gabès) in southern Tunisia to their garrison at Ammaedara (Haïdra) – right across the Musulamians' traditional routes between their summer and winter grazing grounds. The new road was therefore a provocation. Like Jugurtha before him and many another of the Empire's most dangerous enemies, Tacfarinas had learnt the art of war from the Romans themselves; he added gifts of his own. Tacitus tells us that Tacfarinas 'had deserted from service as a Roman auxiliary. His first followers were vagabonds and marauders who came for loot. Then he organized them into army units and formations, and was finally recognized as the chief, no longer of an undisciplined gang, but of the Musulamian people – a powerful nomad tribe on the edge of the desert. Taking up arms, they brought in the neighbouring Mauretanians, under their leader Mazippa . . . Tacfarinas retained in camp an élite force equipped in Roman fashion, which he instructed in discipline and obedience; while Mazippa's light-armed troops burnt, killed, and intimidated.' It was a model guerrilla campaign, with Tacfarinas 'giving way under pressure and then attacking from the rear.' Conventional Roman victories had little meaning in such a war; the survivors simply retreated to the desert to reform and return to make lightning raids where they were least expected and constantly harry the static Roman positions.

The Romans soon learnt that guerrilla attacks must be parried by guerrilla tactics, but Tacfarinas was not easily defeated. Despite frequent setbacks, he 'raised reinforcements in the interior and had the insolence to send representatives to Tiberius [who had succeeded Augustus as Emperor] demanding land for himself and his army. As the alternative, he offered endless war. No personal or national slur, it is said, ever provoked the Emperor more than the sight of this deserter and brigand behaving like a hostile sovereign . . . With Roman power at its height, was this bandit Tacfarinas to be bought off by a treaty granting lands?'

The enraged Tiberius ordered an amnesty in the hope that many rebels would lay down their arms, and the Romans hurriedly taught themselves new methods of war, mobile, light-armed, fast striking, the very antithesis of the solid legionary formations. They even, most unusually, continued fighting in winter. But in spite of some success, including the capture of Tacfarinas's brother, 'enough of the enemy were left to revive hostilities'; and Tacfarinas was still at large.

The fighting flared up with renewed vigour when Juba II died in A.D. 23, leaving Mauretania to his son Ptolemy – 'too young for responsibility,' reports Tacitus with unusual mildness: in fact a debauched and lazy man in his twenties – and the Moors revolted against the tyrannical rule of the new king's favourites. Tacfarinas appealed to all who preferred freedom to slavery to make a united effort to get rid of the Romans altogether, and soon had a new army composed not only of Musulamii and Moors but also of disaffected or dispossessed peasants from Africa Proconsularis itself, and of troops sent by the king of the Garamantes. The Roman governor of the year, however, was a man of energy and military gifts called Dolabella; and within a few months, having induced the unwilling Ptolemy to join the fight, his troops surprised the enemy in their encampment at Auzea (Aumale), some fifty miles south-east of Caesarea, in a dawn attack: they 'were dragged to death or captivity like sheep', and Tacfarinas himself was killed. With his death, the heart went out of the rebellion. It had lasted seven years.

The revolt of Tacfarinas was not the last of the frontier uprisings, but it was the last serious one which the Romans had to face, so far as is known, for more than two hundred years. There were plenty of others, for the antipathy between desert and sown was chronic, but they were better 'contained'; the Romans now knew the kind of warfare they could expect, and had learnt that mobility was more important than brute strength. There was another important reform. In A.D. 40, in the third year of his reign, the Emperor Caligula took the Third Augustan Legion out of the control of the proconsul, who was appointed annually by the Senate and could not provide continuity of command (nor necessarily military experience), and entrusted it to a legate chosen by himself for his professional capacities as a soldier. For form's sake, the legate was under the proconsul; in fact he was in complete control, not only militarily but administratively, of the whole region where Roman troops were garrisoned.

At the same time, Mauretania was annexed to the Empire. Juba's son Ptolemy, who had no heir, was the last king. He had been officially recognized as *socius et amicus* of Rome for his part in the war against Tacfarinas; now he was to be rewarded for his presumption in appearing at an imperial function in a style even more ostentatiously luxurious than that of his cousin Caligula (they were both descended from Mark Antony). The Emperor, his jealousy inflamed by greed, had him put to death and seized his kingdom, though not without trouble. Aedemon, a freedman loyal to Ptolemy, raised a rebellion in protest, which took Caligula's successor Claudius some three or four years to put down. But the rising is of note as the occasion of another Roman expedition to the far south. In pursuit of the Moors retreating to the desert, C. Suetonius Paulinus (celebrated as the conqueror of Boadicea) led his troops into the typical *reg* of the Sahara, all bare rocks and black gravel. Though it was midwinter, his troops suffered from heatstroke and thirst. He turned back after ten days' march; henceforth the western desert was left to its own people.

There were also expeditions across the central Sahara towards the end of the first century A.D. The first was a disciplinary foray in A.D. 69, when the Garamantes from the Fezzan pillaged the territory of Leptis Magna. Later, the Romans mounted two exploratory campaigns: one under Septimius Flaccus, a march of some three or four months into 'the midst of the Aethiopians' (perhaps as far as the Tibesti mountains), the other under Julius Maternus to the land of Agisymba (unidentified), 'where the rhinoceroses foregather' – probably Lake Chad. These remarkable journeys had no known sequel, except that there appear to have been close ties between the people of the

Fezzan and the Romans from that time onward. At Germa, the capital, four hundred and thirty miles south of Leptis Magna, is the most southerly Roman monument in Africa, first noted by an English traveller in 1826, a magnificent mausoleum probably dating from the late first century A.D. Even more interesting is the complex of canals and subterranean aqueducts built to collect rainwater, which were discovered in the 1930s by an Italian archaeological expedition. There are other Roman remains which suggest not merely links with Rome, but Roman residents – not rulers or administrators, but technical experts, perhaps, lent to advise the inhabitants on irrigating and farming their unpromising country. A settled, farming community was less likely to plunder the richer territory to the north. At one time, when Roman power was at its greatest, the Sahara may have formed a vast, semi-independent feudatory state, although the Romans certainly made no serious attempts to conquer it and rule it directly. Trans-

Leptis Magna, Libya: the arch of Trajan seen through the arch of Tiberius

Saharan trade was always left to the caravans of the Garamantes.

From now on Roman Africa consists of Mauretania as far south as Volubilis (divided for administrative convenience into Mauretania Tingitana and Mauretania Caesariensis); Numidia as far south as the Aurès mountains; and Africa Proconsularis with the narrow coastal strip of Tripolitania. Between the first and third centuries of our era these regions were fundamentally peaceful, especially the fertile north-east.

*　　*　　*

To be a soldier posted for half a lifetime to a garrison on the frontier was, for decades at a stretch, boring rather than perilous. The desert tribes outside the borders probably numbered no more than a hundred thousand, at the most; during the course of centuries, many must have been drawn to settle inside the province themselves. There was resistance, of course, every time the Romans pushed their frontier further south; sometimes they pushed it south to suppress raiding parties; but such extensions probably brought new settlers, or, as much of the land was mountainous and unfit for dry farming, a certain amount of transhumation, duly regulated, was permitted across the border. In the interior, some precautions had to be taken against sudden raids from isolated mountain communities. The cities of the west, civilian as well as military, were walled: at Volubilis, the territory of the Baquates tribe reached almost to the gates, and others were occasionally besieged. But the same must have held true of many of these tribesmen also: they were gradually drawn under the Roman influence. More remarkably, others, in mountain communities, kept entirely out of the way. The Romans did not disturb them, and the Arab invasions also passed them by. Their descendants to this day live in villages in the Aurès or the Khroumirie, speaking their pre-Roman, pre-Punic languages and following their ancient Berber customs. In the Kabylie mountains pottery is still made to a pre-Punic geometric pattern. Rome had very little effect on the

Hexagonal mausoleum at Haïdra (ancient Ammaedara) in Tunisia, once the Third Augustan Legion's headquarters

far west, the Arabs hardly more; in Morocco a third of the population is still Berber-speaking. In southern Tunisia, at Matmata and Maknassy, there are even pockets of a Stone Age way of life, troglodytes living in underground warrens; Herodotus knew of them, but the outside world was brought to them not by Roman legionaries or camel-borne Arabs but by tar-macadam, carrying the tourist buses from Gabès.

In the north-east, in spite of occasional reports in the ancient authorities and inscriptions of skirmishes and raids, trouble was exceptional. The unwalled cities, the vast olive groves of the second century, the vulnerable aqueducts – all are silent witnesses to the tranquillity of the countryside. Twenty-six thousand men would not otherwise have been enough to hold a long frontier and police a difficult interior. (Britain, far smaller, needed four legions.)

Defence and security, the protective skin of Roman Africa, were not the only concerns of the Third Augustan Legion. The army also supplied the sinews.

4   The conquest of a country

So-called bridge of Trajan, near Béja, probably built under Tiberius in A.D. *29 : it carried the road from Carthage to Bulla Regia and Hippo Regius*

There is a legend that a Roman soldier fell in love with a Berber princess, who, as proud as Dido, wanted nothing to do with him; she would never marry him, she said, until the waters of Zaghouan flowed to Carthage. The impossible condition was fulfilled, the fifty-mile aqueduct which still strides across the plain of the River Miliana was built; the Roman claimed his bride, who threw herself in despair from the summit. The story perfectly illustrates that the Roman genius for the art of the possible extended to the incredible. They saw possibilities where none had seen them before. Where others had seen them but had been overfaced by difficulty, they saw only a job to be done, and did it. Carthage needed more water.

Of course great roads and aqueducts and irrigation systems had been constructed before; pyramids had been built, fifty-ton blocks of stone quarried, transported, dressed and carved and set on end for palaces and temples; but the Romans were the first to realize that the techniques developed by their predecessors could be applied on a vast scale, and extended to the remotest corners of the Empire or the smallest needs of everyday life. The sheer size of the Roman conception required an imaginative leap which took civil engineering right beyond the dictates of immediate necessity or religious awe, beyond palaces and temples and royal tombs and processional ways. Magnificence had been hitherto the prerogative of kings and priests; the Romans made it secular. Their genius was firmly grounded in an infinite capacity for taking pains, but it was more than that. They applied their minds and skills to mastering their environment to an unprecedented degree. If something was necessary, or even desirable, and

The first-century A.D. nymphaeum (a fountain dedicated to nymphs) beneath the Djebel Zaghouan: from here, a fifty-mile aqueduct carried water to Roman Carthage

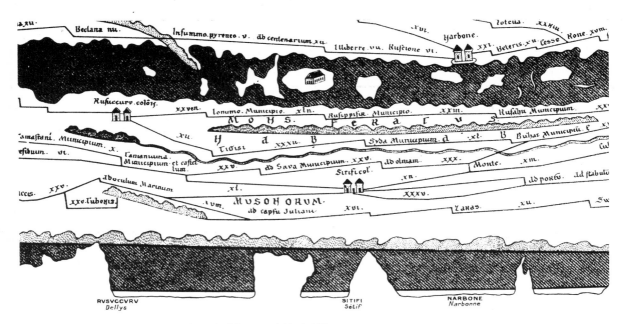

Part of the Table of Peutinger, showing the south of France and North Africa

if it was possible, then they did it, however difficult; and took the doing for granted.

The surveyors and civil engineers of the Roman world were the legions. The Roman army was not only an army of soldiers, but an army of sappers. For in order to conduct war properly, they needed communications; above all roads and harbours. In order to prevent war breaking out, they needed camps and fortifications; and these needed a proper water supply. In order to keep some track of their conquered territories, and to organize the redistribution and taxation of property and to make the collection of corn tribute possible, they needed to survey them.

Nothing reveals the Romans' methodical thoroughness better than the great survey of the new province of Africa which was put in hand by Scipio immediately after the sack of Carthage. It was more than a survey, for at the same time the land was divided into basic agricultural units by means of ditches or roads. In Africa, this unit was about eight hundred yards square, so that there were four to the Roman square mile. Traces of this vast digging operation can be seen from the air over the greater part of Tunisia; they extend right to the edge of the desert and the borders of the Chott Djerid. Only mountains, forests and marshes were ignored: the Romans did not attempt to turn into agricultural land what was uncultivable or not needed. What astonishes is the inclusion in their land

Remains of the aqueduct crossing the valley of the oued Miliana, some twenty miles south of Tunis

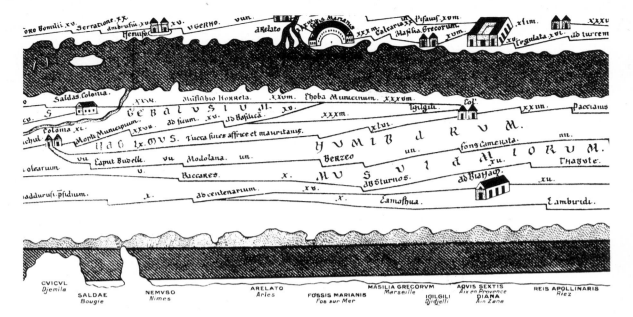

CVICVL
Djemila · SALDAE
Bougie · NEMVSO
Nimes · ARELATO
Arles · FOSSIS MARIANIS
Fos sur Mer · MASILIA GRECORVM
Marseille · IGILGILI
Djidjelli · AQVIS SEXTIS
Aix en Provence · DIANA
Ain Zana · REIS APOLLINARIS
Riez

system of large areas, particularly in the south, which look today as if they have never known cultivation; but the Romans must have found them worth their while or they would not have been included.

This survey and division of the land was the work of the army surveyors. If much of the hard labour was done by slaves or auxiliaries, it was all supervised by the Legion. It must have taken several centuries for all North Africa's farmlands. It took one hundred and sixty years in Africa Proconsularis. But once the bulk of the province was covered, the work must have kept pace with the gradual penetration of the military to the south and west.

The roads were closely linked with the survey, often serving as boundaries of newly-mapped territories, and guide-lines for further division. They, too, followed the army. The Carthaginians had left behind them roads linking their capital with its neighbours, there were a number of roads in Tripolitania, and others between the larger towns; to begin with, the Romans must have made use of these, patching them up as need be. But their view of the function of roads was more systematic than that of any people before them. They saw that a road linking two minor towns was itself of minor importance, unless it also formed part of a logical net-

work of roads covering a whole province. That logic was first military, second administrative – for the collection of corn and taxes – and only a very poor third, though very useful, for the benefit of the inhabitants.

The two hundred mile Tacapae-Ammaedara military road which the Third Augustan Legion had constructed by A.D. 14 was the first road of which there is an epigraphical record, part of the network of roads in Africa which, by the middle of the third century, totalled some twelve thousand miles. Few traces of this network remain. Away from the cities, only one road was paved with flagstones, the main route from Carthage through Ammaedara and south-west to Theveste (Tébessa), a garrison which became the Legion's new headquarters some time in the first century. The rest – though properly constructed of three or four well-drained layers of large stones, smaller stones and gravel, one or more bound with mortar, laid out in a trench perhaps two or three feet deep – had to make do with a surface of packed earth and large pebbles. Like most monuments of man exposed to the weather, roads, even the best, require upkeep. The modern metalled roads of the Algerian mountains subside under the winter rains often enough; it is scarcely surprising that more than a thousand such winters should

51

have washed away the roads of the Romans. Aerial photography has picked out a number, but nearly all in the dry semi-desert country of the south.

Yet the network has been worked out in considerable detail, thanks to the orderly Roman habit of marking their roads with milestones. More than two thousand have been discovered in Africa; others must lie under the surface. Nearly all, especially those of the early Empire, are neatly and legibly engraved with the name of the Emperor in whose reign the road was built and the number of miles from the nearest military garrison, important crossroads or major city. This was done as much for propaganda purposes, to impress the name of their ruler on the travellers who used the roads, as for the record; but the practice has incidentally enabled scholars to date them.

There is another valuable source of information. A people which brought surveying to a fine art certainly had accurate maps for official use. The elder Pliny reports that a great map of the Roman world was put up in Rome in Augustus's day, and at the beginning of the third century Caracalla put on show a vast map of Roman roads. Unhappily, the only surviving map, Ptolemy's celebrated Geography, is no help at all for roads. However, two Roman itineraries have come down to us, both of which offer clues to Roman roads and settlements in North Africa. The Antonine itinerary has no map; it is simply a list of mileages, possibly made for administrative rather than military use. The Table of Peutinger, named after the man who discovered it at Worms at the end of the fifteenth century, is a twelfth or thirteenth century copy of an enormous third century scroll which showed the main roads of the Roman Empire from Great Britain to the frontiers of India. The scale is too small to be very useful, and roads and rivers are only indicated schematically and quite out of scale, but the Table does give the mileages between cities. Most of Mauretania is missing, but the rest of North Africa, in spite of what seems the eccentric omission of major cities like Thugga (Dougga), Mactar, Cillium (Kasserine) and Sufetula

(Sbeïtla), which may be the copyist's fault, has proved in most respects very accurate.

Inscriptions help too. In the middle of the nineteenth century a French general struggling with a detachment of soldiers through the narrow Tighanimine gorge in the Aurès mountains south of Lambaesis (Lambèse) on a voyage of exploration was astonished to find a Roman inscription cut into the side of the cliff: so little was then known about the history of North Africa that he had thought they were the first Europeans to penetrate so far. The inscription, clearly visible at the side of the modern road, records that a road from Lambaesis to Vescera (Biskra) was constructed in A.D. 145 by a detachment of the Sixth Ferrata Legion – which had no doubt been summoned from Syria when the Third Augustan Legion needed reinforcements to subdue resistance as they pushed the frontier further towards the desert.

Africa's roads took more than two hundred years to construct. But by the end of the first century A.D. Theveste (Tébessa), where the Legion was now quartered, was the centre of a spider's web of roads connecting the garrison not only with Carthage and Capsa (Gafsa) and the coast, but with Hippo Regius (now Annaba, formerly Bône) on the coast due north and, to the west, with military posts on the mountainous frontier leading to Mauretania. There was already a garrison at Auzea (Aumale), south-east of Algiers, where Tacfarinas had been killed; now it was linked, through a string of fortresses along the line of the mountains north of the Chott El Hodna, with the Legion's headquarters. Under Trajan, when the Empire as a whole reached its greatest extent, the frontier was pushed well south of the old frontier road which ran from Theveste to the Gulf of Syrte; a new military road was built, on the Emperor's orders, along the rim of the Sahara south of the Nementcha and Aurès mountains. The nomads were now denied a free run even on these semi-barren hills. Other roads linked the southern shores of Lake Triton with the interior of Tripolitania. Hadrian, who visited Africa in A.D. 125, had the Legion's headquarters moved once more, westwards to Lambaesis, so that

The Sixth Ferrata Legion marked their passage through the Tighanimine gorge in the Aurès in A.D.145 with an inscription (above) in the rock-face (right)

it was better placed to defend the whole length of the frontier. The military road inched on. Other roads were constructed to connect it with the old frontier road: the map was filled in. The Vescera-Lambaesis road built by the Sixth Ferrata Legion led on northwards to the coast by way of Cirta (Constantine), where one of the Romans' finest bridges spanned the deep rift which surrounds the city on three sides. A great road ran the full length of the coast, and there were other major arteries inland leading west through Sitifis (Sétif) towards Mauretania; these, too, were connected by minor roads, mostly the responsibility of the local townships.

In Africa as elsewhere the Romans built their roads as straight as possible. They were designed primarily for marching men; the shortest way, even up steep slopes, was best. Up the steepest hillsides, they did build in loops; but they preferred not to, for their carts, having fixed axles, could turn sharp corners

only if the road was heavily cambered or special ruts were cut into the surface to guide the wheels. Straight roads were best, in spite of the fact that the hard horse collar which was generally introduced some centuries later was probably unknown, and hauling a heavy load uphill made the yoke worn by draught animals press heavily against their windpipes, reducing their efficiency by half. (A load hauled today by one animal was hauled then by two.) If necessary, cuttings and embankments were made to smooth out curves or keep the road as level as possible.

Where they had the choice, the military engineers preferred their roads to run along the crests or sides of mountains rather than in the valley. A low road was vulnerable to sudden raids from the surrounding hills; a high road offered a better view. If, in the mountainous country of Numidia, the Romans did have to build a road through a gorge or along a valley floor, modest fortresses would be built well above it to keep a look-out, within sight of each other so that they could signal in case of trouble. Even after the nomad tribes were largely settled and pacified, there seems to have been a certain amount of brigandage on the roads of Numidia and further west. In Tunisia, which was safer, some gorge roads were left unprotected, but elsewhere the Romans left nothing to chance.

*　　*　　*

The Romans also turned their attention to improving those ports which were most useful to them. Even in Africa, all roads led to Rome; harbours were simply staging posts on that one journey. They concentrated on ports with good access to the interior, which were also near the main centres of production. Carthage itself was the major outlet for the corn tribute of the north-east; the three cities of Tripolitania were the ports used for the export of olive oil and luxuries from across the Sahara – possibly Gigthis (Bou Grara) also; there were half a dozen more on the east coast of Tunisia, and, in the north, the marble of Simitthu (Chemtou) was exported through Thabraca (Tabarka); the Legion at Lambaesis used Rusicade (Philippeville);

Tingis (Tangiers) communicated with Spain; Caesarea was the naval base in the war against pirates; and half a dozen others were improved for the export of horses, wild beasts, and the timber and cereals of the west. There were no navigable rivers, and road transport through mountain country was still difficult, so sea journeys from point to point along the coast were standard practice. The fishing fleets which farmed the sea also needed harbours; but when they were for local use only the Romans left them to the inhabitants to maintain.

The Phoenicians had contented themselves with beaching their ships, or, as at Carthage or Hadrumetum (Sousse) where the coast was comparatively unprotected, with building a *cothon* or basin inland, with a narrow access to the sea, round which their ships were put in dry dock. The Greeks, however, had built moles and jetties; and the Romans, whose ships were larger than those of the Phoenicians, brought this Hellenistic harbour architecture to North Africa, sometimes with energetic improvements of their own. At Leptis Magna, they re-routed the oued to prevent the silting up of the harbour, and rocky islands were linked to the coast by

The harbour installations at Leptis Magna

huge moles carrying warehouses, a light-house and other buildings – the ruins of which survive – in order to make a proper deep-sea port. At Caesarea (Cherchel) and Acholla (Ras Botria) the remains of Roman jetties still break the surface a short distance from the shore. A lighthouse was built at Sullectum (Salakhta), an artificial basin at Tipasa. At Carthage, the old *cothon* was large enough for the Romans, and they merely added vast depots. Hippo Diarrhytus (Bizerta) was ignored; it was ill-placed for inland transport, an advantage in early Punic times when the mountains cut it off from tribal raids, a disadvantage for Roman purposes. The *cothon* at Hadrumetum (Sousse) was for some reason also allowed to silt up; while the progressive silting up of the estuary at Utica, presumably too near Carthage, was already severe by the third century (Utica is now several miles from the sea). The main Roman harbours were few.

The Romans also constructed causeways across the sea. The Phoenicians may already have built one linking Djerba to the mainland, but the Romans rebuilt it (the modern road runs on their foundations); they also joined the two Kerkenna islands.

Aqueducts, too, were designed by army architects, and not only for military camps and colonies. The Legion lent their engineers to the cities to supervise the organization of their water supply. A famous inscription describes how an engineer from Lambaesis was called on to direct the building of a tunnel for the aqueduct bringing water to the city of Saldae (Bougie): how, having directed the workmen to start tunnelling from both sides of the mountain, as was usual, he left them to it, but had to be summoned back when it became clear that the tunnellers had missed each other in the depths of the earth. The existence of the inscription suggests that mistakes of this kind were a rarity.

'With so many indispensable structures for all these waters you are welcome to compare, if you will, the idle pyramids or all the useless, though famous, works of the Greeks,' wrote the pragmatic Roman who was in charge of Rome's eleven aqueducts. Nothing constructed in Africa compared in scale with

Roman bath at the oasis of Gafsa (ancient Capsa) in southern Tunisia

the capital's water supply, nor in size with the Pont du Gard which carried water to Nîmes and the aqueduct of Segovia in Spain. But the same spirit inspired the building of African aqueducts twenty, thirty, even fifty or sixty miles long. And since Roman hydraulic skill never enabled them to apply the siphon principle except for small alterations in level (in any case the necessary lead was very expensive), those aqueducts had to be built with a continuous gradual slope the whole immense distance. Their design called for absolute precision from both architects and masons; the fall of water had to be regular, and neither too sluggish nor too rapid. No doubt a certain variation was tolerated, but if a nearby source was too high the aqueduct had to take a longer, roundabout path in order to reduce the incline and lower the pressure.

Wherever the Legion set up a permanent camp they built it to last. Not that it always has lasted: Ammaedara (Haïdra), which was their headquarters for less than a century, was soon overlaid with civilian dwellings and later Byzantine fortifications, and now lies in ruins. But the rigid rectangular grid which the military planner imposed on Roman Theveste can still be clearly traced on the street map of modern Tébessa, though the Legion itself was quartered there only a few years and the town left to civilians. Roman camps were model towns: the streets ran at right angles, living quarters, stores, temples alike were built of stone, all was orderly, precise, squared off, the minor garrisons of the far west as much as the major garrison at Lambaesis. The Legion was quartered here from A.D. 81, and one of the best-preserved buildings of Roman Africa is Lambaesis's Praetorian hall, roofless but with the walls standing to the second storey. Round it can be plainly seen the rectangular grid of streets.

The most famous of the Legion's towns in Africa was not strictly military, however; for though Thamugadi (Timgad) was briefly their headquarters, the town that survives was built after they had moved on to Lambaesis, a day's march away, for its veterans and their families. But more perfectly than any other it reveals the military mind at work: the aerial view of Timgad is justly famous for it shows, within the walls, the typical geometric pattern following the logic of ruler and set square. At ground level severity is relieved by the tilt of the site: the streets march straight up it and over the crest regardless, but the eye is deceived into a pleasant impression of variety.

The Legion usually built camps and veterans' towns on rising ground, choosing a spur overlooking the plain. It is difficult to believe that it was only for prudent reasons, that they were wholly indifferent to the wide

Praetorian hall at Lambèse (ancient Lambaesis), for centuries the main garrison of the Third Augustan Legion

Timgad (ancient Thamugadi) from the air. The theatre and the forum can be clearly seen; so can the erosion of the surrounding hills

horizons so many of them enjoy. But even the veterans' towns did, after all, have a paramilitary purpose; a soldier who had served his twenty-year term was an experienced man still in the prime of life, and if now he turned to family life and farming his own plot of land, it was sensible that he should do so where his military experience would not come amiss if the need arose. Timgad was on the southern frontier; Cuicul (Djemila) was founded in the heart of the old tribal country of Numidia; other veterans' colonies were built alongside native townships in the Kabylie mountains and in the west. Old soldiers never die: the veterans of the Legion remained, in a very real sense, *en poste* until the end of their lives. Even if their role was inactive, their mere presence contributed much to the *pax Romana* which was technically the responsibility of their former brothers in arms.

Not unnaturally, the most elaborate fortifications were in the south, where a frontier road guarded by modest fortresses and the occasional garrison was not enough. The province was defended not so much by a frontier line as a frontier zone, some twenty or thirty miles deep, known as the *limes*. It is here that the Roman gift for the rational exploitation of unpromising territory is most strikingly demonstrated, as well as the economy of means which enabled her to hold so huge an area with so small an active force. The frontier was largely defended by farmers.

In the middle and late 1930s aerial photography – both civilian and military – was undertaken in the semi-desert country south-west of the Aurès mountains. What those photographs revealed led to two archaeological expeditions just before 1939; after the war, their work was continued by Colonel J. Baradez, and his discoveries were published in his book *Fossatum Africae*.

The empty country was crammed with the faint remains of fortresses, roads, farms, villages, canals and waterworks of all kinds, and a vast ditch-and-dyke earthwork. They were part of a great complex of frontier settlement in southern Numidia. The Roman province had no natural barrier to the south; this replaced it. The *fossatum* or ditch was constructed, not continuously but in vulnerable areas, across some five hundred miles, perhaps more. Traces of a similar *fossatum* have also been found south of Volubilis, and of another in Tripolitania.

Part of Numidia's *fossatum* seems to have been intended to protect the inhabitants of the farms and villages from the tribes of the Zab mountains, well behind the nominal frontier. There was a *fossatum* even further north which protected the wheatfields of Sitifis from the inhabitants of the forests of the Bou Taleb range north of the Chott El Hodna. The remainder was a defence against the south. It was not a formidable obstacle; just enough to discourage all but determined invaders, or hold them up until military help could be fetched. Corn was safely grown right up to the Bou Taleb 'reserve'. It is not certain when the sections of the *fossatum* were constructed; in Numidia perhaps early in the second century, in Tripolitania probably very much later – in which case the agrarian settlement it

Aerial view of totally barren ground on the northern edge of the Algerian Sahara, showing remains of walls built in Roman times probably to prevent any rainfall from flowing away too rapidly

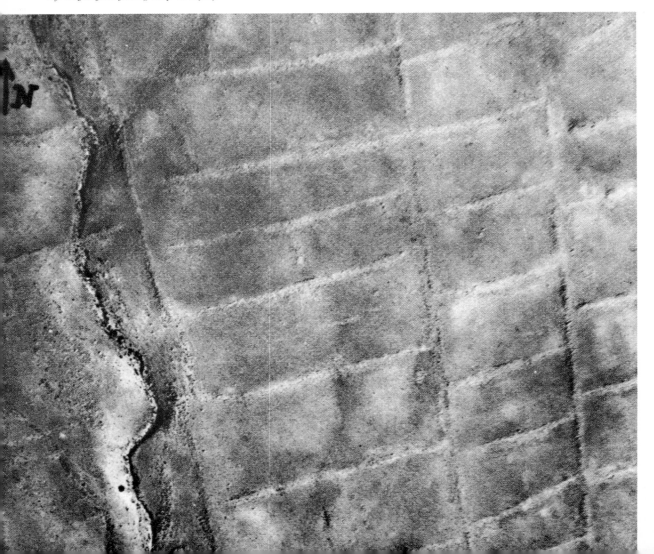

protected certainly preceded it. In Numidia the *fossatum* was guarded by a huge number of fortified towers and small fortresses: in one ten-mile stretch there were sixty. There were as many as this, Baradez believes, because they were manned by the inhabitants of the villages. The region must have supported a quite sizeable population.

All this was the work, either directly or indirectly, of the Third Augustan Legion and its auxiliaries. Where Caesar and Augustus and their immediate successors had founded cities for their veterans, or attached them to older townships, it suited later Emperors, especially as the more fertile parts of the province filled up with the increasing population made possible by prosperity, to settle their veterans on the frontier itself, where their experience made them not merely a reinforcement but a substitute for regular troops. And a man who had spent his whole life on the frontiers had an attachment to the place; he was probably happy enough to settle down there. Meanwhile, everything he had learnt during his years with the army of building, of water-management and of co-operative effort, could be devoted to his own property. On the *limes*, in return for the duty of defence, he had no taxes or tribute to pay.

Fort of Zebaret, south of the Chott El Hodna—one of hundreds of photographs in Jean Baradez' Fossatum Africae *showing Roman military and hydraulic works in what is now desert*

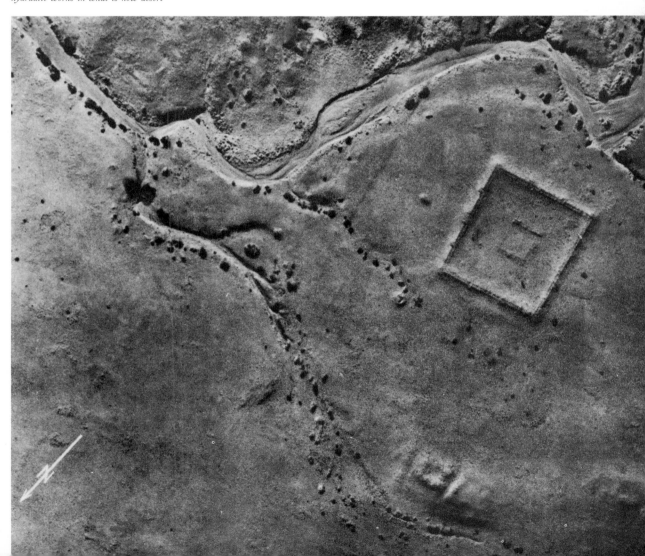

It was not a totally dry country, although it could not support large centres of population. But even as far north as Lambaesis the rain could not be relied on, even in winter. The author of the *Historia Augusta,* a collection of lives of the Emperors, says that Hadrian was particularly loved in Africa because when he arrived to visit his army in A.D. 125 rain fell for the first time in five years. Three centuries later, St Augustine was reminding his parishioners how lucky they were compared to those who lived in the south: 'Here, God grants us rain every year . . . there, He sends it rarely, if in great quantity.' Rain fell, in fact, but intermittently – and violently. In Tripolitania, floods swept one concrete Roman barrage hundreds of yards downstream. In the Aurès, there was frequently snow on high ground. Although enough sank to be tapped for wells it tended

Irrigation channels of c. 1800 years ago, south-west of the Aurès mountains

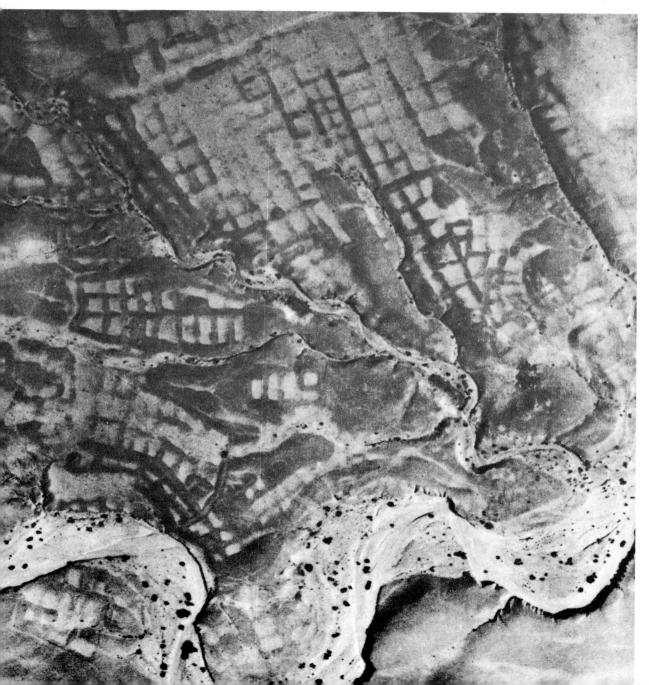

to run off over the dry ground and flow in a flood down the beds of the few rivers towards the desert, where it was lost to evaporation. It was the same all over the desert fringe. The land was not infertile, or the nomads would not have wanted it for grazing. It merely remained to use every drop of water that fell.

It was essential to prevent the water disappearing as fast as it came and to prevent any snow melting in a sudden flood. In parts, especially around Theveste, the Berbers of Numidia had themselves already begun this task, but its vast extension belongs to the Roman period. Traces have been found of whole hillsides terraced not for cultivation but to hold rainfall or melting snow long enough for it to sink in gradually and fill the water table for wells. Horizontal walls were built along the slopes, at intervals of thirty yards; similar ones can be seen today on hillsides throughout Tunisia. These walls have the secondary function of preventing erosion, for the washing away of soil is a serious problem.

Sudden rushing of water down the oueds was prevented by damming them and constructing water channels to feed the water to crops and trees where it was needed. Enormous numbers of these barrages have been found in what is now semi-desert: there were sixty in the neighbourhood of one tiny settlement in Tripolitania. Elaborate regulations were worked out for the fair distribution of the water: similar regulations exist today in the palm groves of the oases. Wells were dug, and such was Roman technical skill that they could tap a natural water vein even in a predominantly mineral water area, or sink a well to a depth of fifty or sixty feet. Artificial basins were built to collect rainfall, and cisterns to hold it. The *limitanei* practised in miniature, but with an even more compelling motive, what was practised in the more populous and more fertile regions with a higher rainfall.

It would be wrong to imagine a kind of green belt the whole length of the frontier; there were never enough people to develop it all, and there was not enough water, except in western Mauretania where in any case Roman penetration was not so thorough. The only farming most *limitanei* could manage was dry farming: widely-spaced olive trees and a few hard-won subsistence crops. Yet the remains of dozens of small mills and olive presses have been found in what is now barren land, and even the stumps of olive trees. There may also have been some fruit trees and vineyards.

The pattern of frontier life varied from place to place; south of the Aurès, the inhabitants huddled together in tiny hamlets behind their *fossatum,* taking turns to man the watch-towers; in Tripolitania, perhaps from the first century on, the *limitanei* tended to live in vast farms, sometimes built round courtyards, which were themselves fortified rather than protected by a *fossatum*. The cultivated areas were merely oases in the surrounding scrub.

The waterworks these ex-soldiers turned small farmers constructed were an impressive achievement. They were handed on to their children, and extended by civilian settlers and even, as time passed, by hungry nomads who came to steal and stayed to farm and, by following the arts of peace, acquired a vested interest in peace-keeping. It was not only soldiers and ex-soldiers who defended the frontier.

The Emperors themselves recognized the value of these frontier settlements, and continued to encourage the granting of land to veterans, under the eye of the Legion. Yet soon these veterans were not Romans from other parts of the Empire. Soldiers were not allowed to marry during their military service; but by the time they retired they had usually contracted a common-law marriage with an African woman, and settled down with her and their children. From the beginning of the third century soldiers could live with their families outside the camps. These children grew up in townships beside the camps, in colonies of veterans or on smallholdings along the *limes*: what more natural than that the Romans should have looked for recruits to the sons of old soldiers, already half Roman by language and adoption? After the first generation or so, it was an African army which Romanized the furthest corners of Barbary.

5 Granary of the Empire

Game of dice: pottery lamp in the museum at Tébessa

The prosperity of Roman Africa was not based on the pioneer economy of the Saharan fringe, though that pioneering was a symptom of it. Making the desert bloom was a striking testimony to the success of Roman methods, but the real wealth was won, as it had been won for four hundred years, from the regions further north where winter rain could be relied on.

Imperial policy was dominated by the agricultural situation in Italy. Italian agriculture had been devastated first by the Hannibalic War and then by the social wars of the last fifty years of the Republic, and the dispossessed peasantry had flocked to the overcrowded capital. The new proletariat needed food, and Italy could no longer keep herself in corn. Corn had to be provided by the provinces, notably Egypt and Africa.

The previous inhabitants had already discovered that corn grew readily enough in the broad river valleys of Tunisia and on the plateaux of Algeria and the far west, and both the Berbers and the Phoenicians had learnt to improve on nature by crop rotation and irrigation where it was needed. Pliny the Elder reports that the country was so fertile that one grain would produce a stalk bearing a hundred and fifty (and three times this figure had been known, it was claimed). As an average yield, this was clearly over-optimistic; all the same, African harvests were prodigious. By Caesar's day, Africa Nova alone, the old Carthaginian territory, produced nearly fifty thousand tons of grain every year. Now, with the extension of Roman rule, there was the prospect of far more.

To encourage the growing of corn in Africa, and at the same time to protect the olive groves and vineyards of Italy, the cultivation of olive trees and vines in Africa was at least technically forbidden under the early Empire, probably under pressure from Italian landowners anxious to preserve a source of revenue, but also because the prospect of a starving Roman mob inspired real terror in the Emperors. All suitable land was to be put under the plough, and the inhabitants set to tilling and sowing and reaping. No doubt the mixed farming economy which the Carthaginians had built up on their estates had been literally trampled underfoot during the wars, and there was little question of actually uprooting healthy trees and plants. The historian Sallust, who went out to govern Africa Nova in 46 B.C., had declared firmly that 'the soil produces good crops of grain and good pasture, but is unsuitable for the cultivation of trees,' which is not true, so it suggests that he saw none. The only olive groves of any importance were in Tripolitania – and they were left undisturbed because much of the land was too dry for wheat. The cattle and market gardens which the soldiers of Agathocles had admired in Cape Bon had been replaced by corn and barley; according to Pliny, the country was given over to the worship of the harvest goddess, and certainly the sanctuaries which survive from this period were all dedicated to Ceres. A hundred years after Caesar's day, the province of Africa – which now included Tripolitania and Numidia – produced nearly half a million tons of grain annually, a ten-fold increase.

Roman North Africa was fundamentally a farming economy. The Carthaginians had built their fortunes on a virtual monopoly of the maritime carrying trade; their farms, at least until the last few decades before their destruction, had simply fed their own population. The nomads lived primarily off their livestock, which provided them with milk products and wool and leather for clothing, and hunting for their meat (their livestock was their capital, too valuable to kill for food); again, any crops they raised in the damp beds of oueds during the brief season they pitched their tents in one place were for themselves. Even the efforts of Masinissa and his kind only made the Numidians and Moors comparatively better off; they did not turn the Berber kingdoms into exporting nations. But under the Romans Africa began to export foodstuffs on a vast scale; and she kept it up for centuries. Much of that food was the statutory *annona* or tribute – for which she got no return in money or other imports. It says a great deal for her agricultural wealth that even after the tax-gatherers had taken their tithe she still had a

Peasant picking up a windfall of apples: detail of a second century Four Seasons mosaic from La Chebba, Tunisia, now in the Bardo Museum, Tunis

sizeable surplus to sell abroad.

In theory the land now belonged to the *senatus populusque Romanus*. Naturally the Senate and people of Rome could not exploit it themselves, although individual senators were quick to buy up a quantity of confiscated estates on the cheap. The land within the survey, which gradually included all land devoted to settled agriculture, was therefore let in their name in return for tribute.

The system was extremely complex. Many of the small farmers, the ex-nomads who had been 'fixed' on good agricultural land by the Carthaginians or the Numidian and Moorish kings, were left in possession of their small properties in return for a proportion of their harvest, although as time passed these small properties tended to be sub-divided between heirs until they were so tiny that they were unable to support the new generation. Poverty, as in other societies, then forced the inhabitants to sell out to richer neighbours and reduced them to the status of serfs working on other men's land.

The old Phoenician cities and Numidian townships which had not been razed to the ground for taking the wrong side in the wars were allowed to keep their city territories, which were divided into allotments belonging to the better-off inhabitants. The municipal authorities were responsible for the collection of the *annona*.

In some of these townships, colonies of veterans or Italian immigrants were settled, so the city land had to be extended or re-divided to give the newcomers their allotments. But most army veterans and other colonists from Italy were settled in townships on good land confiscated from Carthaginian and Numidian landowners, or expropriated from the tribes who were still grazing their flocks on the richer hills within the province. These new settlements, too, were endowed with a surrounding territory of varying size divided into individual parcels of land which followed the regular pattern of the survey system. These Roman *coloni* no doubt paid a more modest tribute than that required from the conquered natives.

New towns and old alike, except for a handful on the coast which had a cosmopolitan admixture of merchants and shippers and traders of all kinds, were basically settlements of landowning farmers with their families and servants. Although the accidents of inheritance impoverished some – while it enriched others – by and large these farmers, whether Roman colonists or the better-off

Berbers and Phoenicians, employed or sub-let to serfs who were little more than slaves. These, who worked the land, sometimes lived in the towns, on the fringes or in poor quarters; but most of them lived on the land, huddled together in the small hamlets of mud-walled *gourbis* which can be seen throughout North Africa to this day, or, worse, in caves or straw huts, in desperate poverty, wearing skins and supplementing their wretched diet of barley and millet with snails and crickets. They had no rights of citizenship in the cities to which they were attached, and – though the point is obscure – may have had no legal rights under Roman law, especially in the Phoenician and Berber towns.

Only one in six North Africans lived in the towns; directly or indirectly, and usually directly, their wealth was founded on the labour of the remaining five-sixths of the population, the rural poor. But the majority of the rural poor did not work on municipal territory. For although the territories of the townships sometimes adjoined each other, they were usually more like islands in a sea of the estates or *saltus* (called *latifundia* if they were large enough), which belonged either to rich citizens of Rome or, increasingly, to the Emperor himself, who acquired them

Team of oxen: detail of second century mosaic of rural life, now in the Bardo Museum

by confiscation or by inheritance. (Romans without heirs frequently left their property to the Emperor.) Large areas, especially in Tunisia which was already well-cultivated and where most land had been confiscated from the conquered Carthaginians, had been bought up by speculating Roman noblemen; they had seen in Africa an admirable prospect of easy money, especially since their power at Rome in the latter days of the Republic was such that they largely evaded the exactions of tribute-gatherers and could export their corn for the best price they could get. These estates were an investment; the owners did not live on them, any more than the Emperor lived on the imperial domains.

Perhaps both kinds of estates were exploited to begin with by slave labour, under the supervision of an imperial agent or, in the case of rich Romans' land, a bailiff; or by companies of tax-farmers. Large numbers of Carthaginians and other Phoenicians had, after all, been enslaved after the fall of Carthage. But the Romans soon learnt to be wary of exploiting conquered territory by setting armies of slaves to till the soil until they dropped; the slave revolts which punctuated the last decades of the Republic originated in just such gangs of down-trodden men. By the first century A.D. the pattern of the Roman exploitation of Africa had settled into something more like medi-aeval villeinage. The large estates, both imperial and private, were, like the municipal lands, divided into allotments. Apart from a modest 'home farm', which might house the agent or bailiff and was probably still worked by slave labour, the land was let either directly to the peasants who tilled it, or to *conductores* or tenants, who in turn sub-let it to peasants. In both cases the peasants occupied the land in return for one third of their produce and a few days' work a year on the home farm. One theory has it that Nero, in the mid-first century, put to death six Roman senators who had acquired huge estates in Africa because they persisted in the habit of employing slave labour in gangs; but it seems more likely that he coveted their wealth, for a drastic alteration in

ownership – whether the parcelling out of the land into peasant allotments was a new development or not – would mean that he could extend the territory on which he could enforce the collection of the *annona*.

The lot of the peasants was hard, even with a tiny parcel of land which they could think of, if not call, their own. Farming in the ancient world, however methodical, was not industrialized, and required a vast labour force because it was as much as a man and his family could do to produce enough for themselves and, on top, half as much again for the *annona*. Though their lives grew easier with increased prosperity, the actual toil of farming was never simplified by the invention of machinery of any kind, and when the bad times came it was they who were required to produce the extra taxes, or who suffered in the occasional localized crop failure.

Fortunately, there was a vitally important side-effect of the judicial fiction that the provinces belonged to the Roman people and not to individual landowners; it meant that the law could regulate the relationship between landowner and tenant, which it could not do in Italy. An agrarian law of 111 B.C. had already given the provincials security of tenure in return for a part of their harvest; by the first century A.D. they could sell or leave the land they occupied as they wished, and with it their homes, on condition that the new tenant did not interrupt its cultivation, and its provision of tribute, for more than two years.

Scrupulous regulations governed the *annona* they had to contribute, and this applied to imperial and private estates alike. An inscription cut on an altar dedicated to Trajan in A.D. 116–7 on one of the imperial domains, at Henchir Mettich in northern Tunisia, lays down that the peasant shall 'give to the owners, lessors. or stewards of this estate . . . one third of the wheat from the threshing floor, one third of the barley from the threshing floor, one fourth of the beans from the threshing floor, one third of the wine from the vat, one third of the oil from the press, one sextarius of honey from each hive' (of which they were not allowed to have more than five).

Another famous inscription from the imperial Saltus Burunitanus (near Souk El Khemis) shows that the lessor, Allius Maximus, with the connivance of an imperial procurator above him in the administrative hierarchy, had attempted to demand more than the normal six days' work on the home farm from the peasants of the domain, and, when they had complained, had sent soldiers to seize and torture them '. . . and this forces us unhappy men to seek your divine aid. We ask, therefore, most sacred Imperator [Commodus] that you succour us; that in accordance with the clause of the Lex Hadriana we owe not more than two days' work per year of ploughing, two of cultivating, two of harvesting . . . So that through the kindliness of your majesty we, your rural workers, born and raised on your estates, may no longer be harassed by the lessors . . .' The Emperor's instruction to the procurator is also recorded: 'In view of the law and of my decision, procurators shall not demand more than thrice two days' work lest any unjust exaction be made by you . . .'

The peasants had rights, at least some of them knew it, and the Emperor was prepared to listen to them. No doubt peasants were frequently browbeaten by their superiors; no doubt justice was not always done to them, especially in the depths of the countryside, far from the towns and the opportunity to lay a complaint, and perhaps the knowledge that it was possible; but they were *petits propriétaires*, with security of tenure, fixed taxes, and a right of redress, even if not all were so fortunate as those who lived on the Saltus Burunitanus.

But some peasants had no land, no fixed residence. Theirs was the hardest lot of all, obliged to hire themselves out by the day as and when they could; living in straw huts in the fields, travelling the country in gangs, like nineteenth-century navvies or modern Irish building workers, to help with the harvest on the large estates. Yet they, too, could hope for better things by helping themselves.

The son of one such homeless peasant of the second century, in spite of his miserable start in life, rose quite high in the Romano-African hierarchy entirely by hard work as a farm labourer (although he himself did acquire a tiny property, perhaps by inheritance from a relative, or by acquiring a sub-tenancy on Mactar's city territory). This man was a harvester of Mactar, and he left behind him when he died in the third century an inscription in verse on his tombstone (now in the Louvre) which records pride in his rise, if not to fame – his name is unknown – at least to fortune:

'I was born of poor parents; my father had neither an income nor his own house. From the day of my birth I always cultivated my field; neither my land nor I ever had any rest . . . When the harvest-gangs arrived to hire themselves out in the countryside round Cirta, capital of Numidia, or in the plains of the mountain of Jupiter, I was the first to harvest my field. Then, leaving my neighbourhood, for twelve years I reaped the harvest for another man, under a fiery sun; for eleven years I was chief of a harvest gang and scythed the corn in the fields of Numidia. Thanks to my labours, and being content with very little, I finally became master of a house and a property: today I live at ease. I have even achieved honours: I was called on to sit in the Senate of my city, and, though once a modest peasant, I became censor. I have watched my children and grandchildren grow up round me; my life has been occupied, peaceful, and honoured by all.'

He was not the only African who told a similar story. But it was possible for a family's fortunes to change dramatically from one generation to another as much by accident as by effort. One Sicinius Aemilianus of Zarath in Tripolitania, who in later life achieved a minor immortality as one of those who accused Apuleius of black magic, had only one small field in his youth and was so poor he was obliged to cultivate it himself, although he belonged to a rich family. But the family was also large, and sub-division of the property between them all had reduced him to virtual penury. Then an epidemic carried off most of his relatives, and he found himself wealthy.

The market in land was free, and a generation or two of sub-division, or of buying up from neighbours who had to sell, meant a great variation in the size of properties, even on the imperial estates. Those who got into debt and failed to pay what they owed 'on the threshing floor' would have to give up their land, which could then be let to one of their fellow tenants, who thus increased the size of his holding, or to a landless peasant like the harvester of Mactar.

*   *   *

A land divided into allotments cultivated by a host of peasant proprietors: it does not sound the most efficient way to turn North Africa into a granary, and it would certainly be quite wrong to imagine that the province bore any resemblance to the wheatfields of Arkansas, even in the first century A.D. when the main crop of the thousands of allotments in the cornlands of North Africa was wheat. The use of a simple wooden plough drawn by a donkey and an ox (or a woman, said Pliny) gave little scope for that kind of mass production. The rural population must always have grown other crops and raised domestic animals. There is little mention of them in the statistics; they were mostly a private sideline for their own use. The extra produce may have amounted to no more than a diminutive vegetable patch tended by the women of the family, a fruit tree, perhaps poultry, a sheep or a goat; the better off must have had a donkey, perhaps an ox as well. The tenants with sub-tenants under them, and the farms of the imperial and private administrators, must have had all these things. With transport expensive and slow, in spite of the new Roman roads, town and country alike had to raise as much as they needed for themselves. Many grew barley, cheaper than wheat, for themselves; animal-owners grew it for their animals. Large numbers of beasts of burden were necessary not so much for ploughing as for the transport of the vast quantities of grain to Carthage for enshipment to Ostia. The prohibition against vines and olive trees was almost certainly a dead letter, as far as local consumption was concerned; the moment there was enough security to grow plants

which needed years to come to maturity, some peasants at least, if they had a few square yards of land to spare near their homes, must have begun to cultivate them for themselves and their families. All but the poorest must have had a couple of sheep or goats for milk and clothing. And it is unthinkable that the Roman administrators in the towns or on the estates would have been content with a diet of couscous and bread. By the beginning of the second century a mixed economy was commonplace: the imperial tenants of the Saltus Beguenses had bees, for instance, besides a variety of crops.

There is one corner of North Africa which is still farmed according to the second-century Roman system – and perhaps it can be traced even further back, to Punic practice. For some reason, the region between the Sousse-El Djem-Sfax road and the coast was spared the worst depredations of the Arab invasions of the eleventh century. Hidden behind their modern cactus hedges are a multitude of small fields lovingly cultivated to the limit of what they will bear by a surprisingly large population. Yet it is not, by its nature, the most fertile part of Tunisia, for the soil is thin and the rainfall low. The inhabitants live in villages founded in the insecure middle ages, where in Roman times they were probably more widely dispersed in hamlets among their properties. But the actual organization of the land, sub-divided between its innumerable owners, is a striking survival from Africa's golden age. The island of Djerba, too, though it suffered more from the Arabs, is cultivated today in what must have been the Roman manner: there are a dozen or so small villages, and scores of scattered farmsteads, each with their olive groves and palm trees and small fields of crops half-hidden by banks and hedges.

Even in the first century, the pattern of land exploitation was not the same all over North Africa. In Tripolitania, olives were always the main crop; the land was too dry for more than a modicum of hard-won wheat and barley. In the hills of the west the famous Numidian horses and mules were bred for export, and sheep for their wool. Round

Carthage itself, there was more horticulture than agriculture: the figs which reached Trimalchio's dinner table in the *Satyricon* of Petronius came from its market gardens, like other exotic fruit and vegetables such as pomegranates and truffles which were much to the Roman taste; and artichokes were certainly grown in quantity for the citizens of Carthage. The forests, too, were not ignored. Those of Algeria and Morocco were hunted by the army for wild beasts for the amphitheatres of Rome – and, once they were built, those of Africa – and their rare woods were much prized by Roman pluto-crats: Cicero himself had paid thousands of pounds for an African citrus-wood table top carved in one piece.

Meanwhile, all over Roman territory, there were still large areas of nomad occupa-tion. The former grazing grounds of the Musulamii between Madauros and Theveste (Tébessa) were taken over after the crushing of the revolt of Tacfarinas for a town terri-tory, a saltus (the Saltus Beguenses), and a private estate; but the Musulamii themselves were granted a 'reserve' nearby. The tribe of the Musunii Regiani were allowed to re-main near Thelepte (Feriana), and land was set aside for the Nybgenii near the city terri-tory of Tacapae (Gabès). There were other tribal areas in the unsurveyed, unregistered hills and forests further west. They continued to live off their flocks, yet they, too, were prepared to hire out their labour to the farmers to earn money or grain to eke out their livelihood; they sometimes came great distances, even from beyond the frontier, to set up their straw huts in the fields for a few weeks at harvest-time and help bring in the wheat – a practice still followed by the Bedouin, whose temporary straw shelter strongly resembles the *mappalia* of the seasonal hired hands illustrated in Roman African mosaics. The Romans, no horsemen them-selves, raised the famous *ala Numidica*, the cavalry auxiliaries, among the inhabitants of the hills of the Maghreb, as the Carth-aginians had recruited cavalry there before them, for service in other provinces of the Empire. By the second half of the first century, the Third Augustan Legion was raising recruits for service in Africa among the nomads. There was little, any longer, to fear from them. Their pacification had begun, and they were beginning to settle in tribal townships of their own.

* * *

Regular winter rains, mild springs without frost, long ripening summers unthreatened by sudden storms: Africa was blessed in its climate, and its harvests were reliable. If there were bad years, whether from drought or locusts, they were rarely ruinous; there is no record of widespread famine, and there was always wheat for Rome. After barely a century of direct Roman rule, the province had displaced Egypt as Rome's principal supplier of corn: two thirds to Egypt's one third. For more than three hundred years, Africa sent about half a million tons of corn to Rome every year. Not the least advantage from the Roman point of view was that the sea journey from Africa was so much shorter, and therefore both cheaper in transport costs and less liable to shipwreck. The Emperors could congratulate themselves on their policy of leaving the exploitation of Africa to thousands of individual Africans, and enlisting the self-interest of their subjects in the prosperity of their tiny properties.

So could the Africans. There was enough to meet the *annona*, and there was enough to feed themselves. And with the coming of settled agriculture, with an assured yearly crop, the population began to rise. In the nineteenth century, with the introduction of modern agricultural methods, the popu-lation of French North Africa doubled in the hundred years after 1830; and although no Roman censuses for Africa survive it is likely that, for much the same reason, the population of Roman North Africa also doubled between A.D. 50 and 150, and con-tinued to rise for at least another half-century. By the beginning of the third century it probably numbered between six and seven million and was possibly as much as eight million. (It was only with the destructive invasions of the Hillalian Arabs in the eleventh century, when the security and settled conditions necessary for farming, particularly in the dry regions where the upkeep of dams and canals is essential to life, finally vanished, that numbers declined to their pre-Roman level. In the mid-nineteenth century Le Kef – the ancient Sicca Veneria – perched defensively on its bluff, was the only sizeable community in the upper Bagradas valley, which had once supported dozens of thriving cities; there was scarcely a village besides.)

The increased population had two major consequences: the rapid growth in size and numbers of the cities of Africa, and the dramatic extension and alteration of agriculture. There were more mouths to feed,

Goatherd playing his pipe; fat-tailed sheep in the background. Detail from second century mosaic from Oudna (ancient Uthina)

Descendants of the fat-tailed sheep can be seen today

but because the *annona* demanded by Rome was not increased the burden was spread over a wider area and a larger number of people.

In the first century, according to Pliny, all the glory of the country was in its grain harvests. In the second, pressure of numbers – combined, possibly, with the exhaustion of even that well-phosphated soil in certain over-cropped areas – dictated the spread of agriculture to less fertile land unsuitable for wheat: the hillsides and wooded heaths within the cornlands, and the dry regions to the south. Much of the glory was now to be shared by great groves of olive trees.

This policy was actively encouraged by the

Emperors. At the end of the second century the first of the provincial Emperors rose to the purple. This was Trajan, a Spaniard, a capable and far-sighted administrator who ruled the Empire as far as he could for the benefit of all its subjects. By this time, too, Italian agriculture had declined yet further; Italy was no longer producing enough olive oil and wine for her own needs, let alone those of the rest of the Empire. The rules against the growing of vines and olive trees were reversed. The peasants, even on the imperial domains, were officially encouraged to bring into cultivation uncultivated land on the fringes. The Henchir Mettich inscription previously quoted makes clear that, in return for the fixed shares to be given to the owners or lessors, 'permission is given to those who live on the estate of Villa Magna Variana, that is of Mappalia Siga, to bring under cultivation those fields which are unsurveyed on the terms of the Lex Manciana, namely that he who brings the land under cultivation have provisional title.' Another inscription from Aïn El Djemala shows that the peasants were allowed to plant vines and olive trees for themselves both outside and inside the domain. The peasants are appealing to the imperial administrators: 'We ask, procurators, that . . . you grant us those fields which are swampy and wooded, that we may plant them with olive groves and vines in accordance with the Lex Manciana, on the terms applying to the neighbouring Saltus Neronianus . . .' Hadrian's procurators reply: 'Since our

Caesar in the untiring zeal with which he constantly guards human needs has ordered all parts of land which are suitable for olives or vines, as well as for grain, to be cultivated, therefore by the grace of his foresight the right is given to all to enter upon even those parts of said land which are included in the surveyed units of the Saltus Blandianua and of Udensis [and others] . . . and which are not exploited by the lessors.' New occupiers had the usual right to leave the new property to whom they wished, and must in return pay a rent of a third part of the produce. But anyone planting olive trees or grafting them on to wild olives need pay no part of the crop for ten years. An instruction

Another detail from the Oudna mosaic. This barn is the only building to be seen on the domain—the owner lived in the town

Hunting wild boar. From the evidence of this mosaic from Oudna, now in the Bardo, it was a 'mixed economy' estate

to the imperial agent is added: 'If any fields lie fallow and are untilled, if any wooded plots or swamps [exist] in this district of *saltus*, [do not hinder from cultivating the same] those who desire [to do so] . . .' Nothing makes clearer the identity of purpose of the Emperor and his rural subjects.

In this way, uncultivated hillsides and heaths were cleared, terraced, and gradually planted with orchards, olive groves and vineyards, or stocked with cattle and horses, sheep and goats. There is no reason to suppose that matters were much different on the city territories, or on the private estates. A famous second-century mosaic, now in the Bardo Museum in Tunis, shows a

typical private domain in the valley of the Miliana at Uthina (Oudna), just off the road between Tunis and Zaghouan. There are wheatfields, which were the source of its wealth still, but also olive trees and pastures for sheep and goats; there are cattle and horses, a donkey, and, in the surrounding scrub, partridge, wild boar, and even panther. There were probably no game reserves as there were in Italy: there is a possibility that game birds were raised in the farmyard along with other domestic poultry. (Hunting, particularly of gazelle and of hare, which is a favourite theme in other mosaics, was important for rich and poor alike, the former for pleasure, the latter for food, and for both to protect the crops from the depredations of gazelle and wild boar.) The mosaic was found in a town house; there is no villa on the domain, only farm buildings. Perhaps it was near enough to Uthina for the owner to dispense with a hunting lodge; perhaps his bailiff too lived in the city. In either case the really significant fact is the presence of olive groves and meadows in the corn country. There was now enough labour from a rising population to make use of hitherto unused land.

It was particularly in northern Tunisia, where the larger estates were, that mixed farming of this kind flourished. The wetter plains south of Algiers and in the far west in Mauretania continued to concentrate on cereals, just as in Tripolitania olives were always the main produce.

But the land left uncultivated within the

Fourth-century A.D. *mosaic from Dougga (ancient Thugga) of Eros, a charioteer, now in the Bardo Museum*

saltus and the city territories was not enough to satisfy the pressure of population. There was a gradual expansion west and south, undertaken by all classes, from the rich citizen of Hadrumetum who founded a stud farm for racehorses in the hills of Numidia to the peasants pushed out of their fathers' modest properties by quantities of brothers, who settled in the south beyond the well-watered regions. Forests were cut down, both to supply wood for fuel and timber and to make room for farming and stockbreeding. (It is ironical that the Roman occupation set in train the erosion which is now so conspicuous over large areas of the Maghreb, when the Africans of the time took such care with their barrages and dykes to prevent it: but once the waterworks were allowed to decay by the Arabs, there were not enough tree roots to prevent the winter rains carrying away the topsoil for ever.) The tribal reserves were hemmed in yet further, or pushed south, and although there were constant clashes between nomads and farmers, and occasional outbreaks of more serious fighting, many tribesmen themselves took to the settled pasturage and farming which need less elbow-room.

It was in response to this migration that Trajan pushed the old frontier north of the Aures to the south of that mountain range. A military road was built from the oases of the Chott Djerid directly west through Ad Majores (Besseriani) and Vescera (Biskra). His successor Hadrian, who visited his army in Africa twice during a reign spent in energetic travels round the Empire, founded the army outpost at Gemellae, well to the south of the old *limes,* to keep an eye on the tribes of the desert; both inspired the network of roads running west towards Mauretania Tingitana from Oppidum Novum, a town largely peopled by veterans. Hadrian moved the Legion's headquarters to its final, westernmost home at Lambaesis. Within the new frontier it defended, more and more of the Maghreb was brought into cultivation until, by the end of the second century, Tertullian was writing: 'Smiling estates have replaced the most famous deserts, cultivated fields have conquered the forests, flocks of sheep have put wild beasts to flight . . . certain proof of the increase of mankind!'

The agent of this civilian colonization was the olive tree. It is impossible to exaggerate its importance to the prosperity of Roman North Africa for, if the wheat of the province enriched the conquerors, the oil was to enrich the native inhabitants also. It was one of the main commodities of commerce in classical times, for in the ancient world olive oil was as much used in cooking as it is round the Mediterranean today; there was no other soap, no other base to fix perfume, and it was virtually the only fuel for lighting. Most of the countries to the north of the Mediterranean were able to grow all the olive trees they needed, now that they had a taste for Roman comforts. But Italy did not fulfil her own needs, and Africa was able to fill the gap, and in so doing earn money for herself.

Along the southern frontier and in the now largely desolate steppes of central Tunisia olive trees were planted. The nomads were pushed out now not for the sake of wheat but for the sake of oil. The olive tree does not require much water – less, in fact, than the palm tree. Only, if rainfall is slow, it requires space for its roots to spread wide. The whole of the area round Thysdrus (El Djem) became a vast olive grove, with trees planted some twenty or thirty yards apart. It could support a large and thriving population, but not a *concentrated* one: a man's work covered a larger area than in corn country. Thysdrus itself, in spite of the enormous amphitheatre which could have held sixty thousand spectators, had a population scarcely half that size; but it was at the centre of an area of prosperous peasant villages, whose inhabitants could come into the city for the spectacles or the chariot-races, or for market days to buy the other food they needed with the money they earned from the sale of their surplus oil, although their place of work was too far for a daily journey. Further west, round Cillium (Kasserine) and Sufetula

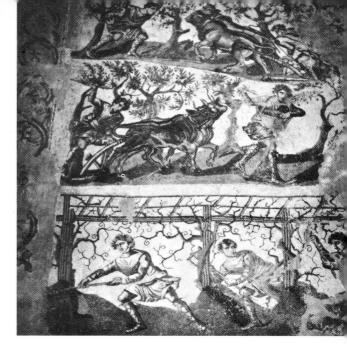

Celebrated mosaic of the early third century A.D. showing cereal-growing under olive trees, and viticulture. Note the curious throwing action of the sower—still used by modern Algerians when broadcasting seed. In the Cherchel Museum

the plough since Carthaginian times, and had been exhausted by over-cropping. It is also remarkably hardy: in the hills of Numidia, it was planted well above the three thousand feet contour (much higher than it is planted today), in spite of the danger from frost. It was even planted on land that was more suitable for wheat. Along the whole length of the east coast, it virtually ousted grain, and there is a famous mosaic pavement from Caesarea (Cherchel), in the comparatively wet, lush west, which shows an early third-century estate dominated by olive trees and vines, with corn growing in their shade.

Spectators at the circus: detail from fifth-century mosaic from Gafsa (ancient Capsa) now in the Bardo Museum

Chariot race: late second-century mosaic from Carthage, now in the Bardo Museum

(Sbeïtla), the olive trees were more widely spaced, the population necessarily more scattered, and the cities smaller. But again, the wealth of their public buildings is out of all proportion to the number of people who actually lived there. In the south, still drier, there were no towns except garrison towns; the peasant smallholders were even fewer. Other crops were grown, of course, and livestock raised for local consumption, but in modest quantities. The olive tree was king.

Nor does the olive tree need fertile land. In north-eastern Tunisia, it was planted not only on ground which had never been cultivated, but on land which had been under

The great virtue of olive-culture is that, although one may wait ten or more years for the tree to bear fruit, it requires little upkeep and little labour for a good return. For the peasant, this meant that taking over virgin land on the borders of the domain where he worked his smallholding was not an impossible burden; and he could look forward to being able to sell his surplus olives in the local market when his trees at last began to bear. The *pax Romana* and the agrarian laws enabled him to be confident that the trees would still be there, and still be his, that far ahead. The large landowners had enough capital behind them to buy large tracts of land for olive groves, and then wait years for their long-term returns. For them, too, the saving in labour was an important consideration. There was still slave labour in Africa, but it was declining sharply for two reasons: most slaves were manumitted after a number of years' service, and the source of supply of new slaves, as part of the booty of war, was drying up. The Empire had virtually given up foreign conquest. So there was now little competition for free labour from slaves. The career of the harvester of Mactar shows that hired hands were beginning to be expensive, for to rise to the position of censor he must have amassed a large capital. He did not make it out of his own field, which cannot have been too large for his family to cultivate in his absence; he made it as a reaper 'for another man' and then as 'chief of a harvest gang.' For those twenty-three years, his wages must have been substantial – perhaps as much as those of a legionary. Those who owned land in Africa must have lobbied at the imperial court for the right to grow olives every bit as fiercely as the Italian landowners had once lobbied to prevent them.

* * *

The wealth of Africa was in its primary agricultural products; there was very little industry. The grain was threshed by the peasants themselves on the domain threshing-floors when they paid their tribute; perhaps there were municipal threshing floors also. In any case, the work was not specialized.

But machinery, however simple, is necessary for the extraction of olive oil. Wooden presses, which were probably common in well-wooded areas, have not survived, but no doubt most peasants had for their own use a primitive press similar to those still used by the Berbers. What have survived are countless stone oil presses; not only single presses, but whole factories – ruined but recognizable – some with as many as a score. The surplus for sale was too great for the peasant to press himself. And because transport was expensive the oil had to be extracted before it was transported to its destination in amphorae. A peasant could still make a modest profit on his olives, enough to enable him to buy what he did not grow himself; and much more substantial profits were made by the middlemen.

Ruins of 'factory' for production of olive oil at Brisgane, near Tébessa

Olive grove near Tarhuna, Libya

Traces of potteries have also been found, especially on private domains in the poorest olive country, where the landlords may have found them a useful way of increasing the return on their investment in large tracts of land. The commonest articles of domestic use found in Africa are the little rose-red lamps made of the local clay. With oil plentiful and cheap, all but the poorest could afford to have artificial light, and there was a steady market for lamps. It was never distinguished pottery; as in Carthaginian times the finest work was imported. But lamps from Hadrumetum (Sousse), for instance, have been found in Sicily and Sardinia, and even in Italy. Amphorae and votive statuettes were also manufactured, and some bricks also, though most bricks appear to have been imported from Italy.

The only city of Africa which could remotely be called industrial was Simitthu (Chemtou), where the ugly henna-red marble so much prized by the Roman world was quarried. Africa was rich in quarries, which provided both stone – the cliff quarry at El Haouaria, from which stone was cut for Carthage, is one of the most impressive sights in Tunisia – and marble, in the enormous colour-range of the *tesserae* used in the mosaics; but since, like the mines, they all belonged to the Emperor and were largely worked by slaves they brought little profit to the Africans themselves. There was some mining also, for copper, lead and iron, but it remained a minor part of the economic life of the time.

The importance of wood has to be assumed: though copses and woodland on the domains were cleared by the peasants themselves, or by such slaves as there were on the 'home farms', there must have been some kind of gang-labour to cut the quantities of wood needed, in both Africa and Italy, to supply fuel for the public baths, which consumed enormous quantities, and timber for the construction of buildings.

Leather and textiles also leave little evidence behind them. The spinning and weaving of the wool of domestic animals was naturally for local use; but Africa had long been celebrated for its fine textiles, and it continued to export them. Dyeing with the purple of the murex shell was a source of wealth for the inhabitants of Meninx on the Island of Djerba and for Chullu (Collo) on the north coast; besides dyers, fullers and curriers, tanners and shoemakers have left records, and there must have been ancillary trades. Most of this activity was in no sense industrialized; for one large tannery found at Tipasa, dozens of one-man artisan workshops have been identified by archaeologists.

The same is true of the modest manufacture of metals. Hardly a mention of them survives – a rare inscription here or there of a blacksmith, a goldsmith, a silversmith. One can imagine them sitting in their tiny shops in the side-streets of the cities, just as their modern descendants do in the souks of Tunis.

The one major industry of North Africa, the one which has left the clearest and most impressive evidence behind it, absorbed wealth rather than created it, except indirectly. The building and upkeep of five or six hundred stone cities, countless aqueducts and twelve thousand miles of roads must have called for substantial numbers of builders and masons. The Third Augustan Legion and its veterans built a handful of the cities and roads of the province; others were built by veterans from other provinces; the vast majority were built by the natives. Virtually nothing is known of their organization: perhaps they travelled the country in gangs like the harvesters; perhaps they were recruited from the local inhabitants themselves, both slave and free, on a permanent or temporary basis. They were certainly not imported from abroad, for the old Punic unit of measurement, the cubit of twenty inches, rather than the Roman foot of twelve, was commonly used, and the walls of town houses – upright orthostat blocks every few yards filled in with small stones or bricks set in mortar – seem to owe more to local lath-and-plaster antecedents than to standard Roman methods.

But if wealth was spent on building cities, and the waterworks and roads which supplied them, it was made there also: on the buying and selling, the processing and transporting of Africa's rural produce.

Remains of industrial building at Tipasa—for what purpose remains uncertain (dyeworks, tannery, pottery have been suggested), but possibly for the production of a popular delicacy made of fish

Ancient tannery in modern use at Fez, Morocco

6 The six hundred cities

Two sides of the Roman genius: visible column and unseen sewer at Sabratha

The harvester of Mactar grew up and spent his working life in the countryside; but as soon as he had enough money he went to live in the town. There was no question, then, of him or any other rich African wanting to become a country gentleman, living in a mansion in the middle of his land. The very rich might have a suburban villa in order to escape the heat of the towns in the height of summer, or possibly a hunting lodge in the hills; but even the proconsul's villa was in the suburbs of Carthage, hardly more than a mile or two from his palace in the city itself. The Carthaginians had made permanent homes of their country houses; but the Roman-African rich of the first three centuries were essentially city-dwellers. Indeed, certain towns like Volubilis seem to have been inhabited solely by the rich and their hangers-on. The great country villas which are so familiar from the mosaics of North Africa all belong to the late third and early fourth centuries A.D., when life in the towns had become a great deal less agreeable.

But in the golden age of the High Empire the Africans took to city life with an enthusiasm unparalleled anywhere else in the Roman Empire. Neither Gauls nor Spaniards nor Britons showed themselves so eager for the amenities of Romanization. In the cities of the east, with their memories of a greater past and their resentment of an exploiting conqueror, Greeks, Jews and Asiatics bewailed the loss of their former independence. But, to the better-off African, Roman rule meant not subjection but opportunity – not merely to become a Roman citizen, but to help govern his city, to join the imperial bureaucracy, to be freed perhaps from the usual taxes and tribute, and even, if he were rich enough, to become a senator in Rome itself.

There were three kinds of city in Roman North Africa: the old Phoenician towns, almost all on the coast, which had always had a sizeable immigrant population and were throughout the Roman period much the most cosmopolitan; the Roman-built garrison towns and veterans' colonies, like Lambaesis and Timgad, built on virgin territory on or near the frontiers; and, by far the greater number, the modest cities of the interior, which were essentially market towns which grew out of Berber villages and hamlets. There was some overlapping, of course; Carthage was rebuilt as a *colonia* by the Romans, and many veterans' colonies were settled in other Phoenician towns, while market towns developed over the course of time next to garrisons, or replaced them when the Legion moved on.

By the third century, there were five or six hundred cities. Two hundred of them were in the rich farmlands of northern Tunisia, in places no more than six or eight miles apart; in the valley of the River Bagradas (Medjerda) there was virtually ribbon development along the main road from Carthage to Theveste (Tébessa). Few were cities as we think of them today, for their population was too small, mostly between five and ten or fifteen thousand; some of them had even fewer inhabitants. Probably only Carthage ran to a six-figure population, and Leptis Magna, the second city of North Africa, had perhaps eighty thousand. Another dozen or so had between twenty and forty, most of them major ports like Sabratha in Tripolitania, Hadrumetum (Sousse) in Proconsularis, Utica, Hippo Regius, Hippo Diarrhytus and Caesarea on the north coast. The only inland cities of comparable size were Juba's old capital in the far west, Volubilis; Cirta, long the capital of the kings of Numidia and for centuries past colonized by Italian immigrants, which was strategically placed on a major crossroads; and Thysdrus (El Djem), in the heart of the olive groves of Tunisia. There was a scattering of cities with nearer twenty than ten thousand inhabitants; the rest were no bigger than large villages.

They were cities not by virtue of their size but by virtue of their function, and the privileges granted by Rome. Very few started as cities: there were only seven in the days of the Republic – Phoenician towns like Utica which had sided with the Romans, and new Roman colonies. The remainder achieved city status when they had grown large and prosperous enough to govern themselves, administer their own justice, and collect

Roman amphitheatre at Mactar, central Tunisia—converted into rough and ready homes by modern inhabitants

Corner of the market at Timgad. It was built by a private citizen, Sertius, who also put up statues of himself and his wife Valentina

their own taxes, for it suited the Emperors to delegate most of the burdens of rule to their subjects. There was a whole hierarchy, from the true city or *colonia*, whose inhabitants were full Roman citizens largely exempt from taxes; through the *municipium*, whose government was also modelled on that of Rome, with a council similar to the Senate and two duumvirs elected, like the consuls, for a year, but whose inhabitants had lesser rights and were not necessarily Roman citizens unless they or their forebears had been magistrates or had received citizenship as a favour from the Emperor for other services; right down to the Berber villages. These, too, with increasing population and wealth, could aspire to higher status.

As the nomads found their grazing areas restricted, many of them took to more settled forms of stock-raising, and to farming, under the leadership of their hereditary chiefs. They, too, built villages, and the Romans recognized them by granting the chiefs the titles of *princeps* or *praefectus*, even, occasionally, *regulus*. Numbers of smaller cities originated in this way, and developed in time into Roman *res publicae*. Others developed on the *saltus*: landless labourers and small-holding peasants built their homes round the main farm buildings; as land on the fringes was brought into cultivation, there was extra produce for sale or exchange, and the land-owners, whether private or imperial agents, founded a weekly market. Groups of *saltus* arranged between them a cycle of market days, so that each village held its market on a different day: a custom enshrined in the names of their present-day counterparts, for Souk El Arba means Wednesday market, and Souk El Khemis Thursday market. Local trade combined with a rising population attracted traders and merchants from outside, gradually the village grew larger and richer, with a bourgeoisie of its own, and acquired its own municipal territory from the domain: it made no difference to the Emperor, by now much the largest land-owner in the province, whether he collected his taxes and *annona* through his agents or through municipal authorities. If the township was on a main road, so much the better;

here a *mansio* might be built by the army, at which the *annona* was collected and where the army and the imperial functionaries could collect their share before the remainder was despatched to the coast. This meant more trade, a larger middle class, and artisans like potters and shoemakers to cater for the needs of men with money to spend.

Most of the villages which grew into cities were in the plains of Tunisia and Algeria; in the far west of Morocco, where the nomads still had unrestricted grazing grounds and farming itself was hardly above subsistence level, and in the dry south and in the Tripolitanian hinterland even villages were fewer. But remains of plenty of substantial towns have been discovered in the wild mountain country of central Algeria, where modern towns are few and far between, and villages an impoverished huddle of shacks.

For the natives eagerly followed their new masters' example: their towns were built of stone, and embellished with handsome and often grandiose temples, forums, market places and public baths. Though the Emperors sometimes donated money for public buildings – what remains of Leptis Magna, for instance, was largely built by its native son Septimius Severus – in hundreds of cities the money for building was provided by new-rich citizens. In the ancient world there were few investment outlets for profits. Some rich men invested their money in shipping, which was extremely lucrative, and was the source of many African fortunes in the coastal cities; the profits still had to be spent. There was little industry to invest in – money was not used to finance an industrial revolution which could, eventually, have raised the basic standard of living of the very poor. Instead, it was spent on conspicuous consumption and, like the Suffolk and West Country wool fortunes of the English middle ages, on buildings.

Auditorium of the theatre at Leptis Magna

All the natural competitiveness of the rich second-century African, frustrated by the *pax Romana* from its traditional expression in war, was poured into the improvement of his native city, into a determination to rise in the local hierarchy to the highest magisterial posts, and into the pursuit of prestige in the eyes of his fellows.

The typical R
a long way fro
down at Timgad
to an older town
but when the pre
the former stre
When a market t
or a garrison, th

Gorgon

Gymnesium

Auditorium and frons scaenae of the theatre at Djemila (ancient Cuicul). The eroded hills behind were once flourishing farmlands and orchards

structed without much semblance of order on the perimeter, doubtless on the sites of the earliest camp followers' shacks as and when they were pulled down to make way for improvements. Berber villages were on the crests of hills; when the slope was sharp, the main street was obliged to zig-zag from one end of the town to the other. It would have been impossible to impose much order on the abrupt site of Thugga (Dougga), an old native settlement, and even at Cuicul (Djemila), which was founded by veterans of the Third Augustan Legion, although the main road runs straight along the narrow spur on which the city was built, expansion meant that the streets had to fit in as best they could with the lie of the land on either side. At Lambaesis, the garrison was built with admirable regularity; but the town which grew up on the rising ground to the south could not be compressed into the same mould.

Nonetheless, the core of a Roman town had a pattern. The two principal roads, the *decumanus maximus* and the *cardo maximus*, which were its arteries to the outside world, crossed at right angles in the centre. All the other streets of the city were, ideally, built parallel to one or other of these. Like the agricultural land, cities followed the original survey system of the province (the *cardo maximus* of Carthage, which ran south-west out of the city to become the main road to Theveste, seems to have been its base-line, from which were calculated the innumerable parcels of land in the survey).

At the main crossroads was the forum, which was the heart of a city, the square where public life was visibly lived. This, like the main streets, was always paved (though wheeled traffic was forbidden), frequently colonnaded against the sun, and the site of the *curia*, or city hall. Just as in Athens and the city states of the Greek world, the comings and goings in this open place in front of the seat of local government played a vital part in fostering the sense of community, and collecting news and trade from the further world. Sometimes, as a city expanded, a second forum was built, as at Cuicul and Thubursicu Numidarum (Khémissa) and

View of the gymnasium, with the great baths complex on the left, from the top of the nymphaeum at Leptis Magna. The baths and gymnasium were built in the first century A.D., the nymphaeum—one of the city's most splendid monuments—at the end of the third, by Septimius Severus

Leptis Magna; but the most important forum remained that which contained the *curia*. Often an inscription records the name of the private citizen or Emperor who donated the money for it; the old forum at Leptis Magna was built in 1 B.C. by Annobal Rufus Tapapius (whose Phoenician descent is obvious from his name, and who had plainly not suffered from the Roman conquest), while the new forum was donated three centuries later by the Emperor Septimius Severus.

The forum was also normally the site of the basilica, or court of justice; usually there were shops and 'bars' as well, and on market days it commonly served as a market place.

Gorgon's head from the forum built at Leptis Magna by the Emperor Septimius Severus

Special market places were, however, built in the wealthiest cities. The one at Leptis was built by the same Annobal Rufus Tapapius, with booths along the sides and two kiosks in the middle for the officials who settled disputes or collected taxes and generally saw to good order. Timgad's market was also donated by a private citizen, who erected statues of himself and his wife there, and Cuicul even boasted a separate cloth market, as well as a food market. The latter still has a *ponderarium* of standard weights and a table with circular standard measure cavities. Temples were built to various gods and Emperors – whose cult was of great importance – and even to abstractions such as Concord, which must have seemed invested with magical powers in that once war-torn land. The richest cities built capitols – temples dedicated to the three principal gods of the Roman pantheon, Juno, Jupiter and Minerva. Many must have had libraries, although only one, at Timgad, has been identified. Streets, forums and marketplaces were infested with statues of emperors, gods, and leading citizens anxious to impress themselves on their neighbours: many were well over life-size. Those found at Bulla Regia

Statue of Valentina from the market of Sertius, now in the Timgad Museum

make a visit to the gallery in the Bardo which now houses them a claustrophobic experience.

Of all Rome's provinces, Africa is today the richest in examples of the triumphal arch. It was built more as a kind of monumental street furniture than as part of the outer defences of a city, for which, with its open arches, it would have been useless. Surmounted by long-vanished bronze statues of gods or Emperors, frequently in chariots pulled by horses, they were permanent rèminders to the inhabitants of Roman might. Often they were erected at the approaches to a city, some distance away; sometimes they formed a kind of roundabout at some public place. There is a fine triple arch at Timgad, other generously columned arches at Cuicul; even a tiny hill-top city like Tiddis, near Constantine, has its own modest arch across the main street. But the finest is the magnificent four-way arch at Leptis Magna, though denuded of its processional friezes (now in the Tripoli Museum) which are the high point of Roman African sculpture.

One of the two kiosks in the market place at Leptis Magna

At Ammaedara (Haïdra), at Mactar, at Cillium (Kasserine), on the edge of the desert, in the depths of the countryside, the traveller is constantly astonished at the sight of vast, pedimented, pilastered mausoleums inscribed with the career of a man or a family in whose memory they were erected. Rich Africans were not content with a dedication in a marketplace or a forum to remind posterity of their existence. They also built these elaborate memorials, perhaps on the land which belonged to them, for themselves and their families. Some think it may have been a hangover into Roman times of the old African ancestor worship, and that surviving relatives may have made an expedition, on feast days or anniversaries, to worship at the tomb of the head of the family.

The Romans built for pleasure on as grand a scale as they did for piety or government. Some two dozen theatres have been found in North Africa; others no doubt have yet to be discovered; still more, of wood, must have perished. No city of any size was without one. Usually they were cut into a hillside; where

Fine mausoleum inscribed with a 110-line poem at Kasserine, Tunisia

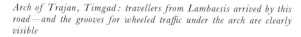

Arch of Trajan, Timgad: travellers from Lambaesis arrived by this road—and the grooves for wheeled traffic under the arch are clearly visible

no slope was available, the semi-circle of seats was built up over huge curving galleries, as at Sabratha. This theatre has been restored by the Italians to something approaching its original splendour. Here, between the imposing double-storeyed *frons scaenae*, its architectural style as much Renaissance as Roman, and the exquisite bas-reliefs of the screen, modern revivals of classical tragedy are sometimes staged. Roman African audiences, however, clamoured for entertainments like the pantomime which Apuleius describes in *The Golden Ass:* musical comedies with half-naked dancing girls, clowns and mimes. The theatres of the time were more palaces of varieties than temples of dramatic art. They were as popular as the cinema in our own day, and leading actors enjoyed the reputations of film stars – even though, as a profession, acting was looked down on, and actors could not hope, even had they wished, to become city dignitaries. To finance a free show was expected, however, from aspiring magistrates; the city of Cirta even had its own permanent acting company. It was a mark of imperial favour when Caracalla lent his finest actor, Agrippa, to Leptis Magna.

The theatres were not the only places of public entertainment. The Legion brought with it a taste for gladiatorial combat, and for fighting with wild beasts, and almost no garrison was without its modest amphitheatre. The civilian population took to these cruel spectacles with avidity, and they soon became the recognized method of putting prisoners, criminals and, later, Christians to death. One of the earliest and finest North African mosaics, from Zliten in Tripolitania, shows just such a scene of carnage: two naked prisoners strapped to little carts are thrust forward into the jaws of wild beasts. There is a musical accompaniment to drown the shrieks of the victims: a small orchestra, which includes a woman player. Many amphitheatres must have been of wood, but with increased prosperity were replaced by stone constructions. The most famous is the

Temple of Juno Caelestis at Dougga built between 222 and 235 A.D., *just before the sudden conversion of the bulk of the population of this part of Roman North Africa to Christianity at the end of the third century*

great amphitheatre at Thysdrus (El Djem), which rivalled in size the Colosseum at Rome itself. Only Carthage had an amphitheatre as large, but by the third century few of the more prosperous cities were without one of their own. Nearly thirty are known.

Chariot racing was also followed with as much enthusiasm as motor racing today. A leading charioteer was the Grand Prix winner of his day, and won fame, fortune and considerable social status, however humble his origins. The leading horses were im-

The semi-circular library at Timgad

Part of the frieze from the four-way arch of Septimius Severus at Leptis Magna, now in the Tripoli Museum

mortalized in the mosaic floors of their owners' homes. The elongated circuses, where the races were held, have scarcely survived, except as sites; five have been discovered.

Naturally, the richest cities had the greatest number and variety of public buildings, donated either by private citizens or by the Emperors. But scarcely a city worth the name was without its own public baths, and preferably several different establishments; Timgad, for instance, had thirteen. They were as important in the social life of a city as the forum and the *curia*. This was one Roman import which made more difference than any to the ordinary comfort of the inhabitants. They offered coolness and cleanness in that stifling climate, and also companionship: they were like clubs, where a man might agreeably spend the whole day and be sure of meeting half his acquaintance. Women could use them on ladies' days, or bathe in separate rooms. The poor too could bathe there – for the rich donated money for

Oven where fuel was burnt to heat air for baths at Timgad

Tables with standard-measure cavities in the market place at Leptis Magna

The amphitheatre at El Djem (ancient Thysdrus), central Tunisia and (below) where warm air circulated under the floor of baths at Timgad

their running costs and the baths were often free, sometimes every day, sometimes on certain days of the week only.

Public baths were built in considerable style. Cleanliness rivalled godliness, and indeed the remains at Leptis Magna and Carthage, in their size and solidity, seem more like cathedrals than other secular buildings of the time. This is partly because they had vast vaulted ceilings. The huge barrel vault had been made possible by the Roman discovery of a concrete from which all air had been expelled (which was not improved upon until the advent of Portland cement in the nineteenth century), and the sophisticated skill with which they used it. Certainly the baths were utterly unlike the temples of the day, four square and sturdy with pediments and pitched roofs; for where temple architecture concentrated on an

89

imposing outward appearance, with marble-columned porticoes and fine flights of steps, the men who built the baths were primarily concerned with the interior: the exterior simply followed the internal spaces. From the outside, they must have looked like giant versions of the modest barrel-vaulted houses to be seen all over North Africa today.

Inside, there were various baths – hot, cold, tepid; plunge baths and steam baths. Latrines were provided for both men and women, and there are still fine examples, whole rows of them, at Leptis, Djemila and Madauros, which once were continually flushed. There were exercise rooms where

young men could wrestle; rest rooms; even small shops and bars. Naturally not all were so elaborate, and only the richest had columns of imported granite from Egypt or Corsican marble; but lavish mosaics and marble facings on floors, walls and ceilings were general. Beneath the main rooms was all the apparatus of water supply and water heating: furnaces, conduits, drains, hypocausts, and fuel stores.

No inscription records the names of the architects of these monuments, for they were built to the greater glory of the gods or the Emperors, the donors or the cities. Architecture was a trade like any other, and without

The frigidarium, or cold bath, at Leptis Magna. The statue is of Apollo, but has the face of Hadrian's favourite, Antinous

much prestige in the Roman world since it was left to underdogs like Greeks and Orientals. Much of Leptis Magna, which bears striking similarities to the Roman cities of Syria, may have been built by Syrian architects – especially since Septimius Severus, who was responsible for many of the buildings that survive, was married to a Syrian princess. Probably many cities were built by the same architect; and there are signs of an African 'school' by the second century. Most of it was basically provincial jobbing architecture, but in a style far superior to any the Carthaginians had followed.

Latrines attached to the baths at Leptis Magna

Fountain in the principal street of Djemila (ancient Cuicul), Algeria

Mosaic of Neptune, god not only of the sea but of inland waters, and a popular subject of mythological art. Now in the museum at Sousse.

Mosaic of wrestlers in the Bardo Museum, Tunis

There are at least two hundred and fifty days of sun every year in North Africa. In summer the heat can be suffocating, and in parts very humid. Shade and water are vitally important. The Romans made living conditions as comfortable as possible. Public baths were only part of their response to the challenge. Streets and private houses were also well provided with water; there were public fountains in forums and market places (a fine example is at Djemila), and many cities had great *nymphaea*, or water basins, with fountains and statues, often sheltered by a portico: the *nymphaeum* at Leptis is one of the most remarkable among that crowd of splendid ruins.

Running water was frequently laid on to private houses. Occasionally water was siphoned up to first-floor level. Not that water was actually laid on to the kitchen, where it would have saved the household staff fetching and carrying it; there was no shortage of domestic servants, and that kind of labour-saving never occurred to the Romans. Water was primarily for the use and enjoyment of the master and his family – sometimes for private baths, above all for fountains in the inner courtyards.

This lavish use of water was made possible by the most scrupulous water-collection. Every Roman house had its own cistern, in which rainfall was collected: one constantly stumbles into their barrel-shaped remains, used now as garden sheds or chicken huts, in the gardens of houses all round Carthage. Wells were sunk, sources tapped, the local oued dammed to form a reservoir. Water was stored in underground reservoirs. Private enterprise, however, was not enough; water management was a municipal responsibility. Public baths used vast quantities, and needed it at greater pressure than could be provided by wells. As towns grew, local wells and carefully hoarded winter streams were soon exhausted. Water had to be imported, sometimes from great distances, by aqueduct. Because water was so important, it was treated with some reverence: often splendid colonnaded monuments surrounded the distant mountain source where it was tapped, as at Zaghouan, which supplied Carthage, and the beautiful marble 'temple' outside Timgad; and fine 'water houses' were built to store the water in the cities. Dedications to Neptune, who was the god of fresh water as well as the sea, abound. From the water houses an elaborate network of canals led to every part of the city, sometimes overground, sometimes under the streets. In one residential quarter of Volubilis the underground conduits have been traced in great detail: each house was fed from the municipal supply, and a similar network of drains carried away sewage. Volubilis was, like Timgad, a planned city, but the visitor to almost any excavated Roman city in North Africa will detect somewhere, from the hollow ring of feet on the stone, the presence of a water channel beneath the flagged street.

There is no record of North African city dwellers dying of thirst: the quantity of baths suggests that they had all they needed.

(Right) Arch of Caracalla at Djemila

92

Small water channel leading under a roadway at Timgad

But they had it because, either with the army's help or following the Roman example, they took the trouble to get it.

Certain cities had their *raison d'être* in water: Hammam Lif near Tunis, for instance, was in Roman times a spa, as it is today. Apuleius went there to take the waters. Carpi (Korbous) in the Cape Bon peninsula was known as the African Baiae.

Shade was as important to health and well-being as water. Often there were public gardens, and cemeteries were always planted with trees. Trees were sometimes grown in the streets, which were usually very narrow – often only one chariot-width, even the main streets of major towns (just as they are in modern Arab villages); the buildings on one side shaded those on the other. The forums and some streets were lined by arcades against the sun, most public buildings had generous open porches, and private houses were built facing inwards round an inner courtyard.

This house plan, which was originally Hellenistic, probably reached North Africa in Punic times; but it suited the climate so well that, of all the architecture of the ancient world, it is the only type of building to survive the Arab invasions. The Arab *dar* is its direct descendant: virtually blank-walled against the glare of the outside world, or using the outside wall for tiny one-room shops as the Roman Africans did, the only light inside coming from the open courtyard in the middle.

Occasionally an extreme solution was adopted. At Bulla Regia, near the Algerian border of Tunisia, houses were constructed

Underground house at Bulla Regia, above ground and below

underground. The streets were at first-floor
level, and stairs led down into the earth.
(Even at this depth, there was a proper water
system: that, and the mosaic floors and
columned courtyard, is all that in practice
distinguished them from the troglodyte
dwellings of Matmata.) Often, too, on
sloping sites, houses were cut back into the
hillside.

Very few private town houses were large.
Most men's lives were lived in public or out
of doors – either on their land if it was near
the city, or in the curia and the forum, or
in the market place. Leisure, too, was
frequently devoted to public amusements;
so the Roman Africans spent their money on
public comfort, and their houses were fairly
simple. Yet the site museums are full of
mosaics taken not only from the baths and

the temples and curias but also from private houses – which, when they were not paved with marble, were often decorated with mythological scenes, portraits of the four seasons, and scenes from daily life: banquets, spectacles, hunting, fishing, and the agricultural life of the domains. This passion for interior décor is a major source of our knowledge of the life of the time. Many mosaics, especially of mythological scenes, were local copies of well-known eastern models; others were designed and made up in squares abroad, and then imported to be laid by local workmen. But some North African mosaics have no affinity with other Roman mosaics. No doubt many a new-rich landowner or merchant commissioned mosaics in the international style; but here and there a local craftsman developed a style of his own. (At Djemila, where the museum boasts some of the most original, a minor provincial school seems to have developed.) The best work is distinguished by a lively naturalism, where the artist has used his eyes as well as his sense of fitness to depict what he saw and knew for himself: a chariot race, oxen ploughing, the trapping of wild beasts.

Central heating for an underground house at Bulla Regia: warm air circulated through the ducts in the angle of the wall

Agriculture, not unexpectedly, was a favourite theme; so, too, was the sea, and heads of Neptune and marine scenes are found inland as well as on the coast. The celebrated mosaic now in the Bardo which shows twenty-three different types of ocean-going vessel was found at Medeïna (Althiburos), nearly a hundred miles from the sea.

Third-century mosaic of Ulysses and the sirens, found at Dougga and now in the Bardo Museum

Fishing—a constant theme of Roman mosaics. This one is in the Bardo

Mosaic from El Djem of the early third century A.D. The subject is a banquet—held to celebrate the games in which the bulls in the foreground were taking part

Most marine mosaics, however, followed conventional models of the day; but their popularity suggests that many a rich citizen of the interior owed at least a part of his prosperity to investment in shipping.

If town life was sweet for the rich, it was also more agreeable for the poor, whether they lived in their masters' households, or in their little one-room workshops, or in tenements (as at Carthage) in a poor quarter, or in hamlets and villages near the cities. They, too, could visit the baths, see life and exchange views in the market place and forum, flock to the theatre or the games or the chariot racing. If they did not have much money to spend, much was available to them free. They could share some, at least, of the pleasures of Roman life.

Some of the increased prosperity came their way even more directly. Many rich men kept open house, and it was often possible for a poor man to pick up a free meal, or at least hope that a man anxious for election would give a public banquet in which he would be able to share.

Meanwhile, the rich who were so conspicuously devoting themselves to the good of their cities were hoping to be rewarded not only by the gratitude of their fellow citizens, but by that of the Emperor. They began to seek, and to find, a wider fame.

7 Careers open to talent

View of Leptis Magna. The ruined theatre is on the skyline

In the nineties of the first century A.D., a literary jury at Rome reached a unanimous verdict: the prize for poetry should be awarded for the first time to an African, P. Annius Florus. But the young man never received it. At the last moment, the Emperor Domitian, who had instituted the prize, refused to ratify the jury's decision. It was unheard of – unthinkable – that a provincial should carry off his prize from under the noses of Italian competitors.

The Emperor's veto caused a sensation in Roman literary circles; Florus himself said later that his rage had nearly driven him into insanity. It was also absurd: it was flouting the temper of the times. For Italy's economic decline was matched by political and cultural decline: the old colonial Empire, with Italy at its head, was changing into an Empire where the separate provinces had more and more influence. Provincials were even about to sit on the throne of the Caesars. Not two years after Domitian's death in A.D. 96, the Spanish Trajan succeeded to the purple. The pre-eminence of Italy was over. For those with eyes to see, it had long been obvious: Spanish influence in Rome had been strong for some time.

For most of the second century Africans were to dominate the intellectual life of the Empire. There had already been harbingers: the playwright Terence, who reached Rome as the slave of a senator in the second century B.C., was a Berber. His owner, won over by his beauty and charm, freed him and gave him an education; and he left his African origins so far behind that he became a friend of the Scipio who destroyed Carthage. (To him we owe the phrases 'homo sum; humani nil a me alienum puto', 'hinc illae lacrimae' and 'quot homines tot sententiae'.) Manilius, too, a poet of the early first century A.D., was probably African. More significant for the future, though, was the career in the middle of the century of Cornutus, a teacher of rhetoric and philosophy at Rome; for it was as leading orators and philosophers, and above all jurists, that the Africans of the Antonine Age played a leading part in the life of the Empire. Even Apuleius, the greatest of them, was – among a variety of other things – an orator and advocate, who prided himself more on being a *philosophus Platonicus* than on being the author of *The Golden Ass*.

Even a modest city provided a decent education for the sons of the rich and those sons of the poor whose gifts attracted the patronage of munificent citizens. Apuleius himself went to school in the small town in Numidia where he was born; two hundred years later, St Augustine also spent part of his schooldays in Madauros, and was helped to further education by a rich friend of his father's. Local schoolmasters were respected citizens, comparatively well paid out of municipal funds; if cities vied with each other in the splendour of their public monuments, they also took pride in the renown of their local grammarian.

Surprisingly, for so practical a people, Roman education was devoted almost entirely to the written and above all the spoken word. Arithmetic was taught, as well as reading and writing, in the elementary schools; but thereafter the aim of schooling was to turn an educated man into an orator. Rhetoric and grammar were the main subjects; the teaching of other subjects was left to the rhetoricians, for there was little specialization. Indeed, the local schoolmaster might also be the local doctor.

In these circumstances, there could be no serious study of history or science, of music or of poetry. Such science as there was was lifted wholesale from books; and original research was virtually unknown. Apuleius, with his exceptional curiosity, dissected fish and made optical experiments with mirrors; but to his compatriots such activities smacked of black magic. The great Roman historians of the Republic and the Augustan age were read, or dismissed, for their prose style. When it was not simply a pastime, literature was studied for its moral examples. It was the education of pedants; style without reference to subject matter was everything.

Still, it was better than nothing. Ordinary soldiers could read; so, very likely, could peasants like those of the Saltus Burunitanus, who had before their eyes the imperial laws in inscriptions. In the cities of the Empire and their surrounding territories, literacy among the poor was higher under the Romans than it was to be again until the end of the nineteenth century.

It was certainly better than what had gone before. The Latin language is a marvellous instrument for the expression of both thought and feeling; and the freedom and liveliness with which Africans like Apuleius learnt to use it suggest that their ancestors had little literature because their languages, Punic and Libyan, lacked flexibility and vocabulary. Latin gave Africans a tongue. At a time when Latin was declining in Rome in favour of Greek, and the nobility spoke the language of their erstwhile enemies (the Romans were the first people to teach a foreign language as part of the regular syllabus), rather as Tsarist aristocrats spoke French at home, African scholars and lawyers and writers gave it a new lease of life. The great Christian apologists of Africa, Tertullian, St Cyprian and St Augustine, played an important part in ensuring that the language of the Catholic liturgy bequeathed to the Middle Ages was Latin and not Greek, its original language.

After school, clever boys went to Carthage for further study. 'What better or more certain title for praise,' Apuleius wrote years later of his *alma mater,* 'than the celebration of Carthage, where every citizen is a cultivated person and where all devote themselves to all fields of knowledge, children by learning them, young men by showing them off, and old men by teaching them? Carthage, venerable mistress of our province, Carthage, divine muse of Africa, Carthage, prophetess of the nation which wears the toga?' By this time the population of Carthage probably numbered a third of a million; it was as large as Alexandria, Antioch and Seleucis; only Rome was larger. It was not, in any technical sense, the capital of Africa, since the Mauretanias and Numidia had their own capitals which were the seats of independent Roman governors; but only Africa Proconsularis had a proconsul as its governor, and his seat, Carthage, was also the major port for trade. It was no minor provincial town, and it was, and remained, an intellectual capital.

Even so the rich young men of North Africa went abroad to complete their education. The 'universities' of Athens and Rome were full of them. The Roman Empire was international, and in nothing more than this. Its schools taught Latin and frequently Greek, and a man could make himself understood in one or other language from one end of the Empire to the other. For the upper classes there was no language barrier, and for no one a national barrier.

Indeed Africans were achieving positions of considerable prestige in the life of the capital, especially during the reign of Hadrian. Florus himself, whose career as a poet had begun so stormily under Domitian, became a famous Roman rhetorician. Old slights forgotten, he had devoted himself to extolling the glories of Rome. The poet Juvenal, who died during Apuleius' youth, had already described Africa as the 'foster mother of advocates' and if he meant that all Africans were naturally litigious, there were plenty of professionals among the barrack-room lawyers to add force to his dictum.

In the middle of the second century, two of the most renowned lawyers in Rome were African-born. Marcus Cornelius Fronto was born at Cirta (Constantine), at the beginning of the century; and although he was probably descended from the Italian immigrants who had always formed a large minority of the population of the old Numidian capital, he proudly claimed descent from Libyan nomads. He had been east to complete his education, and by his early twenties had established himself in the capital, where he rapidly became more Roman than the Romans themselves. His devotion to Latin took the form of a scrupulous pursuit of the *mot juste,* a pursuit which too often led him into artificiality and archaism. But his enthusiasm for perfection made him much in demand as a teacher, and he had considerable success at the bar. Hadrian, who shared some of his literary tastes, appointed him tutor to the adopted sons of his designated heir Antoninus, one of whom was the future Emperor Marcus Aurelius. Imperial patronage no doubt helped Fronto to become the centre of that intellectual circle which Aulus Gellius (also perhaps African-born) describes in his *Attic Nights*. It also helped him to wealth and status: he became a consul in A.D. 143, and had the refusal of the proconsulship of Asia. He married a close friend of Marcus Aurelius's mother, and was able to buy the gardens in Rome of the legendary Maecenas. His friendship with Marcus Aurelius was lifelong, although the future Emperor disappointed his tutor by turning to the Stoic philosophy, with which Fronto had little patience. Marcus Aurelius speaks of his integrity, and their correspondence, which came to light early last century, is full of mutual affection. The over-conscientious pedagogue (Aulus Gellius describes him breaking off a conversation with the architect who was building him some baths, in order to discuss at length – in spite of being tormented by gout – the correct usage of *praeter propter*) was clearly redeemed by courage and sweetness of character.

The other great African lawyer of second century Rome was Salvius Julianus, born L. Octavius Cornelius at the turn of the century into a knightly family, probably of Hadrumetum (Sousse). While still very young he became head of one of the schools of law at Rome, and made himself very useful to Hadrian. He became a senator, and was commissioned by the Emperor to disentangle the legal position between the inhabitants of Rome and visiting strangers in civil actions. He also became a governor – of Germany and of Spain – and proconsul of his native Africa in A.D. 168.

Young Roman boys were also flocking for their secondary education to the classes of a Carthaginian. This was Sulpicius Apollinaris, who was the leading grammarian of the capital. The future Emperor Pertinax was one of his pupils.

If education was one way to a distinguished career, wealth was another. Many Africans were now rich enough to be admitted to the Roman knights class; there were perhaps three or four equestrian families in the average-sized African city, and members of these families could make careers for themselves in the imperial administration or as officers in the army. There was no racialism in the Roman Empire; these new rich, after

a generation or two, certainly felt themselves the equals of Roman bureaucrats in the proconsul's suite at Carthage or in the administration of the imperial domains. Other, richer Africans, like provincials from elsewhere, were being admitted to the senatorial order (much depleted by the executions and confiscations of Nero and the Year of the Four Emperors in the sixties of the first century A.D.). These local plutocrats were of modest fortune compared to the millionaires of Rome itself; but there were huge profits to be made in shipping, which the Romans (only exceptionally a seafaring people) left in African hands, and the *navicularii* of the ports were grand magnates. Their work was so important in the eyes of the Emperors that they were frequently excused the expenses of civic duties, and enjoyed a privileged position at Ostia, the port at the mouth of the Tiber which Hadrian enlarged to handle the *annona* for Rome.

The first African to become a senator had been a citizen of Cirta, who was ennobled by Vespasian in the seventies of the first century A.D. A hundred years later, there were a hundred African senators. Many of them emigrated to Rome, there to pursue conventional Roman political careers, and there grew up a powerful African lobby. Their influence at court was soon stronger than that of any other province. They remained loyal to their native cities; individual senators frequently became the patrons of their birthplaces, interceding with the Emperors to raise them from *municipium* to *colonia*, or pleading for favours for compatriots newly arrived in Rome. A young African coming to trade or study there would find himself among willing friends and allies.

Meanwhile Africa itself, feeling its own strength, was no longer a culturally unregarded province. It had its own rich men, its own hierarchy, its own Romanized civilization. Students were beginning to come to Carthage not only from all over Africa, but from other parts of the Empire, to learn from the teachers of the 'university'.

The best-documented career – and in many ways a typical one – in this new-rich, newly confident society is that of the greatest of second-century Africans, the mercurial, many-talented Apuleius. Born in Madauros around A.D. 125 – the year the Emperor Hadrian had first visited his troops in Africa – he was the son of a municipal *duumvir*. Like M. Cornelius Fronto he boasted of his part-Numidian descent. After schooling in Madauros and Carthage, having been left a fortune by his father, he went to Athens to learn Greek. He also studied Platonic philosophy and was indoctrinated into the mysteries of the goddess Isis, which play such a significant part in his writings. Then he went to Rome where, as he says himself, he set himself to study Latin – a language he certainly already spoke, but perhaps not like a native Italian. It was the period when Fronto and Salvius Julianus were in the ascendant, and the African lobby was at its most powerful. But men such as these,

lawyers and career politicians, were not the sort to hold Apuleius. In any case, he had run through his share of the family money during his years abroad – he was now around thirty – and Rome was no place for the indigent. He was down to his last three slaves: only just enough to keep his head in the air. So it was in Africa that Apuleius chose to make his career; but he was content to do so, even when a turn in his fortunes would have enabled him to return to Rome.

He returned home by way of Oea (Tripoli), where by a happy chance he was introduced by a former fellow-student to the latter's widowed mother, whom he promptly married. Aemilia Pudentilla was rich. She was also much older than Apuleius, and had hitherto shown no signs of remarrying; her suspicious relatives accused Apuleius of obtaining her consent by magic. Brought

Cargo ships and dolphins: detail of second or third century pavement from the Square of the Guilds at Ostia, the port for Rome

Byzantine fortress at Madauros, Algeria—birthplace of Apuleius

before the proconsul at Sabratha, on one of the Roman magistrate's visits to the city to administer justice, he conducted his own defence with wit and skill. The *Apologia* he delivered is one of the works that have survived; it reveals, besides many details of his personal history, how well he had 'set himself to study Latin', his considerable knowledge of both Greek and Latin authors, and how much, both as orator and advocate, he had learnt from the study of Cicero. He got off; and – presumably with his bride – he spent the rest of his life either at Madauros or at Carthage, as a teacher and public orator, devoting himself principally to the interpretation of Plato.

The Golden Ass (Metamorphoses) was his masterpiece. His exquisite version of the story of Cupid and Psyche, which it includes, is immeasurably superior to its known predecessors; and the whole work is the finest of the romances of the ancient world. It owes much to Apuleius's years in the eastern Mediterranean, but the racy style, the uninhibited enjoyment of low life and high life alike, the passion for both the pleasures of this world and the mysteries of the other, are Apuleius' own. As medieval alchemy owes something to Apuleius's scientific curiosity and taste for magic, so medieval romance owes something to this pagan tale; and nearly two thousand years later, it is still read with pleasure.

*　　*　　*

Literature, law and politics were not the only careers open to talented Africans. More astonishing and indeed spectacular was the military career of the Moor Lusius Quietus, who was certainly a pure Berber – 'from the unknown desert', said one ancient authority. He was the chieftain of some Moorish tribe, still nomadic, on the fringes of Mauretania, whose father had already fought for the Romans against Aedemon after the murder of Ptolemy by Caligula, and had been rewarded with a Roman name and Roman citizenship. The son was promoted to equestrian rank by Domitian for military achievement at the head of his Moorish cavalry, but was soon cashiered for insubordination. His gifts as an officer, with the formidable *goums* under his command, were, however, too striking to ignore; and Trajan reinstated him to fight on the Danube against the Dacians, whose mounted warriors were too much for the standard Roman legions. The Emperors, in their wars against the northern barbarians, were forced to rely more and more on other barbarian horsemen to repel them, and Lusius's bare-headed cavalry are immortalized on Trajan's Column in Rome.

Lusius was awarded a triumph for his Dacian campaign, and the governorship of Mauretania. Then he was given the command of regular Roman troops in Trajan's Asiatic war, for which he was promoted, though rather irregularly, to the Senate. This move incensed his new colleagues: it was early days for a barbarian to appear in the highest councils of the Empire. But Lusius went from strength to strength. A ruthless rearguard campaign against the

Parthians brought him another triumph and the governorship of Palestine, a much more important province than Mauretania; and finally the consulship itself. It seemed as if nothing could stop him.

But the Spanish party was too strong for him. When Trajan died, his old favourite Hadrian was entrusted with command, and the Emperor's widow hurriedly announced that Trajan had adopted Hadrian as his heir just before he died. With Trajan dead and Mauretania two thousand miles distant, Lusius had no allies and, because of the terror he inspired, no friends. Hadrian had his troops disarmed and, when Lusius's cavalry rebelled against the Romans, had Lusius himself put to death.

Lusius was not the only African to whom the Emperors entrusted high military rank. They avoided nomad chieftains, however; Lusius's successors were already Romanized. Trajan gave command of the First Alpine Cohort to a soldier born at Thuburbo Maius, later entrusted him with the supervision of the unloading of the *annona* at Ostia and its transfer to Rome, and finally made him governor of Mauretania. One of Marcus Aurelius's best generals was a citizen of Thibilis (Announa), to whose son the Emperor gave his own daughter in marriage. The man who conquered Scotland for the Romans and built the Antonine Wall, Lollius Urbicus, was a citizen of Tiddis, a township of barely nine acres in the mountains just north of modern Constantine. One family of a city near Thugga (Dougga) produced two prefects of the Praetorian Guard – which by this time meant not merely the command of the troops at Rome itself but virtually the premiership of the Empire. Aemilius Laetus of Thina (near Sfax), who rose to the prefecture during the disastrous reign of Marcus Aurelius's son Commodus, actually turned king-maker.

Since the assassination of Domitian in A.D. 96, the Emperors had at least not died by the swords of their subjects. By chance, Marcus Aurelius was the first of the second-century Emperors to have a son. His predecessors had chosen as their heirs the most promising member of the Roman Senate, a

Private house at Thuburbo Maius, Tunisia

Preceding page: Temple of Septimius Severus, Djemila

Above: Fresco of Nilotic scene in the Hunting Baths at Leptis Magna

Right above: Central heating ducts and mosaic in the Hunting Baths

Right below: Exterior of the Hunting Baths

Above: Remains of olive press at Volubilis   Right: The theatre at Sabratha

Above: The Baths of Antoninus at Carthage   Overleaf: Punic stele

Left: Frieze in the theatre at Sabratha

Remains of Christian chapel at Tiddis, a hill-top city near Constantine

practice which, while it might seem more open to argument as a method of succession than primogeniture, had distinct meritocratic virtues. The next of kin is often not the best man.

Given the choice, however, Marcus Aurelius favoured his next of kin. Commodus was far from being the best man. Marcus Aurelius hated war, but dutifully spent his last years with his army on the northern frontier. Commodus hated war too, but his duty was his last consideration; he never paid any attention to the Empire and its problems. The imperial bureaucracy, by now an efficient international civil service, was left to administer, the army was left to fight; while Commodus indulged in excesses that recalled those of Caligula and Nero. He corrupted the discipline of the Praetorian Guard; he squandered the imperial finances on vulgar extravagances; he put to death senators who complained that he had made a treasonable peace with the Germans; and spent most of his time in the amphitheatre, where his cruel tastes – which included taking part himself in the arena – sickened even the hardened inhabitants of Rome. 'Little chick', Fronto used to refer to Commodus in letters to Marcus Aurelius. Grown up, the little chick referred to himself as 'Amazonius' or 'Exsuperatorius'.

He met his deserts in A.D. 192. He and his African prefect Aemilius Laetus shared a mistress, Marcia, who, discovering that Commodus intended to have Aemilius Laetus put to death, poisoned him. The Emperor died unmourned by Senate or people, and the African became effectively master of Rome. He and his Praetorian Guard, with the Senate's agreement, chose a career soldier called Pertinax (the former pupil of Sulpicius Apollonaris) to be Emperor. Pertinax had been governor of Britain, and was at that time proconsul of Africa; once on the throne, he showed every sign of becoming a strong and efficient ruler in the old Antonine tradition. Laetus soon discovered that the new Emperor intended to put a stop to the petty plundering and corruption which Commodus had permitted the Praetorian Guard. He decided to get rid of him. Eighty-seven days after Pertinax's proclamation, the Praetorian Guard murdered him and put the Empire up for auction to whichever senator would pay them the highest bribe.

But it was Laetus' undoing. The 'winner', Didius Julianus (perhaps a relative of the African Salvius Julianus who had been a leading lawyer a generation earlier), though he reigned for an even shorter time, took the occasion to have Laetus and his mistress put to death. Meanwhile the legions in the provinces, enraged at the presumption of the Praetorian Guard, had proclaimed their own Emperors. Two of the three candidates were African.

*   *   *

In the first century a citizen of Leptis Magna, the son of a Punic father who had been granted Roman citizenship, bought himself a property in Italy, near the old Etruscan city of Veii. His son, one Septimius Severus, became a well-known rhetorician and a friend of the poet Martial, who congratulated him that nothing in his looks or his speech betrayed his Punic origin. He was wholly Italianized. Back home in Leptis Magna his cousin, another Septimius Severus, became the leading citizen of his native city when Trajan granted it the status of *colonia*, and his family were raised to the equestrian order. Two of his sons followed their relative to Italy, where they entered the Senate and became consuls, no doubt with help from their influential connections. The third, who took little part in public life, remained in Tripolitania. It was a son of this provincial branch, another Septimius Severus, who became the ruler of the Roman world. All his life, he never lost his African accent, and

Arch of Marcus Aurelius in Tripoli, Libya

Septimius Severus (right), Julia Domna, and their sons (one head is damaged): painted wood panel in the Staatliche Museum, Berlin

his Punic-speaking sister, visiting him in Rome, shamed him with her broken Latin.

As a knight, Septimius Severus started his career in the financial service of the Empire. His powerful cousins, however, helped him and his brother to enter the Senate quite early in life. He had a love of hard work and great gifts for organization, and by the time he was forty-five he had had a successful but fairly modest career, having been legate at Lyons and proconsul of Sicily. During the early years of the reign of Commodus he had prudently withdrawn from public life in order to acquire a late education at Athens. He became a consul in A.D. 190; but since it was a year when there were twenty-four consuls, and in any case the real power was now in the hands of the prefects of the Praetorian Guard, it was not a striking promotion.

That very year, however, an economic crisis and shortage of food precipitated a revolt of the Roman mob who, recognizing the realities of power, demanded the head of the then Praetorian prefect, a Syrian. The Syrian was succeeded by the African Laetus, who was anxious, in order to secure his own position, to fill important military posts with fellow Africans. There were three principal army commands at that time: Britain, Upper Pannonia, and Syria. Distant Syria

Laetus left to a nonentity, an Italian called Pescennius Niger; Britain he secured for Clodius Albinus, who came from Hadrumetum; and Septimius Severus was appointed to Pannonia. Commodus hardly cared what was happening. What had been implicit for some time was soon to become clear: the army was the real master of the Empire – or those legions which were able to impose their will. It was Africans who made it clear, and an African who profited.

When Pertinax was murdered three years later, in A.D. 193, both Niger and Severus were proclaimed Emperor by their armies as soon as the news reached them, and it was rumoured in Rome that Clodius Albinus entertained similar ambitions. Severus was nearest to the capital and seized his chance. He made a forced march to Rome, where Didius Julianus had been hurriedly murdered when news of Severus's arrival in Italy reached the city. *Force majeure* obliged the Senate and the Praetorian Guard to recognize him as Emperor. Severus at once disbanded the Praetorian Guard, and reconstituted it mostly with his own provincial troops, to safeguard his rear while he dealt with his rivals. Keeping Albinus quiet with false promises of the succession, he turned east, where he defeated Niger in A.D. 194. The Senate, who disliked Severus as an upstart and a threat to their order, began to intrigue with Albinus, who was from a senatorial family. Albinus rapidly realized that Severus's ambitious Syrian wife would never allow him to succeed in place of her two sons, and himself set off for Rome with his legions. Severus defeated him near Lyons in A.D. 197, and he committed suicide.

Back in Rome, Severus had put to death twenty-nine members of the Senate who had supported Albinus. Many of them must have been Africans themselves, and the executions broke the back of the African lobby. Ironically, it was never again to have such influence as it had done under the Spanish Emperors and during the reign of Marcus Aurelius. Though Severus later introduced other Africans into the Senate, senatorial power had so declined in the face of his military dictatorship that it made little difference. The Senate was at a discount, because Severus favoured his own equestrian order. Army officers increasingly took over major civil governorships from the senatorial order, and the higher ranks of the army were staffed with *equites* from Africa and the east. He depended on the loyalty of the army to himself personally, and even his civil administration was more like a general staff than a bureaucracy.

Septimius Severus did not forget his origins. Leptis Magna owed him a host of splendid monuments, largely financed out of the quantity of property confiscated from those in various parts of the Empire who had supported his rivals. He reorganized the frontier defences of Africa in A.D. 203–4. He made Numidia officially a separate province under the legate of the Third Augustan Legion, encouraged the soldiers to acquire a stake in the land by permitting them to marry and live on plots outside the camps, and seems to have organized the frontier smallholders into a peasant militia grouped round *centenaria*. He promoted the establishment of garrison outposts beyond the *limes*, threatened since the time of Marcus Aurelius by more serious attacks from the desert by nomads – possibly camel-borne.

Severus himself despised African culture – he derided his rival Albinus for his liking for 'old wives' tales and literary nonsense like those Punic Milesian novels of his beloved Apuleius – and felt himself to be thoroughly Roman, well versed in Latin and Greek authors and in law. He struck the Romans, however, as wholly alien, cruel and superstitious in spite of his concern for the improvement of the law: 'the Punic Sulla', some of them called him. Through his strong-minded and clever wife, Rome had its first taste of an older east than Greece: Julia Domna was the daughter of a family of priest-kings of Emesa in Syria, and their sons were as Semitic as she was. Severus felt that the intrigues of Rome corrupted their moral values, and to save them from themselves took them with him on the last campaign of his life. He died in A.D. 211, after three years in Britain fighting the incursions of the highlanders. Strange to think of this native African, who until he grew up had never seen snow, lying on his deathbed in York, where the icy winds of February blow straight from the Urals. Stranger still to think of his exotic family transplanted to the life of the camps, in that damp, thickly-forested land where, in Strabo's words, 'the mist holds on for long, so that in the course of a whole day the sun will only be visible for a few noontide hours.'

The sons Septimius Severus left behind him were no more successful than Marcus Aurelius's. The megalomaniac Caracalla murdered his brother, and was murdered in his turn, like Commodus, by the prefect of the Praetorian Guard, again an African. This Macrinus, for want of a better candidate, was acclaimed Emperor: Lusius Quietus was avenged, and a Moor was at last on the throne of the Caesars. But not for long. Julia Domna, who had been virtually Regent during her son's incapable reign, did not give up easily. She saw an opportunity for pushing the dubious claims of two of her Syrian great-nephews, grandsons of her sister, by pretending that the elder was a bastard son of Caracalla. Her plot succeeded; Macrinus was deposed, and for four years Rome was treated to the spectacle of a teenage Emperor acting as hereditary priest to his Semitic *baal* and marrying a Vestal Virgin. Affront could go no further; and when he was assassinated the women of the family quickly substituted his more moderate cousin Alexander, whom the army murdered, together with his mother, in A.D. 235. So ended the African dynasty, in Oriental mysteries and petticoat government. During the next half century there were twenty-six Emperors, only one of whom died a natural death, before in A.D. 284 Diocletian at last stopped the rot. The third century was a time of anarchy.

Some of the causes of the long-drawn-out disintegration of the Roman Empire were already apparent in the reign of Marcus Aurelius. It had stopped expanding in Trajan's day. The Republic had grown rich on the spoils of the cities of the east, Augustus

(Right) Marble bust of Septimius Severus in the site museum at Djemila

had financed the reorganization of the army and the bureaucracy from the loot of Egypt, his successors had profited from the increase and exploitation of the natural wealth, primarily agricultural, of the provinces he had bequeathed to them. The limits had been reached. Growing pressure from the barbarians in the north in the second century A.D. meant higher costs in soldiers and money, and there were to be no new resources to meet them. It meant higher taxes and dangerous expedients like the debasement of the coinage. The extravagances of Commodus aggravated the crisis, and the civil wars in the north and east which followed his murder put a heavy strain on a tottering structure. Severus's strong arm policy and the stability which, somehow, the Syrian princesses had maintained during the reigns of his successors only staved off more serious decline.

Africa, meanwhile, free of major wars, was still quietly bringing under cultivation the huge tracts of virgin land within her borders. Higher taxes were largely absorbed by a greater population and increasing agricultural production. For her, the second century and early third were the high peak of her prosperity under the Romans. The effects of the crisis of the Roman world only hit her in the middle of the third century, after she became the cockpit of an imperial contest. An expatriate African had played king-maker, an expatriate African had won the crown; now Africa herself played the king-maker. The results were disastrous.

On the death of Alexander Severus the Thracian giant Maximinus had been acclaimed Emperor by the Rhine army which he commanded. He was the first professional-soldier Emperor, and he recognized as clearly as Septimius Severus where his support lay. He doubled his soldiers' pay. More money had to be raised somehow, and taxes were increased; his critics complained at the time that he even confiscated the cities' public funds and temple offerings.

In Africa the imperial procurator set about the new tax-gathering with zeal, particularly in the whole area round Thysdrus, where the inhabitants had just demonstrated their prosperity by building their enormous amphitheatre. 'Among other violent exactions,' reported Herodian, a contemporary, 'the procurator in question had condemned certain wealthy young men of good family and attempted to confiscate all their ancestral fortunes at once.' Enlisting their peasants, the young men murdered the procurator and routed his soldiers. 'The deed done, the desperate young men realized that their only salvation was to venture even greater daring, to make the proconsul of the province share their enterprise and raise general rebellion.'

The proconsul was a rich landed proprietor said to be descended from the Gracchi on his father's side and Trajan on his mother's. The young Africans rightly thought that 'he would welcome the imperial office as a culmination of his career, and the Senate and Roman people . . . would welcome a man of noble birth who had ascended to Emperorship by appropriate degrees' – a dig at the hated Maximinus. After some hesitation, the aged Gordian, associating his son Gordian II with himself, accepted the supreme honour, and the Senate and the European provinces acknowledged his claim.

Unfortunately they reckoned without Capellianus, governor of Numidia and legate of the Third Augustan Legion, who remained faithful to Maximinus. He killed Gordian II in battle, whereupon Gordian I committed suicide. They had reigned for scarcely two months.

The future of the *imperium* was now out of African hands, but Capellianus took revenge. He executed half the aristocracy of Carthage, killed prominent supporters of the Gordians throughout the province, and allowed the Legion to pillage the unprotected countryside as they wished. There was perhaps in this an element of the hatred for the rich olive-growers of the frontier peasant-smallholder – from which class the army was recruited; but all suffered. Parts of the country never fully recovered. Its prosperity was so damaged that the new tax burdens – which were to grow heavier – were impossible to meet.

The loss of confidence is strikingly reflected in the archaeological evidence. The quantity of buildings erected by private donors had risen dramatically during the second century, and had continued steadily, on a lesser scale, throughout the Severan period. After the death of Alexander Severus, however, all such building virtually stopped for half a century. The only monuments put up were gifts either from the Emperors or from imperial governors. It is possible that the Thysdrus amphitheatre was never used by its builders.

There was another serious consequence of the Gordian *débâcle*. A change of fortune brought Gordian I's young grandson, nephew of Gordian II, to the purple in July A.D. 238. One of the first actions of his principate was the disbanding of the Third Augustan Legion for its part in the overthrow of his elder relatives. That same year, a garrison established in the desert by Severus forty years before, at Castellum Dimmidi well to the south of the Numidian *limes*, was withdrawn. The military left behind them, to be covered by the encroaching sand, a quantity of fine objects now in a museum in Algiers, for, like other

regiments in important outposts of other empires, they had done themselves proud; but it was the beginning of the end. The province was contracting, territorially as well as economically.

*   *   *

Meanwhile the cares of the world were beginning, for many Africans, to take second place to the things of the spirit. On July 17, A.D. 180, seven men and five women from Scilli had been brought before the proconsul Saturninus in Carthage for refusing 'to swear by the genius of the Emperor'. The proconsul begged them to 'have no part in this madness.' But they persisted in their refusal and, when Saturninus offered them time to reconsider, one of their number replied: 'When the right is so clear, there is nothing to consider.' Their refusal cost them their lives. When the sentence of death was pronounced, 'they all said "Thanks be to God".' They were the first known Christian martyrs of Africa. It was the dawn of a new age.

Copper or bronze head of a duck in the Constantine Museum

8 The new religion

Hitherto, the official Graeco-Roman pantheon of gods, with Jupiter at their head, had been accepted readily enough by Romanized Africans alongside their old gods. Every sizeable city had a capitol for the worship of Jupiter, Juno and Minerva; Ceres and Neptune, Mars and Liber Pater (Dionysius), Venus and Mercury, Apollo and Aesculapius – all had their devotees. So had Oriental gods like Isis and Mithras, whose cults were spread throughout the Empire by merchants and soldiers and bureaucrats, and which the Romans had themselves adopted from their former enemies in Egypt and Persia – just as, in Hannibal's day, the worship of the gods of the Carthaginians had been introduced to Rome. If the grandest of old Roman families looked upon the eastern mystery religions with disapproval, the Romans in general regarded all gods, in the philosophical spirit of the time, as manifestations of the same divine principle, and therefore to be tolerated and even worshipped. When in Rome, do as the Romans do; with admirable broad-mindedness the Romans suffered this principle to work both ways. And among the poor and uneducated, superstition prompted what philosophy taught the upper classes: a ready acceptance of new gods, new invisible powers to be propitiated.

The old local gods did not disappear with the arrival of the Graeco-Roman gods. In the African countryside the peasants continued to worship the local genii of woods and sources, caves and mountains; and sometimes even educated city-dwellers worshipped in the new Roman temples and followed the Berber cults of their forefathers without any sense of incongruity. If the gods were jealous, it was not of each other. They were more like patron saints, or the *marabous* of the modern Maghreb.

The Punic religion, too, survived. But in part at least it underwent a significant transformation. The city-dwelling Africans were adopting Roman-style names and learning the Roman language (without which any career outside a small town was increasingly impossible); if they themselves were being Romanized, their gods should be Romanized also. Tanit became identified with Juno-Caelestis, Baal with Saturn, Shadrapa with Bacchus, and Melkart with Hercules. They were virtually indistinguishable. It was the Romanized versions of Shadrapa and Melkart whom Septimius Severus, in deference to his origins, adopted as his presiding deities. The enormous quantity of ex-votos dedicated to Saturn by the poor, and the disappearance of the Punic script by the end of the second century, suggests how far, at least in the neighbourhood of the cities of Africa, this Romanization extended. Yet the popularity of Saturn (whose name thinly disguised his original identity as Baal), in preference to Jupiter or Minerva, say, also reveals the strength of old loyalties. For Romanization, whether religious or cultural, was far from complete. It scarcely touched the old nomad hinterland. Many of the rural poor continued to bury their dead curled up and painted red, and went on speaking Libyan or a bastardized Punic long after the latter had ceased to be a written language. As late as the fifth century, St Augustine was urging his fellow-clergy to learn the 'Punic' spoken locally in order to make themselves understood by their parishioners. (Not that this is unusual: more than six hundred years after Wales fell to the English monarchy, and nearly a hundred after the coming of the railways, some of its inhabitants still spoke only Welsh.)

Linked with the worship of Baal was the Punic practice of naming children after the god: Given of Baal or Iatanbaal, Honoured by Baal or Hannibal. Hamilcar was similarly derived from Melkart. With Romanization, the Africans took Roman names but they were names formed on the old pattern and closely connected with worship, whether of Saturn-Baal or, later, the Christian God. Saturninus and Saturus recur constantly; so do Honoratus (Honoured by God), Donatus and Adeodatus (Given of God) – the latter was the name St Augustine gave his own son. Rogatus, Fortunatus, Concessus – no one would take such names for Italian Latin. They have vanished utterly from modern North Africa; but in their place, the Arabs – also a Semitic people like the Phoenicians – name their children Abdullah or Muhammad, Slave of Allah, or his Prophet . . .

In the most Romanized parts of the province, the well-off adopted Roman-style open-air cemeteries, where the vaults were furnished a good deal less sumptuously than had been to the Carthaginian taste; and after a thousand years in which their national costume had been virtually unchanged, they took to the toga. Their womenfolk followed the hairstyles of the ladies of the imperial family – unwittingly publicized by the official statues of succeeding reigns – and wore, even to sleep in, the Roman *mamillare* or *strophium* (breast cloth or band). But for Africans outside the upper classes the toga never became more than a kind of court dress, worn for ceremonial occasions and tomb-stone portraits only. They remained attached to the Oriental sleeves and lively colours, the bangles and baubles, which the Phoenicians had long ago brought with them. To this day the rural population remains faithful to this style of dress – or to an even more ancient garment, the hooded Berber *burnous* of the North African shepherd which first appears in pre-Roman rock engravings. The toga – even the simple tunic – might never have been.

Even in the greater cities, where Romanization was naturally more successful, it took a long time. Two hundred years after the death of Julius Caesar, the future Emperor Septimius Severus, born into a leading family of the second city of the province, was learning Punic in his nursery; and at the turn of the second century, when he was in a position to do so, he even made Punic one of the 'official languages. Old habits died hard, in religious matters as in language. In the temple at Thuburbo Maius dedicated to the new worship of Aesculapius, with whom was now associated the Punic god Eshmoun, the injunction to abstain from pork and beans and from the pleasure of bath and bed for three days before admission to the sacred precinct was merely a temporary version of the permanent vows of the old Punic priesthood. But, both in the cities and the countryside, the unreformed Punic religion survived alongside the new. For not all its adherents welcomed its Roman garb. The *kohanim*, its priests, watched with dismay

Statue in the Tripoli Museum

as the Roman language was introduced into its rites and their knowledge of Punic was no longer indispensable, and as new temples to the Romanized gods were built on the sites of the prophets of old. They retreated to neighbouring heaths and forests, from where they stirred up the faithful against these

Arch of Caracalla at Tébessa, an early third century four-way arch, set in ramparts built by the Byzantines, with modern inhabitant in hooded burnous

hateful innovations with all the fervour of supporters of a losing cause. Some, it was said, still practised the infant sacrifice which the Romans had been at such pains to stamp out; one second-century proconsul hanged some *kohanim* who were alleged to have sacrificed children in a sacred wood near Carthage. They fomented unrest: another proconsul – the future Emperor Pertinax – had to put down what appears to have been a religious rising in Carthage itself.

There were political and social undertones to this religious discontent, no doubt, a hard core of resentment against the new order. This resentment never expressed itself in attempts to provoke tribal invasion from the south – the benefits of the *pax Romana* were too welcome for that – but it may have had something to do with the continuing devotion to the old religion and, shortly, the passionate enthusiasm with which, in the third century, Africans of the lower classes, who were the first to suffer from rising taxes and rising prices, turned to the one religion which the Romans could not tolerate, and which therefore offered, as well as hope of better things in the next world, a way of demonstrating against the masters of this.

In this motley host of cults, there was little difficulty about the introduction of Emperor-worship in the first century A.D. What was one religion more among so many? For most citizens of the Empire it did not go against the grain to worship the mortal representatives of a nation which, for all its faults, was god-like in its beneficence and power. The Jews, it is true, refused to do so; from long custom, and because they made no attempt to make converts, the Romans excused them from participating in the ritual worship of the Emperors.

But, for all their other subjects, Emperor-worship was the one cult the Romans took seriously. More than the worship of Rome's national gods, worship of the Emperors was the symbolic bond that united the diverse peoples under their rule. They also organized it seriously. All public office, whether imperial or municipal and however modest, required an oath of loyalty and, except for soldiers, some form of sacrifice to the Emperor, even if it was only a pinch of incense. Not to sacrifice meant not being able to take any part in public life; not to do that signified to the Romans *odium humani generis*, the equivalent of an anti-social attitude.

There were special provincial assemblies, composed of deputies from among the leading citizens of the cities, which met in the various capitals to celebrate with appropriate ceremony the rites of the Emperors. These assemblies had other functions: they were a useful method of sounding provincial public opinion, and they were able, at the end of a proconsul's term of office, either to make him an address of thanks, if merited, or complain of his behaviour. Protests could, indeed, be made from lower down the hierarchy: the younger Pliny records his own and Tacitus's part in the trial of one discreditable proconsul of Africa who had during his year of office condemned seven innocent men to death for money, and against whom complaints had been laid at Rome by a municipal *curia*. (Nor was the equivalent of tomato throwing unknown: Vespasian when proconsul – his reward for conquering the Isle of Wight and much of Wessex – was pelted with radishes at Hadrumetum, where the inhabitants were exasperated by his meanness.) But it was the provincial assemblies which mattered; it was a great honour to belong to them, and it gave the deputies a happy sense of self-importance to journey to the chief city of the province and feel they were involved in deliberations of state. The threat of their publicly-expressed disapproval was also, usually, a useful check on at least the worst excesses of proconsular behaviour, and reinforced the supervisory activities of the imperial procurator who was the Emperor's personal representative in the provincial capitals.

Nevertheless, there is no doubt that their real importance in imperial eyes was as cheer-leaders in the worship of the Emperor. Their chief officer was nominally a priest, the *sacerdos provinciae*, whose principal function was to lead the province in the correct observance of these religious duties. Not that the tone of the ceremonies was reverent, once the official rites of sacrifice to the Emperor had been celebrated: Apuleius, who regarded the honour of being *sacerdos* as the summit of his professional career, organized magnificent games at Carthage. There were processions and feasts, and for the populace the occasions were mostly excuses for behaviour of a kind familiar still in Europe during Fasching or Mardi Gras. Long after Apuleius's day, Tertullian was inveighing against Carthage being turned into a tavern, wine flowing in the mud, and the people 'giving themselves over to outrage, indecency and the pleasures of the libertine.' The Emperor's birthday, in fact, was a good excuse for a party. But the excuse was also the *raison d'être*, a matter of policy; the occasion for the expression, through its representatives, of the province's devotion and loyalty.

So long as allegiance was sworn and formal sacrifice made to the Emperor, his subjects could worship whatever gods they wished. But the remarkable religious toleration of the Romans broke down in the face of Christianity. The other international religions were accepted because their adherents were prepared to sacrifice to the Emperor. Local cults were tolerated for the same reason, or because their devotees were so poor that their absence from public life was to be expected. The Jews were an exception, but were tolerated because their religion was also, in a sense, a local cult. At first those other Jews, the early Christians, were in the eyes of the authorities merely a sub-cult of Judaism, and were protected for several decades by this confusion. Like all Jews, they were allowed to be conscientious objectors.

But the Christians were a light unto the Gentiles, and the Romans soon noticed that this Jewish sect was not confined to Jews, and that it was spreading all over the east and even in Rome itself. Like Judaism, it forbade Emperor-worship, but unlike Judaism it was a missionary religion. It was both international and disloyal – dangerously so, simply because it was international. It was an explosive combination, which the Romans could not ignore. Christianity called in question the kingdoms of this world; and obliging its numerous converts to become conscientious objectors to Emperor-worship it also represented a potentially serious loss to public service and public finance.

Nero had already discovered that this new mystery religion was a useful scapegoat – although few, even at the time, believed that the Christians were responsible for the burning of Rome. (And no one any longer believed the conventional charge that the Christians ate children or indulged in nameless orgies at their secret 'love-feasts'.) But by the second century A.D. the Emperors were obliged to take seriously this canker which was eating the heart out of the public life of almost every province.

The general policy of suppression was formulated by Trajan in his famous correspondence with Pliny, then governor of Bithynia, when Christianity – 'this wretched cult' – had numerous followers in Asia Minor. 'These people must not be hunted out,' Trajan wrote. 'If they are brought before you and the charge against them is proved, they must be punished, but in the case of anyone who denies that he is a Christian, and makes it clear that he is not by offering prayers to our gods, he is to be pardoned . . . Pamphlets circulated anonymously must play no part in any accusations. They create the worst sort of precedent and are quite out of keeping with the spirit of our age.' The punishment was death, but there was to be no witch-hunting, no listening to tale-bearers. The Emperor did not want martyrs, but recantations.

In practice, persecution was erratic. It depended on the whim or temperament of the Emperor, or the arrival of some natural disaster like plague or earthquake, when the pagan crowd would clamour for someone's blood. The noble army of martyrs during the two and a half centuries which separated the first persecution from the last numbered fewer than the victims of the Catholic Inquisition – to name only one of the Church's heresy hunts.

Not the least of the Christian Churches' strengths has been their devotion to the written word, to keeping records, publishing sermons, translating the Bible (the Scilli martyrs had 'the Book and the letters of a just man, one Paul'), writing letters, keeping each other and the world informed. Martyrdom, and with it martyrology, was a vitally important element in the history of the Church. Nowhere was this more true than in Africa.

*   *   *

Nothing is known of how Christianity reached Africa, but its first converts were probably the Jews in the seaports. It was brought by sailors and merchants, perhaps from the east, but more likely from Rome itself: from the beginning it seems to have been a Christianity more Latin than Greek. The first African Pope, Victor I (189–?199), was also the first Pope to write in Latin. From the synagogues it spread rapidly, above all among the poor; by the third century A.D. Africa was the most Christianized province of the west. The followers of the new religion were in a minority, but a substantial one. Only seventeen years after the execution of the Scilli martyrs, Tertullian was claiming in his Apologia, published in A.D. 197: 'We are of yesterday, yet we have filled all that is yours, cities, islands, villages, free towns, market towns, the camp itself, tribes, town councils, the palace, the Senate, the forum; we have left you your temples alone . . . If we abandoned you for some far country you would shudder at your solitude, at the silence, the stupor of a dead world.' Even if he exaggerated, Tertullian wrote in the expectation of being believed.

It was impossible to root out the new sect. The Romans soon discovered that persecution rebounded on their own heads; making an example of individual Christians or groups of Christians did not work. An example was set, certainly, but from the official point of view it was the wrong one. Martyrs did not make recusants of their fellow-believers; they made converts of pagan onlookers.

Many Roman magistrates who had to carry out the persecutions felt great distaste for the task. The proconsul Saturninus, for example, gave the Scilli martyrs as much leeway as he could, urging them to recant, offering them thirty days to consider (which, however, they refused). And it was not long before the imperial officials – and the pagans in general – realized that what the Scillitans said of themselves was true of other Christians also: that they paid their taxes, and held the Emperor in honour even if they refused to sacrifice to him. They were good neighbours and peaceable citizens. So at many times and in many places, the obligation to sacrifice was quietly relaxed.

During some reigns, for decades at a time, there appear to have been no persecutions at all. Even under Septimius Severus, who

decreed that converts should be sought out by the State, a public figure like Tertullian was able to broadcast his faith and opinions to the world and live to a ripe old age without, so far as is known, even being admonished, let alone threatened.

Detailed knowledge of the persecution of Christians we owe primarily to the shorthand writers in the law courts. These *acta*, among which that of the Scilli martyrs is the earliest for Africa, are transcripts of the trials; copies of them were later sold on the side to the faithful, and jealously preserved and re-copied as a permanent reminder of the glorious dead. (During the course of centuries they were, not unnaturally, frequently supplemented by later interpolations and forgeries, usually readily betrayed by the sensationally miraculous content.)

The *acta* sometimes have an additional connecting narrative or explanation – although unfortunately this rarely includes any indication of how the defendants were brought to trial, or why they, rather than their fellow Christians, should have been arrested. But for the most part they consist of simple question and answer exchanges. The strong emotions, whether the faith of the accused or the reluctance of the prosecuting magistrates, shine through the direct speech.

There were also unofficial records, not more moving but often fuller and more dramatic. These *passiones* were usually eye-witness accounts by other Christians, such as the celebrated Letter of the Churches of Vienne and Lyons to their co-religionists in Asia and Phrygia describing the fearful martyrdom of the heroic slavewoman St Blandina and her companions in A.D. 177. The most famous of African *passiones*, however, was largely written by the victims themselves, on the eve of their martyrdom. This was the Passion of St Perpetua and her companions, written, according to the editor who prepared it for publication, by St Perpetua and St Saturus 'with their own hands.' It is one of the most moving documents in the history of African Christianity.

In her single-minded courage, Perpetua is of the company of Dido and Sophonisba and the wife of the defending commander of beleagured Carthage. She and Saturus, with Saturninus, Secundulus and the slaves Revocatus and Felicity, were arrested and tried at Carthage in A.D. 203, during the reign of Septimius Severus, who had decreed that Christians, especially the newly converted and those who had converted them, should be actively sought out for prosecution by the State – a reversal of Trajan's policy a century earlier. There is nothing to show why Perpetua rather than her brother – known to be a Christian also – should have been arrested, but from the editor of the Passion, who provided an introduction and an account of the final horrors in the amphitheatre at Carthage, we learn that she was twenty-two, well-born, well-educated (and Saturus reveals that she spoke Greek as well as Latin), well married and the mother of an infant son. For the rest, he lets Perpetua and Saturus speak for themselves.

Perpetua's father was a pagan, and her story is full of his enraged incomprehension at her profession of Christianity, and her own grief 'for the sorrow that had come on his old age.' But she could do no other than she did; she did not falter.

She describes how they were questioned in the market place: 'There was my father with my child . . . beseeching me: "Have pity on your baby". And the procurator Hilarion . . . said to me: "Spare your father's white hairs; spare the tender years of your child. Offer a sacrifice for the safety of the Emperors." And I answered: "No". "Are you a Christian?" said Hilarion. And I answered: "I am." And when my father persisted in trying to overthrow my resolution, he was ordered by Hilarion to be thrown down, and the judge struck him with his rod. And I was grieved for my father's plight, as if I had been struck myself.'

Her steadfastness did not mean that she had no proper maternal concern for her son. But she took it as a sign of God's blessing that when her father refused, after the trial, to return the baby to her in prison to be fed, 'neither had he any further wish for my breasts, nor did they become inflamed.'

Martyrs were constantly on the look-out for signs of divine favour. The principal aim of Perpetua and Saturus was to describe the visions they were granted. Perpetua dreamed twice of a dead brother who, at the age of seven, 'had died miserably of a gangrene of the face', and whom her visions showed her first in purgatory, unable to drink from a font placed too high, and then, after she had prayed for him, drinking at a font low enough for him to reach; and the wound in his face had become a healthy scar. 'Then I knew that he had been released from punishment.' Her third vision, on the day before the games, was of the heavenly martyrdom to come. Saturus's vision was of himself and Perpetua in paradise, with angels and other African martyrs, in the presence of the Lord: 'We were all fed on a fragrance beyond telling.'

The slavewoman Felicity, who was eight months pregnant, was also granted a sign. The editor describes her distress that she would be unable, since it was illegal in her condition, to meet death with the others, and her fear that she would be executed with ordinary criminals after the birth. Her fellow martyrs therefore 'in one flood of common lamentation poured forth a prayer to the Lord two days before the games. Immediately after the prayer her pains came upon her,' and the baby was born.

Both the women were as spirited in word as in deed. When a prison warder jeered at Felicity that the sufferings of childbirth were as nothing to those she would endure in the arena, which she should have thought of before, she replied: 'Now I suffer what I suffer: but then Another will be in me who will suffer for me.' Perpetua chided the prison governor for ill-treating them: 'Why do you not at least allow us to refresh ourselves, the most noble among the condemned, belonging as we do to Caesar and chosen to fight on his birthday? Or is it not to your credit that we should appear thereon in better trim?' The gaiety of men and women martyrs alike at the public feast on the eve of the games astonished the crowd: many, claimed the editor, were converted, among them the prison governor.

Some have seen in the cruelty of the

"Here are the martyrs Saturus, Saturninus, Revocatus, Secundulus, Felicitas, Perpetua, who suffered on the Nones (7th) of March": inscription found on a tomb in the Basilica Maiorum, Carthage

amphitheatre, in which criminals as well as Christians were torn to death by wild animals, not only a pandering to the blood-thirsty tastes of the onlookers and the reassurance (however illusory) of seeing justice publicly meted out in that ill-policed age, but a revival of the long tradition of human sacrifice. Wild beasts were sacred to the gods, and wore religious ornaments in the arena; their victims were sent to meet them either naked or in the costume of priests, so that their ordinary clothes should not profane the gods. A more ancient superstition hovered in the background: the games took place at set times of the year, ostensibly to celebrate the Emperor's anniversary or victories, but perhaps also to renew the fertility of the earth, and to placate the unknown forces of nature.

The Christian martyrs were, in a sense, the accomplices of their persecutors. Just as the Punic religion had taught that sacrificial victims became divine, so for them death in the arena was a certain passport to paradise.

Perpetua and her companions went to the amphitheatre 'as if they were on their way to heaven, with gay and gracious looks; trembling, if at all, not with fear but with joy.' The editor recounts the end: how Saturninus was mauled first by a leopard, and then by a bear; how Saturus had to face

a boar and the bear before the leopard got him in the throat; how the two women, one with milk dripping from her breasts (which scandalized the crowd), were enclosed in nets and tossed by a maddened heifer. He describes how Perpetua's immediate instinctive action after being tossed was to tidy herself, to cover her legs with her tunic and fasten up her hair – for dishevelled hair, the sign of mourning, was inappropriate to the hour of her glory. Then she pulled the bruised Felicity to her feet, and together they left the arena, their 'turn' over. 'When are we to be thrown to the heifer?' were her first words: she had been in an ecstatic trance throughout the ordeal. She and the other survivors returned to the arena to be executed. Perpetua guided the sword of the gladiator to her throat.

There are strong reasons for believing that the anonymous editor who witnessed this scene was the Father of Latin Christianity himself.

*   *   *

Tertullian, like Perpetua, belonged to a rich pagan family of Africa. He was born at Carthage, probably of Punic descent, around A.D. 155, and was trained in the school of rhetoric where Apuleius had been a pupil thirty years before. He knew Greek and Latin literature well, and studied law and philosophy in Rome. His wife was a Christian, and he was converted in middle age; he may have become a priest. Little is known of his life, except through his writings.

A good deal more is known of his personality. An ardent, uncompromising spirit, who grew more uncompromising with age, he crusaded unceasingly against the evils of this world, whether the sins of the pagan community or the weakness of his fellow Christians. A Roman logic was married in him, sometimes uneasily, to all the wild undisciplined fervour of the African. A steady sequence of pamphlets poured from his pen,

to confound faithless and faithful alike. He attacked Jews and heretics; he denounced military service and attendance at the games. Like other rigorists, his view of the deportment proper to women was harsh. Not only were they to dress with a decent modesty, but they were not to take second husbands. Fornicators and adulterers, he believed, should not be re-admitted to the Church. He himself ostentatiously abandoned the wearing of the toga as too much of a compromise with paganism. To follow all Tertullian's prescripts and to live in the world at the same time would have taxed a saint.

He was also something of a trial to the leaders of the Church. He had little patience

The horrors of the amphitheatre: detail from the famous mosaic from Zliten, Libya, which shows a prisoner strapped to a little chariot being thrust towards a leopard. Now in the Tripoli Museum

with the spiritual pretensions of the bishops, who were just beginning to set themselves up above their flocks and preparing, in their corporate capacity, to build the remarkable organization which was to survive the barbarian invasions and hand on to distant generations the remnants of the classical world into which the Church was born. It did not suit bishops to be told that wherever two or three lay Christians were gathered together in the unity of the Spirit, there the Church was. By the end of Tertullian's life there were some seventy bishops in Africa (the number is believed to have been based on that of the Jewish sanhedrin), and this was now revolutionary doctrine. He also extolled the virtues of seeking martyrdom with too much enthusiasm for comfort: bishops did not care for the idea of losing all the souls in their care, and they themselves had work to do in the Church Militant before joining the Church Triumphant. He vigorously denounced the understandable practice of fleeing from persecution – and unfortunately his views were to lend a glamorous authority to the Donatist schism which plagued the Church in Africa after the Great Persecutions.

Yet none of this prevented St Jerome from including him in his list of Eminent Men of the Church – although he was careful to omit any mention of what Tertullian's beliefs actually were. The African was forgiven everything for his passionate defence of the Faith, for the wit and conviction with which he expressed the basic tenets of Christian belief, and the splendid vigour of a Latin style at once demotic, literate and rhetorical, to which the liturgy of the Church owed, and still owes, an enormous debt. A generation after his death St Cyprian, a greater and a wiser churchman, made a habit of reading Tertullian every day, saying to his servant: 'Hand me the Master.'

*   *   *

St Cyprian himself was the greatest of the bishops of Carthage, the first African martyr-bishop and the man who, more than anyone, organized the African church. His repu-

Sculptured pillar—Christian art from Tébessa

tation in the west was such that the Churches of Gaul and Spain appealed to him as an arbiter. His importance in the development of Church discipline was considerable: like Tertullian, he believed that baptisms were invalid when performed by heretics or schismatics; unlike Tertullian, he believed that contrite sinners, even gross sinners such as apostates who denied the Faith, should be re-admitted to the Church after suitable penance. For in his view the Church, like the field in the parable, properly comprised both wheat and tares.

Cyprian was born into a prosperous pagan family around A.D. 200, shortly before the Severan persecution in which St Perpetua died. Like Tertullian also, he was converted in middle life; indeed, Cyprian had been openly anti-Christian, like most of his class, which had much to lose by turning Christian. (Paganism remained common in the Romanized upper classes, even after Constantine had adopted Christianity as the official religion of the Empire in A.D. 313. In the second half of the fourth century, the family of St Augustine's mother had been Christian for several generations, but his father was still a pagan.) St Cyprian distributed most of his fortune to the poor, and the authority of this educated convert was such that he was soon attending the episcopal councils which were becoming a regular feature of the life of the Church; and only three years after his adoption of Christianity he was elected bishop of Carthage. Such rapid promotion is familiar in the early stages of any new organization; and no doubt in a movement which found its chief support among the poor, Cyprian's social and educational superiority marked him out for leadership. He was already well known as an orator and pleader. His great intellectual gifts emerge clearly in the dozen or so treatises on various aspects of the Faith that survive. The tempestuousness of his master Tertullian has been replaced by a calm, reasonable persuasiveness. He owes something, perhaps, to

another contemporary of Tertullian, the Roman lawyer Minucius Felix – possibly also African by birth – whose *Octavius*, a subtle defence of Christianity in dialogue form, is a masterpiece of sophisticated debate. Cyprian is more straightforward than rhetorical, more concerned with substance than style. His letters, of which some sixty have survived, show the most devoted concern for the welfare of his flock as individual souls as well as for the maintenance of a disciplined, unified Church.

The unity of the Church was the major problem of St Cyprian's episcopacy. He maintained that unity in his own day, but did not lay it on secure foundations: half a century later, both the orthodox Catholics and the schismatics were claiming that his words or deeds were the justification for their own position – which may have been a tribute to his diplomacy, but was by no means a proof of his success.

The trouble arose principally from the perennial tendency of the Christian Church to split into two: the rigorist, evangelical wing (exemplified by Tertullian) and the more moderate believers who were prepared, indeed willing, to make some concessions to the temporal world. The earliest converts,

Christian font, richly decorated in mosaic, found at Timgad

not unnaturally, had been enthusiasts for the Faith, prepared to die for it or at least to renounce the world; but, with the spread of Christianity, weaker or richer brethren were drawn in, who were less willing to give up all they possessed. The increasing number of converts had another consequence: a more formal organization was necessary, to handle donations and legacies, to administer charitable funds, to settle doctrinal disputes and personal rivalries; the clergy also received a stipend. By the time St Cyprian became bishop of Carthage, the Church was beginning to be rich and to acquire property; and the Church itself, as distinct from individual members, was finding a motive for some compromise with the Roman authorities.

For forty years after the death of Septimius Severus and the end of his persecutions there was peace for the Church: the faith of new converts was not tested. But in A.D. 250, when St Cyprian had been a bishop for two years, the first of the Great Persecutions was inaugurated by the Emperor Decius. All Christians were commanded to sacrifice to the Emperor, for which they would receive a certificate, on pain of torture and imprisonment or exile and confiscation of property.

It was soon clear that the quantity of Christians in Africa was now more impressive than their quality. 'Some did not wait to be arrested to go to the capitol [to sacrifice]', wrote Cyprian, 'did not wait to be questioned before denying their Faith. Many were defeated before the hour of battle . . . did not even have the merit of appearing to submit by force . . . many were in such a hurry that the magistrates were obliged to postpone their cases until the morrow.'

The bishop himself had gone into hiding, a prudent step which earned the scorn of Gibbon and would certainly have horrified Tertullian. Cyprian did not believe in apostasy, but he believed discretion to be the better part of valour; and he counselled the other Christians to flee. The Romans could have sought him out had they wished, for he continued to direct the affairs of the Church from his retirement, and messengers could certainly have been followed; but the authorities contented themselves with confiscating his property.

But there were many who thought, like Tertullian, that flight was itself apostasy: calling themselves martyrs, they preferred to suffer for their Faith in prison. In their eyes, the bishop no longer had any spiritual authority.

Meanwhile, the apostates, the *lapsi*, having by one sacrifice to the Emperor earned the necessary certificates, or *libelli*, were seeking re-admission to the Church. St Cyprian, still in hiding but closely in touch, decided that there were so many of them that it would seriously weaken the Christian community to excommunicate them all; and that after a suitable period the question of their re-admission should be considered.

He was forestalled. The martyrs in prison had already begun issuing pardons to the *lapsi*, particularly to their friends and relations; soon they were being distributed wholesale, in an ecstasy of saintly forgiveness. As martyrs, they were, they believed, their bishop's spiritual superiors, and they were not the only ones to believe that: many of St Cyprian's own clergy were recognizing the validity of these *libelli pacis*, and re-admitting the apostates to communion. Church discipline had broken down in the face of this unlikely alliance between 'martyrs', the most zealous, and *lapsi*, the least.

Suddenly Decius died; the persecution was over. Cyprian, his authority badly shaken, came out of hiding and tried to repair the damage. The question of the *lapsi* was to be settled at a council (which eventually agreed that they should be re-admitted, at least on their death-beds after a suitable show of repentance); priests, too, should be forgiven, but not restored to office; meanwhile all should be given pastoral care.

The unnatural alliance was soon broken; for although a number of purists, led by a priest who had been Cyprian's rival for the see of Carthage, formed a short-lived schismatic sect, the *lapsi* and many of the martyrs who had confessed them gradually returned to Cyprian's fold.

It was mainly a victory for diplomacy, but there was another reason for the bishop's

Christian cemetery at Timgad—some of the fifteen thousand gravestones taken from the Chapel of the Martyrs

success: Cyprian had a vocation for good works. During the severe plague which tormented Africa in A.D. 252, he and his priests and helpers succoured Christian and schismatic, heretic and pagan alike. Human charity added its persuasiveness to hope and faith.

Unfortunately, Cyprian's very success in luring back followers and converts of the schismatics created another doctrinal problem which contained the seeds of dissension. Some of them had been baptised while in opposition: should their baptism be recognized? St Cyprian, whose views on the solidarity of the Church were already well known, was adamant: they must be re-baptised, because baptism by heretics or schismatics was a ceremony outside the Church and therefore invalid. To his surprise, however, the bishop of Rome, where persecution had caused a similar problem of discipline, thought otherwise. For him baptism by the schismatics was valid, since the schismatics had left the Church on a point

of order rather than a point of doctrine. Cyprian put the matter to a council of eighty-seven African bishops from all over North Africa in A.D. 256. Their support for him was unanimous, and it looked as if a serious split might develop between Rome and Carthage.

This was averted by the renewal of persecution by the Emperor Valerian, and the martyrdom of both bishops. In A.D. 256 Valerian decreed that all bishops and priests who refused to sacrifice should be punished by exile. In Numidia, nine bishops were sentenced to the mines near Cirta; others were banished. In Carthage, the proconsul sent for Cyprian, and, after the routine question-and-answer exchanges in which the bishop testified to his faith, banished him to Curubis (Korba) on the bay of Hammamet. There he remained for a year, until the next year's proconsul summoned him back to Carthage to face death: Valerian had decided that Christians were to lose their rank and property, Christian women should be banished and all clergy should be executed at once. St Cyprian spent his last night in comfort with his friends and the deacon Pontius, who was to become his biographer. On September 14, A.D. 258, 'the day singled out of all days, the day of promise, the day of God,' he was taken to open ground surrounded by woods, escorted by an immense crowd of Christians, and there beheaded. He had charged his friends to see that the executioner was given twenty-five gold pieces. His martyrdom united moderates and rigorists in his praise; though each party claimed him for their own, the breach between them did not reopen for nearly fifty years.

Six months later two Numidian bishops were put to death and, within the week, two deacons, Saints James and Marian, at Cirta, where the number of the faithful to be dispatched was so numerous that 'inventive cruelty arranged rows or lines drawn up in order, that the blade of the impious murderer might take the beheading of the faithful in a rush of fury.' Their *passio* was cherished by the persecuted Church alongside the *acta* of St Cyprian.

The blood of the martyrs was the seed of the Church, as Tertullian had thundered warningly against the Roman authorities, but the tree grew straight and strong because it was pruned of its heresies. At least part of the strength of Christianity was its doctrinal intransigence. The Faith was not to be watered down by pagan tolerance; heresy was countered by intellectual argument. It was not always nipped in the bud. Africa was fortunately spared the early struggles of the Arian controversy, and Montanism – a sect embraced by Tertullian – though it gained adherents had little influence there; but the unsolved problem of the *lapsi* and re-baptism was dormant, not dead. From it was to grow not merely a minor offshoot but a new branch of the Christian Church, which was finally destroyed only when the whole community of Christians in North Africa was cut down by the Arabs.

The persecutions stopped and for the moment there was an uneasy peace both for and within the Church. Meanwhile, the province had other troubles. The withdrawal of the Legion by Gordian III seems to have been a signal for an outbreak of serious risings on the frontier. The evidence is scanty, but by A.D. 253, when the Legion was restored after a disastrous interval of fifteen years, insurrection appears to have involved not only the Bavares tribe within the frontier of Mauretania near Sitifis but the Quinquegentani of the Grande Kabylie mountains; in alliance, they pillaged Numidia, carrying off amongst others a number of Christian maidens (to save whose virtue St Cyprian was obliged to raise a huge sum in ransom). Order seems to have been restored by A.D. 262. In the late 280s, and also in the 290s, further warfare broke out, for which again there are few details; but the co-Emperor Maximian came in person to repress it. Cities in the interior began, for the first time, to build walls round themselves, and at the end of the third century the Romans had withdrawn from the rich and splendid city of Volubilis, in the far west, leaving Mauretania Tingitana to be governed by semi-Romanized barbarian chieftains. Like a snail, the province was shrinking into its shell; and the shell was cracked.

By then, Africa was suffering almost more from firm government than from the half-century of anarchy which had followed the end of the Severan dynasty. After a period when there had been more than twenty Emperors in fewer than fifty years, and the Empire had seemed on the verge of disintegration, Diocletian had come to the throne; and for a crucial twenty years – his reign lasted from A.D. 284 until his voluntary retirement in A.D. 305 to his great palace in Spalato (Split) – the Empire had strong, centralized government. It worked – at a price. Diocletian's response to the problems of barbarian pressure from outside and over-independent provincial initiative inside was to increase the size of the frontier army (possibly doubling it) and to divide the provinces into smaller and more tractable units. Africa was divided into eight – Mauretania Tingitana, Caesariensis and Sitifensis; Numidia Cirtensis (northern) and Militiana (southern); Zeugitana (northern Africa Proconsularis) and Byzacena (central);

and Tripolitania – instead of the original four. Except for Mauretania Tingitana, which was grouped with Spain – a belated recognition of the fact that North African communications were easier by sea than by land – these provinces were grouped together into the *diocesis* of Africa, under a *vicarius* (who was to prove less powerful in practice, however, than the individual governors).

He also divided the Empire itself, or rather the responsibility for the Empire, by associating with himself a junior Augustus, Maximian, and appointing two Caesars to assist them. This arrangement unfortunately proved as fruitful of discord as the uncertainty of succession in the early days of the Empire. But an unhappy six-year dispute after his retirement was followed by another long reign, that of Constantine, son of one of the two Caesars, who was joint-Emperor and then sole Emperor until his death in A.D. 337.

Modern Europe owes other familiar words besides vicar and diocese to Diocletian. The frontier armies were put under the command of *comites*, or counts, and the troops of the peaceful interior provinces under that of *duces*, or dukes. Occasionally dukes doubled up as provincial governors, though it was the usual policy to separate civilian and military roles. Diocletian also introduced cavalry into the Roman army proper, where earlier Emperors had left this important arm to barbarian auxiliaries.

There was work for the army in Africa: indeed, during the tribal revolt of the late third century which Diocletian's co-Emperor Maximian suppressed, reinforcements had to be brought in from Gaul to help the Third Augustan Legion. Maximian toured North Africa from the Atlantic to the Bay of Tunis, and ordered a general repair of all military roads and of the *limes*, which had fallen into neglect since the days of the Severan dynasty.

Unfortunately the army in Africa disgraced itself after the retirement of Diocletian. There was a struggle for the throne, and it sided with the loser. The winner revenged himself by laying fertile farmlands waste, and by pillaging Carthage and Cirta. Only seventy years earlier another fertile part of the province had suffered in just the same way

when the young men of Byzacena had nominated Gordian I as Emperor. Carthage suffered for a second time in three generations.

Another part of Diocletian's policy had been the conversion of the *imperium* into a form of monarchy, with all the ostentatious trappings of a court – the vast, secretive household, the atmosphere of mysterious royalty; and he had made his capital at Nicomedia, in the richer east. Constantine followed his example – and transplanted the court yet again, to a splendid new city on the Bosphorus, where this new regime, more durable than that of Augustus himself, was to survive for a thousand years as Byzantium.

But it was all very expensive. A larger army, a greater number of provincial staffs, not merely one set of courtiers and bureaucrats but two: they required new supplies of money and men. The history of the later Roman Empire is a melancholy tale of the Emperors' efforts to raise such supplies, crushing when they succeeded and desperate when they failed.

As usual, taxes, in the absence of war booty and industrial or agricultural advance, were the chosen means of raising money. The senatorial class had always been excused taxes; so the burden fell most heavily on the poor who actually worked the land and on the middle classes of the cities who were responsible for tax-collection. It had once been an honour to become a magistrate of one's city, to join the class of *curiales*, an honour for which citizens were glad to pay entrance fees and annual dues; now it was a burden, and obligatory. Even in the second century A.D., Trajan had had to appoint procurators in the cities to supervise the collection of taxes; in the third, magistrates were personally responsible not only for their own dues and taxes, but for any that they failed to collect. The *curiales* struggled to buy or bribe their way into the senatorial class; otherwise they fled to the countryside or another city to escape municipal burdens, or vanished into the army, or the priesthood, or into a lower class.

Peasants also fled, when bad harvests or ill-fortune piled up debts they could never hope to pay off. Tiny freeholdings did survive until the end of Roman times, but many were swallowed up by richer neighbours when their owners were forced to sell. Often freeholders became tenants, and tenants, obliged to pay their debts by selling their rights in their land, became serfs; but the flight from the land, combined with the flight from the cities, was sufficiently serious for the Emperors to try to arrest it by decree. For farming was still a necessary occupation; and municipal taxes had to be paid by someone. Diocletian and Constantine therefore decreed that men should be 'tied' to the occupations of their fathers, whether they were peasant-farmers, artisans, or *curiales*. Such an arrangement also meant that the Emperors could demand from each city, each piece of land, a statutory number of recruits for the army, and a statutory amount of taxation, for which the *curiales* were responsible. Gradually they turned the citizens of the Empire into subjects, and classes into castes.

The poor grew poorer; but the rich grew richer. Not only were they spared taxes or able to bribe their way out of them, but they could profit from the misfortunes of the poor. Every freeholder who sold out to them, every city-dweller who put himself under their protection, added to their wealth in realty or manpower. And the laws which tied peasants to the land were laws they welcomed. For reasons that remain unclear, the population of the Empire appears to have been declining at this period, and landowners were as anxious as the Emperors that the men who tilled their estates should continue to do so for ever. Though the Emperors took advantage of a tied population to demand soldiers from cities and landowners, the richest could resist or buy their way out of even this obligation.

The very pattern of upper-class life was changing. The literary evidence makes plain that the great landowners were at long last living on their estates. Life in the unhappy, hard-pressed cities was no longer the easy, civilized pleasure it had been a hundred years earlier. All those Roman Africans who could afford to do so, and whom office did not keep in the towns, retired out of harm's

way to their country estates, where they built themselves houses and created self-contained little empires of their own. The rich turned into country gentry, and – although large tracts of Africa were still owned by absentee landlords such as the Emperor, the Church, Roman senators or those rich who had many estates – the feudal manor began to supplant the city *res publica* as the basic unit of Mediterranean civilization.

It is to the late third century and the fourth that the great mosaics of African villa life belong. For the first time in representations of the life of the countryside, aristocratic dwellings appear alongside the stables and barns. They are real country mansions, often semi-fortified, and quite unlike the town houses of the second century. They are only exceptionally built round a courtyard; instead, coolness and shade are provided by the long Mediterranean verandah built the full length of the outside of the house. Sometimes, there are adjoining private baths, similar to the Moorish *hammam*. A famous mosaic found at Carthage and now in the Bardo, the mosaic of the Seigneur Julius, shows just such a house, with dome-roofed baths half hidden behind it. The house is turreted at the corners, with its living quar-

Typical North African villa of the fourth and fifth centuries A.D., *with colonnaded living quarters on the first floor. Detail of mosaic from Tabarka (ancient Thabraca), now in the Bardo Museum, Tunis*

The mosaic of the Seigneur Julius, found at Carthage and now in the Bardo. It shows the house and household, the domain and livestock of a country gentleman. Note the first-floor living quarters again—and the domed bath house behind the house

ters on the first floor to afford some protection in case of attack in the troubled times of the fourth century; but as a portrait of rural life the mosaic is redolent of the *douceur de vivre* that was still possible for the rich. The house is surrounded by a pleasure garden; there are cereal crops and olive trees, domestic animals and poultry, huntsmen, servants and farm labourers. The seigneur, in the time he cares to spare from the pursuit of game, watches over his domain; his wife, fashionably dressed in spite of exile from Carthage, gazes at herself in a mirror.

Estates like this one were beginning to develop into self-contained manorial communities. The flight from the cities brought artisans and craftsmen out to the country, to seek the protection and patronage of the only people strong enough to protect them from tax-gatherers and bureaucrats. Africa was on the brink of the middle ages.

At the beginning of the fourth century A.D., Diocletian suddenly renewed the persecution of the Christians. It lasted several years, and was of a savagery which matched that of the Decian persecutions half a century before.

9 A church divided

General view of part of the excavations at Mactar, central Tunisia. The city was founded by the kings of Numidia and, under Masinissa and his successors, attracted settlers from Carthage. In early Roman times, Phoenician influence remained strong; later five Christian churches were built

The crowd which had watched St Perpetua and her companions die in the amphitheatre at Carthage had been hostile to them. Half a century later, the crowd which escorted St Cyprian to the scene of his martyrdom outside the capital had almost rioted in support of their bishop. For by the middle of the third century Christianity had become the dominant religion of the urban poor. During the next half-century, between the persecution in which Cyprian died and the Great Persecution of Diocletian at the beginning of the fourth century, it became the religion of the poor in the depths of the countryside also. It spread from the Romanized cities of the wheatlands to the olive country of the high plains of Numidia and the semi-desert of the south, and to the nomadic interior of the Mauretanias. Very little is known of this change, except that it was paralleled in other provinces in the eastern Roman Empire, where, as in Africa, it coincided with the survival of a native language; but, to judge from inscriptions, it occurred with startling suddenness. Within a generation, the African peasantry was converted from Saturn to Christ. The last securely dated dedication to Saturn is for A.D. 272.

There were also sensational conversions in the professional classes. Arnobius, for instance, a teacher of rhetoric at Sicca (Le Kef) had been such an ardent pagan that he had difficulty in persuading his bishop that he wished to become a Christian. He was obliged to write *Adversus Nationes* to convince him. Another convert was his pupil, Lactantius, to whom Diocletian had given a professorship in Nicomedia; like Arnobius, he was converted shortly before the Great Persecution. Unlike Arnobius, he spent his life outside Africa, but he became the author of *Divine Institutions,* and in A.D. 313 the Emperor Constantine appointed him tutor to his son Crispus.

Eighty-seven bishops had attended Cyprian's council at Carthage in A.D. 256. Fifty years later, there were probably three times that number. Admittedly, the vast majority of African bishops were more like parish priests than heads of dioceses – one reason why Cyprian, with the score or so of Carthage's parishes under his wing, could make himself undisputed primate of the province – and the authority of many, if not most, extended no further than one small town or a few villages, or even one manorial domain. However, every bishop represented at least one Christian community of sufficient size to have its own organization of priests and deacons, and probably its own holy books and sacred vessels.

But the Christianity of the African poor – and even of intellectuals like Tertullian – had much in common with the religion it displaced. The new Semitic God was, for the superstitious Berbers, the old Semitic Saturn-Baal writ large: a God of Vengeance to be feared and propitiated, rather than a loving Father. It was 'a transformed popular religion, rather than . . .conversion to a new religion' (W. H. C. Frend in *The Donatist Church*). Indeed, one of St Augustine's tracts suggests that many fifth-century Christians believed that God was Saturn re-christened; and the old god's nickname, *senex,* the Old Man, may have been applied by extension to Christian bishops. The correct and fanatical observance of ritual, rigorous acts of penance, devotion to martyrs and the pursuit of martyrdom were of fundamental importance, as ritual and blood-sacrifice had been in the old religion. Human suffering still bought the favours of the Divine Power, and persecution was the passport to paradise.

The mass conversion was rapid and easy because it was less of a change than it looked. That does not explain it; but there was a significant social difference between Saturn-worship and Christianity in the third century which suggests a reason. Saturn, though based on a more ancient African god, had become Romanized, respectable, official, with public temples and a recognized place in the accepted pantheon; the God of the Christians had not. His name could be a rallying cry for dissent. And in the late third century there was strong reason for dissent.

Ever since the Gordian uprising had been suppressed so brutally and had been followed by severe tribal fighting in the interior of the province, the cities of the fertile wheatlands had been hard-pressed and declining – in some cases to their former overgrown village structure. But in the olive country of Numidia and the south the late third century onwards was the age of settlement and prosperity for freeholders and leaseholders protected by the Mancian law. Many of the irrigation works date from this period; and the sites of well over a thousand villages founded in the fourth century and later have been listed in southern Numidia alone, a region which is mostly uncultivated steppe today. It was becoming, then, as important a source of olive oil as the groves of Africa Proconsularis and Tripolitania. Its comparative agricultural wealth attracted the attentions of the tax-gatherers, and an unfair share of Diocletian's new demands fell on Numidia.

A rising standard of living is a common prelude to revolt in the history of mankind, the thwarting of new aspirations the spark that lights the fuse. African city life, which had so much to offer men like the harvester of Mactar in the previous century, no longer functioned as a safety valve in the third. The peasantry turned to Christianity.

Hardly had they done so when Christianity itself became respectable. The Edict of Milan, promulgated by the Emperors Constantine and Licinius in A.D. 313, ushered in not only toleration but the long alliance between Church and State. Almost simultaneously, the Church in Africa split in two, and it was from the olive villages of Numidia that the Donatist schismatics, hating the secular authorities and the *status quo* as much as they hated their religious rivals, and hating each the more for their alliance, were to draw most of their support. The instinct for dissent found its outlet after all, and for the remaining century and a quarter of North Africa's existence as a province of imperial Rome its history is that of a people divided against itself, a history written not only in words, of which there were to be many, but in blood. Civil war simmered beneath, and sometimes on, the surface, until it was finally subsumed in the death throes of the Empire itself.

It would be wrong to see in the schism merely a form of social protest, or even a nascent African nationalism: in the far west, where tribal chieftains always exercised considerable authority, the population was converted to Catholic Christianity and not to Donatism. But economic distress and the corruption and oppressive policy of the administrative machine certainly exacerbated religious tension in the potentially more prosperous parts of the province, and confirmed the Donatists in their refusal to yield when the rightness of their cause, both legal and moral, had long been disproved.

The Donatists were not heretics; they believed what the Catholics believed, and their forms of worship and organization were the same. The schism sprang from a difference of emphasis which had already been obvious in St Cyprian's day. Neither side believed that apostasy was not a grave matter; both had condemned the handing over of sacred books on demand to the Roman magistrates. But was a priest who handed over heretical or medical documents, pretending that they were scripture and thus avoiding punishment, also a *traditor?* Was such a *traditor* priest thereby incapable of administering the sacrament of baptism? Did the parable of the field of wheat and tares refer to the Church or to the world – did the true Church admit only the virtuous, and exclude sinners? Was it wrong to have any dealings with secular authority?

To all these questions, to which the Catholic answer – developed over decades of argument – was now in the negative, the Donatists would have answered yes. They laid up difficulties for themselves. They fought test cases on shaky evidence. Some of their leaders turned out to be as guilty of apostasy as any on the other side. They, too, appealed to the Emperors for support – and appealed in vain. They were as vulnerable as any other group which claims moral superiority to the frailties of both flesh and spirit. Had their views on the necessary purity of the priesthood prevailed, whole communities would have been deprived of the Christian communion. It is, as St Augustine was later to argue unanswerably, only God who can divide the wheat from the tares.

Yet it is impossible to withhold sympathy

from the Donatists. The Christians with their vast increase in numbers were no longer a band of dedicated souls; corruption and malpractices were as rife, even in the priesthood, as in the pagan community. And like other evangelicals, the schismatics appealed to something very deep in human nature, which was not merely a question of the poor against the rich. Thousands did, willingly, die for Donatist beliefs; their leaders were, in the fourth century, more distinguished both as Christians and as intellectuals than those of the Catholics; and neither the might of the State nor the genius of St Augustine ever broke their hold on the hearts of half North Africa.

The schism began in tragedy: the Great Persecution of Diocletian of A.D. 303–305. There had already been during his reign a number of isolated executions in Africa of men who refused to serve in the army on the grounds that they were Christians. The son of a veteran was beheaded at Theveste in A.D. 295; a veteran at Tigava (El Kherba) met the same fate for refusing to re-enlist after being converted. In A.D. 298 the centurion Marcellus threw down his arms before the standards of the Legion stationed at Tingis (Tangiers), in the presence of his fellow-soldiers. He, too, was tried and executed, and the shorthand-writer at the trial, one Cassian, who had flung away his notebook and pen with an oath at the injustice of the sentence, of which he complained to the judge, was also beheaded. There were many Christians in the army, and although such crises of conscience were rare, at a time when every soldier was needed – it was the year the Emperor Maximian was in the province to suppress tribal revolts – the dangerous doctrine of 'I am a soldier of God, not of the Emperor,' could not be countenanced.

But in A.D. 303 Diocletian turned against civilian Christians. Possibly at the prompting of the oracles of Apollo, by no means yet silenced, their meetings were suddenly forbidden, their places of worship were ordered to be pulled down and their scriptures burned. Christians were to be deprived of their rank and not allowed to bring court actions. When two fires mysteriously broke out in his palace, Diocletian further ordered the arrest of all bishops and priests.

In Africa this was taken to mean death for all who refused to recant or deliver up the scriptures. Most of the higher clergy persuaded themselves that compromise was to be preferred to martyrdom. Many bishops gave up the scriptures to the magistrates; Mensurius of Carthage handed over heretical works which he pretended were sacred books. At Cirta (Constantine) Bishop Paulus, aided and abetted by his deacons, sub-deacons and priests, gave up various ecclesiastical objects, and after some prevarication disclosed the whereabouts of the scriptures; and the sub-deacon Silvanus officiously brought out of hiding behind a barrel in the library a silver box and a silver lamp. It was all set down in official records. Years later, Silvanus had cause to regret his role in this scene.

But not all their congregations followed the episcopal example. Many of the laity were enthusiastically courting imprisonment, some even declaring they had scriptures hidden which they did not in fact possess. There were genuine martyrdoms: the most moving *acta* of the persecution records the trial of the priest Saturninus of Abitina (where the bishop had turned *traditor*) and his flock of nearly fifty men, women and children, including his own four sons. To almost every question put to them by the proconsul at Carthage, the simple answer came: 'I am a Christian.' Their fate is not known – it is possible that some or all of them died in prison; but their stoical courage under threat of torture was an inspiration to many. In southern Numidia the governor, a convinced pagan, appears to have been given the opportunity to put many to death; those who gave him that opportunity were not forgotten, and their tombs became places of pilgrimage.

Meanwhile the Christians who were in prison began to pardon *lapsi* as they had done in St Cyprian's day. But this time they also unequivocally condemned their own clergy. In Carthage, they were soon openly accusing Bishop Mensurius's deacon, Caecilian, of starving the martyrs of Abitina to death by preventing food reaching them in prison. Whether that was true or not, Caecilian was known to be opposed not only to unnecessary martyrdom, as St Cyprian had been, but hostile to martyrs also. He was tactless enough to make this clear – something St Cyprian would never have done – and was soon the most hated man in Carthage.

The persecution lasted scarcely more than a year, but it left behind it an unbridgeable gulf between the *traditores*, those who handed over, and the anti-compromise party. The latter, which found its earliest supporters among the urban mob at Carthage and in the Numidian countryside, now began to force its own candidates into the episcopacy. The story changes from a tragedy to one with distinct elements of farce. The origins of the schism are remarkably well documented; each side kept detailed records, the better to confound its opponents. Both had plenty of ammunition.

At Cirta, for instance, when the *traditor* bishop Paulus died, the leading citizens wished to elect a less compromised Christian as bishop. Unfortunately they allowed themselves to be overawed by the excited mob, who had set their hearts on a man of the people who had proved his worth by spending the previous few months looting pagan temples. Blinded by enthusiasm, they overlooked the fact that their man was that same Silvanus who had been a *traditor* alongside Bishop Paulus not two years before. Nor did they hold it against him when, on becoming a bishop, Silvanus promptly appointed a certain Victor as a priest in exchange for a bribe.

Silvanus then had to be consecrated, according to custom, by twelve bishops who – on St Cyprian's authority – were 'in a state of grace', which, as they interpreted it, meant bishops who were not themselves *traditores*. However, of the twelve who gathered for this purpose at Cirta in A.D. 305 under Secundus of Thigisis, primate of Numidia (significantly, the Church in Numidia was now strong enough to have its own primate – unthinkable in St Cyprian's day), Secundus himself was suspected of being a *traditor*; four other bishops present, according to the minutes

of the meeting, actually admitted to it; and the notorious brigand Bishop Purpurius of Limata, when taxed with murdering two nephews, replied: 'Yes I did kill, and I will kill anyone who acts against me.' Weakly, Secundus decided that the sins of bishops could only be left to the judgement of God. The *traditor* bishop of a fanatically anti-*traditor* see was duly confirmed in his holy office by other *traditores* and a self-confessed murderer. It was tricky ground on which to fight for a Church from which the tares must be weeded out.

None of this prevented the bishops of Numidia from virtuously protesting when the anti-martyr archdeacon Caecilian was elected bishop of Carthage on the death of Mensurius some years later, in A.D. 312, and consecrated by three bishops, one of whom, Felix of Apthungi, they claimed – wrongly – had been a *traditor*. It was true that the election and consecration had been rather hurried; true, too, that the number of consecrating bishops had been fewer than was usual; but the most serious objection was a point of pride. Since St Cyprian's day, the consecration of the primate of Africa had devolved on the primate of Numidia. His claims, which were not welcomed by the Carthaginian clergy, had on this occasion been ignored. Secundus set off at once for Carthage accompanied by a veritable army of seventy bishops.

The extraordinary intrigue which followed reflected little credit on either side. There were rumours of attempted embezzlement of Church treasures in the Carthaginian camp; an interventor appointed by Secundus was murdered in church; Purpurius of Limata threatened to break Caecilian's head during the service if any re-consecration took place; a wealthy dowager of Spanish birth called Lucilla, who had never forgiven Caecilian for reproving her for kissing a martyr's bone at communion, allegedly bribed Secundus's party to elect one of her servants in Caecilian's place.

However it came about, there were two bishops in Carthage when Secundus finally left for home a few months after he arrived. The schism was now in being, the sides about evenly matched, each convinced that it alone was the true Church. Its history might have been different had Caecilian enjoyed as much popularity as St Cyprian had in similar circumstances – let alone as much quality as a bishop; and had not the anti-bishop Majorinus been succeeded the following year, the year of the Edict of Milan, by a personality as remarkable as all but one in the history of African Christianity.

*   *   *

Donatus led the anti-Catholic Christians – maintaining always that they were the true Church – for forty years. To him the schismatics owed what dignity and strength the movement was able to wrest from its unsavoury beginnings. Not that the scandals were over, or that mistakes were not made, or that the Donatist Church did not acquire its share of worldly goods and worldly ambitions; the schismatics soon acquired a lunatic fringe, were plagued by sub-schismatics of their own (such was the logic of purity) and, like the Catholics, found great difficulty in recruiting for the priesthood. Many of their priests were illiterate rabble-rousers. But Donatism attracted a number of the best intellects of the day, and throughout the fourth century men like Parmenian, Tyconius, Primian and Petilian took the initiative in an energetic war of propaganda. The Catholics were forced into a defensive role, and the mere titles of their tracts suggest men hurriedly plugging holes in the dam of orthodoxy, whenever and wherever it springs a leak; Bishop Optatus of Milevis' *De Schismate Donatistorum*, or the whole string of works written by St Augustine in the twenty years after his conversion – *Contra Cresconium, Contra Epistolam Parmeniani, Contra Litteras Petiliani, De Baptismo contra Donatistas, Psalmus Contra Partem Donati*. The followers of Donatus had to be taken seriously, for their leaders, taking as their text Tertullian's alluring pronouncement, 'Nothing could be more foreign to the Christian than the State', could proclaim themselves the champions of the poor and oppressed.

Very little is known about Donatus himself: none of his works survive, there are no eye-witness accounts. He remains throughout his life a shadowy presence in the wings of the African scene. But the magnetism of his personality can be deduced from its effect on those whom posterity can still see in the centre of the stage. Not for nothing was the schism named after him: his followers – according to St Augustine – resented insults offered to him more than they resented blasphemy, and even his enemies saluted his integrity. He was plainly a born leader and orator, with the power to draw the crowds, and turn those crowds into impassioned disciples: many believed that he performed miracles. His reputation and his sayings survived long after his death, and some have seen in him a forerunner of the holy prophets of Islam who were to inherit, three centuries later, the fanatical devotion so readily awoken in the hearts of the Berbers.

He seems to have come, appropriately enough, from Casae Nigrae, far to the south of Tébessa, on the fringe of the great chotts of the northern Sahara, the harsh and unyielding land which suffered most during Diocletian's persecution. It is not known when or why he arrived in Carthage; but he was active on behalf of the Numidian bishops led by Secundus of Thigisis during their attempts to get rid of Bishop Caecilian. He may have been instrumental in rousing the Carthaginian crowd against Caecilian, and a useful ally for the rich Lucilla in her efforts on behalf of Majorinus. At all events, when Majorinus died Donatus was well enough placed to be chosen anti-bishop in his place. Almost at once, the bishop of Rome, Pope Miltiades – himself an African and suspected of being a *traditor* – found him guilty of rebaptising lapsed clergy and forming a schism.

So far, the activities of the party of Donatus were simply a matter of internal Church discipline. They did not remain so. For they provided the first Christian Emperor with the chance to forge the first link in the long alliance between the State and the Church. Once Constantine was converted, that alliance was perhaps inevitable; but it was the Church in Africa which played into his hands.

Constantine had already decided to take a hand in the dispute. No Emperor could afford to have the major supplier of corn and oil for Rome racked by dissension, whether political or religious. Without enquiring into the matter very closely, he gave his support to Caecilian; property confiscated during the persecution was to be returned to the Church, Caecilian was to be provided with money, his clergy were to be immune from curial responsibilities – and his opponents brought before the magistrates. 'The Devil rewarded the lapsed clergy not only with the restoration of ecclesiastical honours, but also with royal friendship and earthly riches,' the Donatists pointed out sharply, but even they did not realize the momentous significance of Constantine's interference. Indeed, within a few days of the announcement they themselves forged a second link in the chain that was to bind the secular and the religious authorities together, by appealing to the Emperor to hear their side of the story and be their judge. They did not spurn royal friendship until it was at length clear that they would not get it. Meanwhile, the damage was done.

Constantine was taken aback by this com-

Coin portrait of Constantine

munication from Caecilian's opponents, which included detailed charges against the bishop he had chosen to support; he wondered if he had made a mistake. But he found it quite natural to be appealed to; he felt himself directly responsible to his new-found God for the peace and unity of His Church. As he wrote to Pope Miltiades, 'It seems to me very serious that in those provinces which the Divine Providence has spontaneously entrusted to my devotion . . . the population should be found in a state of discord.' He asked Miltiades, with other bishops, to adjudicate; Donatus and Caecilian were summoned to Rome.

The council found in favour of Caecilian; but the Donatists refused to accept the verdict, complaining that 'the bishops had shut themselves up somewhere and passed judgement as convenient for themselves'. They claimed that evidence against Felix of Apthungi, one of the three bishops who had consecrated Caecilian eleven years before, had not been taken into account. Constantine at once overrode the bishops' verdict: there must be a further council at Arles the following year, and the case of Felix should be re-investigated at Carthage. The Christians were no longer masters of their own Church. When the council at Arles confirmed the previous verdict, Constantine again hesitated to dispossess the Donatists: 'I consider it absolutely contrary to the divine law that we should overlook such quarrels and contentions, whereby the Highest Divinity may perhaps be moved to wrath, not only against the human race, but against myself.' Even when his own proconsul at Carthage found Felix innocent of the charge of *traditor* – after a trial which turned on the exposure of a forger – he continued to listen to Donatist appeals. It gave the Donatists a precious opportunity to establish themselves in the eyes of the world. 'What frenzied audacity!' Constantine complained, threatening to come to Africa himself. Instead, however, he suddenly sent for the forger and challenged Donatus and his party that if they could still prove anything at all against Caecilian he 'would regard this as if every accusation which you bring against him has been proved.

Looking down the nave to the apse of the Christian basilica at Tébessa. Built in the late fourth century, it is one of the largest Roman buildings in North Africa

May Almighty God grant peace everlasting,' he added optimistically.

It took Constantine three years – partly because of other problems – to make up his mind finally that Caecilian was the right man to back, and decree that Donatist churches were to be confiscated and their leaders exiled. But those three years had given the Donatists a taste of recognition and – not surprisingly – the hope that Constantine would change his mind yet again. The new decrees had still to be put into effect, and they had no intention of yielding while there was still hope. They announced that they would never communicate with Constantine's 'scoundrelly bishop'.

In this situation, Christians for the first time appealed to the use of force against other Christians. The Church had called in the Emperor, and made a mockery of religious authority; Constantine had made a mockery of the law; and neither religious nor legal sanctions were now enough. The stage was set for the persecution of Christians by Christians.

Caecilian appealed to the army. Fatally, once force was decided on, the operation was conducted half-heartedly. Most Donatist bishops actually remained in possession of their sees; and the deaths that occurred, which included a 'massacre' outside Carthage, merely served to divide the schismatics irrevocably from the Catholics, as might be expected. They also provided Donatus with his most persuasive watchword: the true Church is persecuted, not persecuting.

Nothing, now, could shake the following of Donatus, not even the belated revelation in A.D. 320 that the Donatist bishop of Cirta had been a *traditor* fifteen years earlier. Silvanus, who had not mended his ways, imprudently quarrelled with one of his deacons, had him stoned and excommunicated him. This man, who knew Silvanus's history, appealed to the civil authorities. At the trial, everything came out: the yielding up of the silver box and lamp, the taking of bribes, the embezzlement of money intended for the poor when he accompanied Secundus of Thigisis to Carthage during the campaign against Caecilian in A.D. 312. Many of his fellow bishops were implicated with Silvanus; they were sentenced to exile by the governor. Yet the aftermath of the trial reveals Donatus's strength. Although Silvanus went into exile, Purpurius of Limata, who had also been exiled – and had raged at Silvanus when he first quarrelled with his deacon, 'You will kill us all' – remained cheerfully in office.

The Catholic leaders, struggling to maintain the fiction of unity, had certainly been distressed by the violence involved in their attempts to implement Constantine's decision. So was Constantine, who, if he could not have peace and unity, of the two preferred peace. The following year, though he continued to support Caecilian, he extended toleration to the Donatists, and left the matter to the judgement of God. But, unawares, he had put the Church at a considerable diplomatic and psychological disadvantage. With their connivance, he had judged ecclesiastical disputes, whether directly or through episcopal councils summoned on his authority; he had exiled bishops, seized Church property and forbidden religious meetings. If the Church had acquired a protector, that protector was also its master, and Constantine was now in a position to play a leading role in the Arian controversy which was threatening to disrupt the east. (He took the chair at the Council of Nicaea, and is credited with making a significant amendment to the Nicaean creed.) He was a convert of barely thirteen years' standing, with no theological training; he had not even been baptised. It was a notable triumph.

*   *   *

In Africa, much of the history of the remainder of the fourth century is obscure; but Donatism went from strength to strength. The Donatists proselytized abroad, formed alliances with the eastern bishops against Athanasius, who was backed by Rome, and

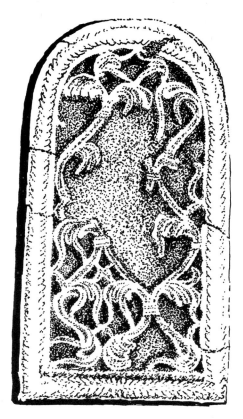

Tracery pattern from a window of a church near Tébessa, probably Byzantine

even recruited in Rome, where they supported a schismatic bishopric for a hundred years. They could thus claim with some justification that they too were 'Catholics'. They attracted many of the educated; they acquired wealth; and they built churches.

Just as, in the golden age of the second century, rival municipalities had vied with each other to create finer cities, so in the fourth the rival Churches struggled to outdo their opponents in the size and splendour of their monuments. There was a difference: the cities had for the most part been built by rich private donors while the Churches must have been largely financed out of the pockets of the comparatively poor, for, until the end of Roman times and in spite of the patronage of the Emperors, most rich families remained pagan. And some of the finest basilicas in North Africa were built by the Donatists in Numidia – at Tébessa, for instance, where the ruins of the church are as impres-

Stables of the hostelry for pilgrims attached to the Tébessa basilica

sive as anything else in the city, and at Timgad, where seventeen churches have been discovered—more than the number of public baths. Even small places often had two or more, though it is not usually possible to tell which denomination erected them. Many Christian mosaics have been uncovered: mosaics cruder in workmanship than the works of the classical period, and far removed in spirit – the figures front-facing, hieratic, symbolic rather than naturalistic – forming a link between the strange processional splendour of the carvings on the arch of Septimius Severus and the glories of the age of Justinian.

By A.D. 330 the Donatists could muster two hundred and seventy bishops. Their strength was such that, in that year, they seized the basilica which the Emperor had built for the Catholics at Cirta, now renamed Constantine in his honour – and kept it, in spite of Catholic protests. Constantine merely gave the Catholics money to build themselves a new one. However, Donatus did not have everything his own way. When, some ten years after Constantine's death in A.D. 337, he appealed to his son Constans for full recognition of the rightness of his cause, the two notaries sent to re-investigate the matter, Paul and Macarius, sided firmly with the Catholics. The Donatists rose in revolt, and found themselves being persecuted more harshly than they had been thirty years before. One Numidian bishop who had raised a private army among the Donatist peasantry was besieged and massacred with his followers in his own basilica; another bishop, who became one of the great martyrs of the Donatist canon, was humiliated and executed, and his followers were flogged; riots at Carthage were suppressed by regular troops; Donatus himself was exiled. Although this persecution did not last long it inflamed enmity. For decades afterwards, Donatist apologists stirred up the faithful with reminders of the *tempora Macariana*.

Donatus continued to lead the schism from exile until his death in A.D. 355 and within a few years the Donatists were as strong as before. They continued to bear witness not so much against the State (they did not hesitate to appeal to the pagan Emperor Julian) as against the world, in the persons of the increasingly corrupt imperial administrators. These, now, were almost wholly recruited from and identical with the great landowning class against whose depredations the old bureaucracy, in the days when it was composed of Romans and Oriental professionals, had taken some stand.

The Catholics, too, offered them plenty of ammunition; the hierarchy appears to have been as corrupt and self-seeking as the secular administration, devoting more time to money-lending and intrigue than to their calling. The Donatists' hopes were revived when Julian the Apostate succeeded his uncle in A.D. 361. Almost his first action as Emperor was to restore exiled Christian leaders of every sect all over the Empire, and if his aim was to create discord among them he succeeded. The surviving Donatist ringleaders exiled with Donatus appealed to him and were granted back all the property which had been confiscated from them in A.D. 347. It proved the signal for an outbreak of religious warfare. The Donatists, half drunk with triumph, set upon their Catholic adversaries in a frenzy of revenge – killing, humiliating, pillaging, looting. Two Donatist bishops led an armed gang in an assault on a Catholic church in Numidia and slaughtered two deacons. In Mauretania, gangs led by Donatist bishops virtually sacked the city of Tipasa. Many Catholics, terrified, turned Donatist themselves. The extremists were in control.

For the religious hatreds of the 340s, exacerbated by worsening social conditions, had led to the rise of what almost amounted to a separate social class: footloose bands of the poorest peasants, similar in origin to the harvest teams of which the celebrated citizen of Mactar had been a hard-working member. Their numbers were swelled by the grossly oppressed labourers and tenants of the *latifundia* of Numidia and Mauretania. To such men, and their womenfolk, Donatism, with its detestation of the established order, and its invitation to martyrdom, made the strongest appeal. It had suited the Donatist leaders, when their rivals could call on the army, to put such forces into the field against them. Neither the Donatists, however, nor the secular authorities were able to keep these bands under control and it is likely that at least some of their outbreaks were provoked by official attempts to 'settle' them on the land: however wretched their gipsy life, they would have exchanged a kind of liberty for the status of tied serfs to which the once-free peasantry had been reduced by the laws of Diocletian and Constantine.

They soon acquired the name of *circumcelliones*, which was a reference to the shrines where they gathered to worship at the tombs of martyrs and collect food. They had their own rude disciplines and communal organization, their own rituals (including drunken orgies), their own battle-cries – of which *Deo laudes* was the most characteristic – and even their own style of dress, a rough habit. 'They lived as robbers,' as St Augustine – a partial witness – put it, 'died as *circumcelliones* and were honoured as martyrs.' They actively courted martyrdom; if a religious skirmish was not available, they would challenge passing travellers to stand and kill them, or be killed; sometimes whole groups would throw themselves over a cliff into salt lakes, or burn themselves alive in an ecstatic fervour. They exerted a terrorist pressure on the hated landlords and usurers; they laid waste villas and churches, sometimes independently, sometimes led by the wilder Donatist clergy; they prevented the collection of debts, and had been known to force rich men out of their carriages in favour of their own slaves, and make them run behind. They might be compared to the outlaws of Sherwood Forest, operating their own kind of rough, Robin Hood justice against the sheriff's men and the feudal barons.

Julian's reign was brief. With the advent of a new Emperor, State and Catholic

Church were once more united in persecuting the Donatists and trying, in vain, to stamp out the *circumcelliones*. Even the Donatists were alarmed at their excesses; one Donatist bishop disowned them, and went into schism with several colleagues. And the great Parmenian, who was Donatist bishop of Carthage from A.D. 363 to A.D. 391, never countenanced violence. They were not so easily got rid of; half a century later, St

Remains of Christian basilica at Henchir El Kousset, near Kasserine. Nearby is a ruined factory for the production of olive oil, also Roman

Augustine's letters are full of them. And to make matters worse, the unhappy province was now consigned to the care of a *comes* who for corruption and greed rivalled the most iniquitous of the Roman governors against whom Cicero had once inveighed.

*   *   *

The story of Count Romanus, immortalized in the pages of Ammianus Marcellinus, eloquently exemplified the horrors which had overtaken the once great imperial administration. His arrival unfortunately coincided with the devastation, after centuries of peace and prosperity, of the city lands of Leptis Magna by the tribe of the Austuriani. It was the first time the barbarians had struck in such strength from this part of the desert. It was Romanus's first duty to protect the province under his command; yet when the citizens of Leptis appealed to him he held them up to ransom, demanding payment in advance of full provisions and four thousand camels. Having had their lands laid waste, the citizens were unable to meet these demands, and Romanus simply took the army away and left them to their fate. The Austuriani raided Tripolitania twice more, emboldened by the lack of defence; olive trees and vines were cut down. The three cities never recovered, and Leptis itself seems to have been deserted within half a century.

But this neglect of duty, shameful though it was, was not what prompted Ammianus Marcellinus to record that 'even Justice herself has wept'. After Romanus's first desertion – he may indeed have depended on supplies, or genuinely lacked money to pay his soldiers – the people of Tripolitania sent envoys to the Emperor to complain. The Emperor sent a commissioner, to enquire into the matter, and to pay Romanus's army. Romanus, however, used the money for his soldiers' wages to bribe the commissioner to give a false report to the Emperor. This done, the original envoys and other leading citizens of Leptis were sentenced to death for having made unjustified complaints against Romanus. When the truth emerged ten years later

(a compromising letter was discovered in Romanus's papers), although the guilty commissioner committed suicide, Romanus escaped punishment.

Romanus's fiscal administration, which was all of a piece with his notions of justice, led to the most serious uprising which the Romans had had to face since the revolt of Tacfarinas early in the first century. In A.D. 372 his inordinate tax demands and the way in which his troops lived off the land – Ammianus Marcellinus maintained that his devastations were worse than those of the barbarians – provoked into rebellion a Romanized native chieftain in the Kabylie mountains south-east of Algiers. This was Firmus, who belonged to the powerful Jubaleni tribe (perhaps descended from King Juba), who had become Romanized landowners but also retained some of the prestige which had belonged to the old princes of Numidia. Firmus quickly found allies among the Donatist peasantry of the high plains, and his revolt spread rapidly as far as Calama (Guelma) in the east, and west to the plain of the river Chélif beyond Caesarea (Cherchel). The insurgents proclaimed Firmus king.

The revolt failed. Although one of his brothers captured Caesarea and held out there for three years, he was finally overcome by one of the great soldiers of the later Roman Empire, the *comes* Theodosius. Firmus himself was halted at the walls of the Catholic city of Tipasa, whose citizens celebrated their victory by adroitly attributing it to the miraculous intervention of a 13-year-old Catholic martyr. (St Salsa's ruined basilica can still be seen on Tipasa's rosy cliffs. The supposed corpse of the saint was, however, that of a sexagenarian matron.)

The Donatists could now be represented not merely as erring schismatics, but as traitors. Yet the persecution which followed was brief, for the new *vicarius Africae*, although an imperial official, was himself a convinced Donatist and the Catholics were naturally unable to enforce the regulations. Both sides were led by moderate men; the passions aroused over the election of Caecilian had long since faded, and a generation had passed since the *tempora Macariana*. They seem to have settled down to live in peace if not harmony. The Catholics, though legally in the right, were still at a moral disadvantage. The most distinguished Christian in the province was the Donatist theologian Tyconius; when his thinking took him beyond the accepted Donatist position towards the Catholic belief that the Church must be a mixture of wheat and tares, to be separated only by God on the Day of Judgement, and Parmenian felt obliged to excommunicate him, it never occurred to him that he should join the Catholics.

The truce lasted barely twenty years. Once more, the Jubaleni tribe set in train the events which brought down on the Donatists the vengeance of the State; but this time, the Catholics were able to inflict a moral defeat on them as well.

The Jubaleni, in the shape of Firmus's brother Gildo, had been restored to imperial favour. Gildo, who had fought for the Romans against his brother, was appointed *comes Africae,* and one of his daughters was married into the imperial family. But after a decade of loyalty to Rome, Berber ambition reasserted itself. In A.D. 397 he held up the corn supplies for Rome. This could not be ignored by Rome, for Africa, since the founding of Constantinople and the diversion there of Egypt's annual corn harvest, was Italy's only large supplier. Gildo was declared an enemy of the State.

This time, the Donatists were made to seem deeply implicated. The most intransigent and fanatical of their bishops, Optatus of Thamugadi (Timgad), had acquired Gildo's support in a private quarrel with an off-shoot of Donatism, had summoned into being his own army of *circumcelliones* – equipped with swords as well as their traditional staves – and was already, according to St Augustine, 'scorching all Africa with tongues of flame'. His new cathedral was the most magnificent in Africa, he himself had an almost royal power, and he was poised to convert the province by force to Donatism. But his reliance on Gildo meant that if Gildo failed Optatus would fail with him.

Gildo proved his own worst enemy. This descendant of the Jubas was as fratricidal as ever his ancestors had been. In a family feud he murdered two nephews. His brother fled to Italy, where he was given Gallic troops to take to Africa to avenge his sons. Gildo's army was utterly defeated by his brother's near Theveste, and Gildo himself died a fugitive. He left behind him estates so enormous that their confiscation by the State required the appointment of a special governor, *comes patrimonii gildoniaci*. Bishop Optatus was executed, and although the Donatists awarded him the martyr's crown, at last, after nearly a century, the balance of power was shifting. For the Catholics now had, in the person of Bishop Augustine of Hippo, a tireless champion.

Basilica of St Salsa, built in the fourth or fifth century, at Tipasa

10 The greatest African

St Augustine of Hippo, as seen in Renaissance Italy by Piero della Francesca. Detail from a painting in the National Museum of Ancient Art, Lisbon

St Augustine belongs to the world. His teaching on free will and predestination, on original sin and the operation of God's grace – largely inspired by his attack on the heresy of the Welsh monk Pelagius, who believed that Christians could earn salvation by virtuous living – was enshrined in countless pamphlets and, above all, in *The City of God*. This book, which he began to write at the age of fifty-eight and finished in his seventies, rapidly became one of the most influential of all theological works. It helped to turn the talents of the most gifted men of his own and succeeding generations away from secular affairs and towards monasticism and the organization of the Church and even, a millenium later, served to inspire the most extreme heretics of the Reformation. It earned St Augustine the title of one of the Four Doctors of the Church. Yet during his life much of his energy was absorbed in combating the comparatively unimportant provincial heresy of Donatism at home in Africa.

He was the son of a Christian mother and of a pagan father, who belonged to the afflicted class of *curiales*, or minor gentry, which suffered most from the depredations of fourth-century tax-gatherers. The family was never well-off; Patricius was obliged to borrow money from a richer friend in order to send his son to university in Carthage. But by upbringing and association St Augustine belonged to the official classes which, however much they themselves hated the imperial administration, nevertheless could not afford to sympathize with the peasantry off whose backs they lived. It never occurred to St Augustine to condemn slavery. He had only a smattering of the local dialect – probably a bastardized Punic – which served further to divide him from the rural population. And his education, his position, and his great intellectual gifts enabled him to satisfy a natural taste for the company of other educated men, not only ecclesiastics but rich landowners, proconsuls and *comites* who belonged to the great world of the Roman masters. Since his Christianity was the approved variety, they in turn could safely give him their friendship.

It might have been otherwise. His birth-place, Thagaste (Souk–Ahras) in Numidia, had formerly been – as far as its Christian community was concerned – wholly Donatist. Catholicism probably made its first converts there during the *tempora Macariana*, in the decade before his birth in A.D. 354. Thus his mother, who bore the un-Roman name of Monica, was a Catholic, and not a Donatist like some other members of her family. Had she been a Donatist, the course of her son's career might well have been very different – and with it perhaps the history of the western Church. Yet African Church history would probably have been much the same: though St Augustine spent half a lifetime fighting Donatism he died believing that he had failed – as indeed, in any but the most technical sense, he had. Donatism survived alongside Catholicism until both were vanquished together by the soldiers of Islam two hundred years after his death. He deprived it finally of its intellectual respectability, but he never broke its emotional hold. The name of its founder remained one to conjure with in Africa – more so than that of Augustine.

*   *   *

The young St Augustine was imaginative, shrewd and ardent. He was as African as Tertullian had been – as far removed from Roman *gravitas* as he was from the cosmopolitan sophistication of Constantinople. His spiritual progress in childhood and early manhood is the best documented of antiquity; his *Confessions* ranks as one of the three or four most naked self-exposures ever written. If the later chapters, with their profound and penetrating analysis of the nature of time, reveal the author's gifts as a philosopher, the more famous biographical chapters show him to have had the psychological perceptiveness, the eye for significant detail and passion for human truth of a great artist. He was also well aware – fifteen hundred years before Freud – of the existence of the subconscious. In middle age, the ascetic in him finally suppressed the artist; but the great imaginative structure of *The City of God* owes a debt to that other St Augustine.

His autobiography makes eloquently plain that, as a young man, he had a genius for, above all, loving and being loved. His relationship with his mother was possessive to a degree that would raise eyebrows today (his father and his brothers and sisters he scarcely mentions), yet it cannot be described as anything other than enriching. Neither St Monica's obvious faults nor her son's demands on her can mar it; nor did it ever prevent him from loving others – the childhood friend whose death caused him to hate 'all the places we had known together, because he was not in them'; the concubine with whom he lived faithfully for fourteen years, and whom he took with him to Italy; the son she bore him, in whom he felt such fatherly pride. His grief for his lost friend and concubine is such that he cannot bring himself to mention their names. Few have written more passionately of the joys of the flesh – even though, having turned his back on them, he harps on their sinfulness with all the over-enthusiasm of the reformed; or more movingly of the pleasures of having like-minded companions with whom to share the study of philosophy. The capacity to give and inspire affection redeems the absence in St Augustine's life of the kind of incident or behaviour which the hagiographer can set up as an example to the faithful, a pattern of Christian living. Even as a Christian and a bishop he could behave extremely badly. Though never much of a scholar in the austerest sense of that word, he had dared to offer criticism to the far more distinguished St Jerome on a point of scholarship; and was forgiven. He dared to make military suggestions to Count Boniface, the most eminent general of the day, along with abusive reproaches about the widowed Count's remarriage; and remained a friend. Without shame, he allowed his richest friends, the Roman St Melania and her husband Pinianus, to be forcibly enrolled parishioners of Hippo, where the congregation had their eyes on their wealth, and then made no attempt to apologize when the visitors remonstrated; yet they soon restored the bishop to their favour. It has been maintained that this undoubted charm had not a little to do with his adopting the doctrine of salvation by grace and predestination. In his own life he received much love that in justice he deserved to lose.

St Augustine started his school career in his home town in the wooded hills of central Numidia; but Thagaste was a small, unimportant place, and at the age of eleven or so he was sent to school in Madauros, some twenty or thirty miles distant, where Apuleius had been born and brought up. His hatred of school is well known. He detested 'one and one make two, two and two make four', and he failed to acquire any competence in Greek. At the age of sixteen he spent a year at home – the year of the celebrated theft of a neighbour's pears which looms so large in the *Confessions* – while his father struggled to raise money to send him on to Carthage. There he won prizes, more friends and mistresses, and indulged a passion for the theatre and the circus.

Clever boys of his day became teachers, or went into the Church. St Augustine – not yet a Christian – became a teacher of rhetoric, first in Thagaste for a year, and then for the next six or seven in Carthage. He was not a very successful one. He could not keep order in the unruly schools of the capital, and his lack of Greek was a handicap. At the age of twenty-nine, accompanied by his concubine and their son, he gave his protesting mother the slip and embarked to try his luck in Rome. He had a struggle to make ends meet. He acquired some private pupils, but he was fortunate after a year to be recommended for a post as a teacher of rhetoric in Milan. There, having been a Manichee for some years and then flirted with neo-Platonism, he recognized his destiny. He fell under the influence of St Ambrose, the princely bishop of Milan, and one day in a garden, after 'a deluge of tears' and a providential reading from the Epistles of St Paul, 'It was as though the light of confidence flooded into my heart and all the darkness of doubt was dispelled'. He was thirty-two.

He returned to Thagaste in A.D. 388 and there founded a celibate community. The monastic movement had started in Egypt a century earlier; he introduced it to Africa. It was a long-held dream. Even before his conversion he and his friends had discussed the possibility of pooling their possessions and living a communal life 'away from the crowd'. They wanted their womenfolk to share it, however; but 'when we began to ask ourselves whether the women would agree to the plan, all our carefully made arrangements collapsed and broke to pieces in our hands and were discarded. Once more we turned to our sighs and groans.' But celibacy, once accepted, enabled the dream to be fulfilled.

The life of retreat did not last long. By A.D. 391 his anti-heretical writings had already brought him a certain fame, and at the instance of a high official who wished to meet him in the expectation of being converted, he went to Hippo Regius (Bône), on the coast. Unhappily for him, the bishop of Hippo was an aged Greek, with little Latin and less local *patois*, whose congregation felt the need of a younger, livelier priest who spoke Latin. Seeing in Augustine the man they wanted they ordained him by force. Augustine was deeply distressed; but a sacrament, however given, had to be accepted as the Will of God. He must have remembered that beloved pagan friend of his youth, who, baptised during a coma, nevertheless rebuked the young Augustine's mockery and died a believing Christian. Thereafter Augustine preached daily at Hippo in his bishop's place; and he became bishop himself in A.D. 395. It was just the time when the Donatists, with the backing of the *comes* Gildo, were at the zenith of their power and influence. In the same year, the Catholics suffered a serious loss: the Donatists kidnapped an able young Catholic lawyer of Constantine called Petilian, and submitted him to forcible rebaptism. Like Augustine, Petilian felt there was no appeal against what appeared to be God's Will, and thenceforth his considerable gifts were devoted to the schism which he now believed to be the true Church. As the Donatist bishop of Con-

stantine, he was to be Augustine's principal adversary.

St Augustine's prodigious energies could no longer be devoted solely to the things of the spirit. The role of bishop required a man of action; and though he managed to write hundreds of sermons and pamphlets, and hundreds of private letters, the things of the world demanded his attention. He turned out to be a natural administrator, with a flair for leadership and negotiation. Hippo was not an important diocese, but Augustine became the closest adviser of the primate of Africa, Bishop Aurelius of Carthage, and, in effect, the principal advocate of the Catholic cause. Together they strove to take advantage of the failure of the revolt of Gildo, and the confusion into which the Donatist party had been thrown. The re-conversion of the Donatists became his life's work as a man of action. That he failed to achieve this after a decade of vigorous propaganda – debates, a stream of tracts, correspondence with individual Donatist clergy – led him to advocate the strengthening of right with might. Like Constantine, he came, with less and less reluctance, to believe in the physical oppression of heretics, taking as his text 'Compel them to come in.'

At first, he believed that 'we must act only by words, fight only by arguments, and prevail by force of reason.' It was his experience of the world which changed that opinion; for instance, 'my own town, which although it was once wholly on the side of Donatus was brought over to the Catholic unity by the fear of the imperial edicts . . . There were so many others which were mentioned to me by name, that from the facts themselves, I was made to own that to this matter the word of Scripture might be understood as applying, "Give opportunity to a wise man and he will become wiser".' As one historian of the period points out (W. H. C. Frend), that 'opportunity' was coercion, 'and this was not so mild as Augustine would lead his readers to think'. It included torture. Although Donatism was an obscure provincial sect, with no progeny, its effects, by changing St Augustine's opinion on this one point, were incalculable. A thousand years later, the perpetrators of the Inquisition could lean on the authority of this Doctor of the Church.

*   *   *

While religious controversy preoccupied the province of Africa, the Empire itself had other, graver problems to face. During the fourth century it had become impossible any longer to keep the barbarian tribes of northern Europe outside the frontiers, even by withdrawing them. In the middle years of the century, when Constantine's sons were on the throne, Gaul was ravaged by the Franks and the Alamans. During the joint reign of Valentinian and his brother Valens, in the late 360s and 370s, the Visigoths had to be permitted to settle peacefully within the Danube frontier. Even Theodosius the Great (A.D. 378–395), the last really effective Roman Emperor with a tough military and social policy, was obliged to allot yet more territory to tribal settlements; and his death ushered in the permanent division of the Empire, and the long minorities of his two young sons, Honorius in the western Empire and Arcadius in the east.

It was Honorius's guardian, the brilliant Vandal Stilicho, who had to deal with Gildo's rebellion. With most of the western provinces in the hands of the Germanic invaders, and poised, in the person of Alaric king of the Goths, to invade Italy itself, the imperial court at Ravenna was more than ever dependent on its African granaries for food: the crime that had finally made Stilicho take action against Gildo had been the seizure of the corn fleet. Once Gildo was defeated, the experiment of allowing a certain amount of self-government by native chieftains was over. The new *comes Africae* was the Vandal's own brother-in-law.

By their association with Gildo, the Donatists had condemned themselves as the party of disunity and rebellion. From now on, the Catholics could count on the political as well as the religious support of the imperial government. They could also count on the support of new allies – the many Roman aristrocrats who were at this time fleeing from the perils in Italy to seek refuge on their estates in Africa. The newcomers knew little of Donatism, and had their own motives for wanting a quiet, conforming peasantry.

Meanwhile the Catholics were doing all they could to get the schismatics declared heretics, so that anti-heresy legislation already on the statute books could be enforced against them. They also tried to set their own house in order. Aurelius of Carthage inaugurated annual episcopal councils to invigorate the hierarchy (it was at the first of these that Augustine had made his name in debate), and bishops from outlying parts spent almost as much time on the road and in Carthage as in their dioceses. The Council of A.D. 401 appointed missionaries to be sent out into the field to reconvert Donatists and other non-Catholic Christians. Where possible, bishoprics were filled by monks from the Augustinian monastery which Augustine had by now founded at Hippo; and Augustine began to recommend Catholic landowners to convert their Donatist peasantry by force.

The Donatists, although on the defensive, were not yet beaten and the scandals on the Catholic side, where embezzlement, simony, quarrels and even sex scandals were rife, fortified their belief in the rightness of their cause. Harassment and persecution were only what they expected; and had not Tyconius written 'In proportion as the just are persecuted, the unjust feast and rejoice'? Persecution was the proof of virtue. They fought back. One Donatist bishop boldly re-baptised eighty families on an estate virtually on the border of St Augustine's diocese. There was much violence, aggravated by gangs of *circumcelliones* who attacked the villas of Augustine's rich friends. Petilian accused the Catholics of being butchers; to St Augustine's chagrin, members of his own congregation could reel off his rival's words from memory. Petilian also took pleasure in reminding the world of St Augustine's Manichee past. The Catholic bishop Possidius of Calama (Guelma), later St Augustine's biographer, was actually captured by *circumcelliones*; and when St Augustine tried to get the rival Donatist bishop of Calama to pay a fine of 10 lb in gold, prescribed by law, he failed – though he later had the sentence confirmed by the proconsul himself.

In A.D. 405, Honorius proclaimed an Edict of Unity, whereby Donatism was at long last declared a heresy. All Donatist property belonged to the Catholics; their meetings were forbidden, those who permitted them were to be flogged; Donatists were not allowed to make wills, receive legacies, or enter into contracts. But the Donatists still did not give in. Indeed, one Catholic bishop took his entire flock over to Donatism, and two towns in Byzacena turned Donatist. Even in Hippo, their pamphlets continued to appear, and the exiled Primian and Petilian, undaunted, took their side of the story to Ravenna. The Emperor gave them permission to return to Africa, and when Stilicho was murdered in A.D. 408, Donatist hopes revived and with them their efforts. The unfortunate St Augustine stood by helpless while a gang of *circumcelliones* introduced a Donatist bishop into Hippo; some of his own clergy defected.

Typically, however, the indefatigable St Augustine was already in touch with Stilicho's murderer, from whom he obtained promises of aid; and fortunately for him the new proconsul Donatus, himself an African, was an ardent Catholic, having been converted from Donatism. But when Donatus, ready to suppress Donatism by any means, introduced the death penalty, St Augustine protested: 'You will help us greatly . . . if you were to repress this vain and proud sect in a manner which does not let it feel that it is suffering for truth and justice.'

That is the key to St Augustine's policy. Throughout these years, though he had come round to advocating the use of force, he believed that it should be seen to be legal – one reason he was so keen to have the Donatists defined as heretics. But, though he wanted the Donatists to be legally in the wrong, he was very anxious not to make martyrs of them. The death sentence was the last thing he wanted. Nor did he always want other penalties exacted: although he took the case against the Donatist bishop of Calama to the proconsul, it was primarily to

get a *legal* verdict against him. When the proconsul confirmed that the bishop had to pay the 10 lb gold fine, St Augustine arranged for it to be commuted.

It is also why he was determined to get the Donatists to a conference, so that the Catholics might meet them in debate and prove, to their faces, that they were legally and morally in the wrong. He wanted the world to know it; he also wanted the Donatists to know it, and be seen to know it. The Edict of Unity of A.D. 405 had been a legal victory, which as usual had been enforced half-heartedly; what the Catholics needed now was a moral and psychological victory. In A.D. 410, Possidius of Calama and another Catholic bishop were sent to Ravenna to plead with the Emperor for a last effort against the Donatists.

Honorius had serious troubles on his hands. Alaric king of the Goths had been defeated at the time of Gildo's revolt, but had reformed his armies and invaded Italy itself at the opening of the new century. Alaric had been followed within a few years by another barbarian chieftain, whom Stilicho had also beaten back. But the barbarians were not to be held off for long, for they were being pressed on by the Huns at their backs; and at the end of A.D. 406 the Rhine frontier had been breached for ever, by a great horde of Alans, Vandals, Suevians and Burgundians, who had poured into Gaul. (By A.D. 409 the Vandals, among others, were in Spain.) Eventually Alaric seized another chance: in August A.D. 410 he took and looted Rome.

The sack of the Eternal City was the most traumatic event in the history of the Later Roman Empire, and haunted the imagination of generations to come, as a symbol of kingdoms come to dust (it also provoked in *The City of God* St Augustine's majestic defence of Christians against the charge of being responsible). Yet it lasted only three days. Before the end of the month, Alaric turned his attention to southern Italy – and the prospect of invading Africa to seize territory for his people there. A severe storm sank or scattered most of Alaric's fleet, and he died almost immediately afterwards; but it was a portent; in twenty years Africa was to succumb to another, and greater, barbarian army.

Possidius and his companion were too set on their own concerns to worry about the implications of what was happening in Italy. And in spite of the danger from the Goths, Honorius found time to listen to the two African bishops. The very day after Alaric entered Rome, the Emperor sent a message to the *comes Africae* Heraclian: heresy was to be put down in 'blood and proscription'. He also sent Count Marcellinus to preside at a conference which was to settle the issues between the two sides once and for all. The result was not in much doubt: Marcellinus was a friend to whom St Augustine had already dedicated one work, and to whom he was to dedicate *The City of God*.

The council which met at Carthage in June A.D. 411 was the decisive encounter between the Catholics and Donatists. The only occasion on which Augustine and Petilian met face to face, it ended in the vindication of the Catholics. Bishops of both parties were summoned to attend from all over North Africa. After an enormous roll-call, punctuated by acrimonious accusations (Donatists frequently acknowledged their Catholic opposite numbers with the words: 'I recognize my persecutor'; once there was an accusation of murder, and one signature was alleged to be that of a corpse), the Catholics mustered two hundred and eighty-six names, the Donatists two fewer. The vital session lasted all day from dawn to dusk on June 8th (the Donatists standing all the time, having refused at a previous session to sit down with sinners). Petilian strove to keep the debate on the identity of the true Church, but was driven by St Augustine to discussing the momentous events of a century before, when the Donatists had failed to prove that Caecilian was not rightfully consecrated bishop of Carthage. The verdict both of the Emperor and of two episcopal councils had gone against them then; they had failed to abide by it, thus becoming the authors of disunity. They had no new evidence which would invalidate Caecilian's consecration; and Count Marcellinus's decision, given by candlelight that very night, went against them now.

Six months later, Honorius made Donatism a criminal offence. But as usual it was one thing to announce proscription and punishment, another to carry it out. Though Augustine had the satisfaction of driving from Hippo his rival bishop Macrobius, Macrobius found alternative employment as leader of a gang of *circumcelliones*. Donatist bishops remained in charge of distant Numidian and Mauretanian dioceses; Petilian, though exiled from Constantine, continued to call Donatist councils; new Donatist priests were ordained. Yet the enforcement was firmer this time; the Roman authorities gave the Catholics constant support. Count Marcellinus seems to have visited Numidia where he held trials of refractory Donatists – although, following St Augustine's advice, he commuted the extreme penalty to hard labour. St Augustine himself at once published a digest of the proceedings of the conference for the instruction of laymen, and backed it up by preaching in Constantine and other places. Even when Count Heraclian was sentenced to death after an ill-judged rebellion against the Emperor, and Marcellinus – apparently implicated – was also executed, the new *comes* followed their policy.

St Augustine's personal intervention failed to dislodge the tough incumbents in distant cities such as Caesarea and Thamugadi (Timgad), but the schism seems gradually to have weakened its hold on the cities of Africa Proconsularis. St Augustine hardly mentions it in the last decade of his life. But the future did not lie with the cities: and Donatism remained strong in the countryside, where its roots were nourished by the fundamental antipathy of the Libyan to the ordered values of the classical world of the Mediterranean.

* * *

The province faced other perils. The nomads of the interior and the south were now a constant source of anxiety. In a Constitution of A.D. 409, the Emperor had addressed the vicar of Africa: 'We have learnt that the lands ceded to *confederates* by the far-seeing humanity of our ancestors, in order to assure the upkeep and protection of the *limes* and the *fossatum,* are sometimes occupied by ordinary tenants. If these satisfy their greedy desires by occupying such lands, let them know that they must dedicate their devoted services to the upkeep of the ditch and the guarding of the *limes,* like those that our ancestors proposed for this duty. If this condition is not fulfilled, let them know that the most elementary justice will be to transfer these concessions [to others] so that these precautions may continue to be observed . . .' It was one of a stream of orders and decrees intended to prevent the province falling apart at the seams. But though the bureaucracy kept its eye on everything, it was with less and less effect.

Later, Count Boniface had to beat off several Moorish raids. But it was not from the desert or the mountains that the conquerors came. In A.D. 416, the king of the Visigoths, who had finally reached Spain after their long journey from the Danube through Greece and up and down the length of Italy, cast speculative eyes on North Africa as a final home for his people. Though he did not come – his fleet, like Alaric's six years earlier, was destroyed in a storm – it occurred to the Donatists that they might have more in common with these barbarians in Spain, all of whom had adopted Arian Christianity during their wanderings and were therefore heretics, than with their Catholic African brothers.

It was another Arian people, the Vandals, who crossed the straits of Gibraltar to invade Africa thirteen years later – not merely an army, but eighty thousand men, women and children. One authority puts the figure at one hundred and eighty thousand. Once landed in August, A.D. 429, they marched virtually unchecked, their ships keeping them company along the coast, to the frontier of Africa Proconsularis. Here Count Boniface, the most brilliant soldier of the Empire (one of 'the last of the Romans' according to Procopius) turned to face them with his army, but it was like commanding a rising tide to ebb. He retreated, after a resounding defeat, to Hippo. He held out there for fourteen

months only because the Vandals were not used to siege warfare. The Empress Regent Galla Placidia eventually arranged for reinforcements to be sent to Boniface from Italy and the east; but his new army was beaten even more decisively, and Boniface retired to seek other laurels in Italy.

The Vandal king Gaiseric made Hippo his first capital, settled his people in Numidia, and negotiated a treaty with the Emperor, whom he allowed to keep the unproductive western provinces of Africa. Technically a *foederatus,* he was actually king in all but name. In A.D. 439, he seized Carthage: the citizens were cheering at the circus as he approached. North Africa was not ruled from Italy again, until Mussolini occupied Libya.

The refugees who had fled to Africa during Alaric's invasions of Italy had turned tail and fled back to Italy, or to the provinces of the east. They were joined by thousands of native Africans, those who had most to fear from a change of masters. One rich senator of Carthage was reduced to beggary in exile before finding a modest post in the imperial service in another province; his daughter was sold into slavery in Syria by merchants who had bought her from the Vandals. Her story is known from a letter written by a bishop in Syria, entrusting another bishop to return her to her father's care. Hundred of exiles were not so fortunate. Nor were those who failed to get away.

*   *   *

During the siege of Hippo, in the August of A.D. 430, St Augustine had died, less concerned over the dismemberment of Roman Africa than over the conversion to Christianity of one obscure physician and the constant study of the penitential psalms which he had had inscribed in huge letters on the walls of his cell, so that he might read them as he lay dying. The City of God awaited him.

11 The Vandal interregnum

Fine mosaic found in the remains of what was almost certainly a Christian church at Cherchel (ancient Caesarea). Probably of fourth-century date, it is now in Cherchel's French church

By the beginning of the fifth century, Africa was the only province in the west which had not been overrun by barbarians. In spite of the miseries of so many of its inhabitants, its fields continued to yield their generous harvests, its olive trees produced huge quantities of oil, its vineyards and orchards were heavy with fruit, and its pastures still supported horses and sheep and cattle. It is true that a survey of Honorius in A.D. 422 suggests that the acreage under cultivation had shrunk, perhaps considerably; but if some land had been deserted by a declining population, it was only the most unproductive, and what remained under cultivation was still splendidly fruitful. The unfailing African sun and the scrupulous upkeep by a hard-working peasantry of the irrigation works which utilized every drop of water combined to sustain the province's reputation for fertility. No wonder Alaric, in ravaged Italy, and the Visigoths and Vandals in disputed Spain, had seen it as a promised land.

The Vandals did not come to destroy, but to settle. The atrocity stories spread by alarmed ecclesiastics are of some of the unavoidable horrors of invasion, the consequences of thousands of newcomers living off the land. And like other conquerors the Vandals were greedy for loot. The Church was rich: like the secular landlords, it was dispossessed of its finest estates, and had to give up its plate, its gold, and treasures of all kinds. But it was unlikely that the Vandals cut down the olive trees and burnt down the vines that were the basis of the prosperity they had every intention of enjoying themselves. These remained, to amaze the army of Belisarius a hundred years later just as, a millenium before, other crops and orchards had amazed the army of Regulus. The worst excesses against the civilian population were, no doubt, the private revenges wreaked by Donatists on their hated oppressors under cover of the invasion.

'The union of the Roman Empire was dissolved; its genius was humbled in the dust; and armies of unknown barbarians, issuing from the frozen regions of the north, had established their victorious reign over the fairest provinces of Europe and Africa.' That was how it struck Gibbon; and certainly the whole of the western Empire was occupied by Germanic tribes under their own kings – Vandals in Africa, Ostrogoths in Italy, Visigoths in Spain and southern France, Burgundians in the Rhone valley, Suevi in Galicia, Franks in northern Gaul and Anglo-Saxons in Britain. But it was not quite how it seemed at the time, at least to the barbarians. Except in Britain, the forms of Roman life remained; the invaders were simply an occupying military caste, who took over the administration. They had all, except the Anglo-Saxons, felt for generations the power and presence of the Mediterranean world symbolized by Rome, an infinitely superior civilization whose benefits they were anxious to share. Contact had been sufficiently close for them all to be converted to Christianity during their journey to the west: a heretical, Arian Christianity, but nonetheless they were as ready as any Roman to render unto Caesar the things that were Caesar's. That included acknowledgement of the Emperor's suzerainty. Even when the last Emperor at Rome was deposed in A.D. 476, the barbarian kings of Europe continued to acknowledge the Roman Emperor in the east, thinking of themselves as his allies ruling in his name. All, on entering the Roman Empire, adopted the Roman language: no Germanic words, except those borrowed later, survive in the Romance languages. All used Roman coins, and employed Roman senatorial families in the task of government. Only on the Rhine frontier and towards the Seine and the Danube did the barbarians 'Germanize' the local populations.

The Vandals in Africa were the one people who broke completely with the Empire, and that may be credited to the particular genius and ambition of their first king. Yet even Gaiseric was only a partial exception. If he dispossessed the Roman landlords in favour of his own people on a scale unknown in Gaul (where a plutocrat like Symmachus continued to run and profit from his estates), he continued to make use of the *conductores*;

he persecuted the Roman Church, but installed an Arian priesthood in its place; he minted Roman coins, made Latin the official language, employed Roman engineers and architects. He and his successors built baths at Tunis, and patronized Roman African rhetoricians and poets and grammarians (one of whom later inspired Milton's description of Paradise), whose work, though much inferior to that of the great writers, was Roman nonetheless. Even more interesting, Gaiseric suppressed the tribal organization of his nobles in favour of an autocracy based on the Roman model.

The Romanization of the conquerors of the west is not surprising, for the tribes can be counted in tens of thousands, or at most hundreds of thousands, in populations of several millions. In Roman Africa, the eighty thousand Vandals found an indigenous population of six or seven million, possibly more. Even if they numbered one hundred and eighty thousand, they cannot have been more than five per cent of the total. It is true that the Romans themselves, like the Arabs later, managed to transform the peoples they conquered with numerically tiny forces; but the barbarians were anxious to be transformed.

The Vandals took to the delights of civilization, whether as *grands seigneurs* on their new domains or as urban notables, with Teutonic enthusiasm. The Greek historian Procopius, writing after their downfall, considered them the most luxurious of all known peoples. 'The Vandals, since the time when they gained possession of Libya, used to indulge in baths, all of them, every day, and enjoyed a table abounding in all things, the sweetest and best that the earth and sea produce. And they wore gold very generally, and clothed themselves in garments [of silk], and passed their time, thus dressed, in theatres and hippodromes and in other pleasurable pursuits, and above all else in hunting. And they had dancers and mimes and all other things to hear and see which are of a musical nature or otherwise merit attention among men. And most of them dwelt in parks, which were well supplied with water and trees; and they had great numbers

of banquets, and all manner of sexual pleasures were in great vogue among them.' They lived, as far as they could, the life of Roman grandees. They were certainly very rich: they paid no taxes on their own lands, either to their kings or to a foreign overlord, and they acquired loot not only from their subjects but by piracy overseas. Their new wealth sapped their barbarian virtues, and the fleshpots of Carthage – as seductive as they had been in St Augustine's youth – proved as enervating to their energies as King Gaiseric had feared, when he tried to close down the most notorious district of the great seaport.

Meanwhile, the Vandal conquest cost Italy the free supplies of corn which she had enjoyed for five hundred years. 'The very soul of the Republic,' said Salvian, 'was destroyed by the capture of Africa.' Mauretania was a poor exchange for the rich heartlands of the old Africa Proconsularis; and in fact the western Maghreb was soon re-occupied by the Vandals, or fell to independent Moorish kings. But Italy's deprivations, from the point of view of the Empire as a whole, were a comparatively minor matter. Much more serious was the threat to Byzantine control of the Mediterranean. Gaiseric was not content with the enjoyment of his new kingdom. He wanted a maritime empire.

Carthage remained an extremely important port in the commercial life of the Mediterranean. Syrians, Jews, Greeks, and no doubt the sharper-witted of the Carthaginian *navicularii* continued to operate fleets of merchant ships there. Huge oil shipments from Africa, now the greatest oil-producing country in the Empire, still found their way northwards across the Mediterranean, where they were wanted not only for cooking and cleaning but for lamps to light the interiors of the new churches of Gaul. But a commercial empire was not what interested the barbarian king. He wanted quicker rewards, and found another use for Carthage's merchant marine. He became a pirate, and for the first time since the Punic Wars the straits of Sicily were no longer safe for the imperial navy. The Empire gained a temporary respite by offering Gaiseric's son Huneric the Emperor Valentinian's child-daughter Eudoxia as a bride. Huneric in fact already had a wife, the daughter of the king of the Visigoths; she was conveniently found 'guilty' of treason and returned to her father with her nose and ears cut off. The various barbarian kings never found it easy to form alliances among themselves; but this was an unforeseen triumph for Roman diplomacy.

Unfortunately his son's new betrothal failed to outweigh the temptations of Gaiseric's position of strength and his huge fleet. The king's thoughts turned to fresh conquest. 'Every year,' wrote Procopius, 'at the beginning of spring, Gaiseric invaded Sicily and Italy, enslaving some of the cities and razing others to the ground, and plundering everything.' Even Illyricum and the Peloponnese were not safe from his raids, and at one point he appears to have harassed his fellow barbarians in north-west Spain. He also seized, and this time occupied, the Balearic islands, Sardinia and Corsica. The western Mediterranean was soon a Vandal lake.

Gaiseric's greatest coup was something the Carthaginians had never brought off: the looting of Rome. In the summer of A.D. 455 he invaded Italy with an army of Vandals and Moors, and spent fourteen days in the capital collecting as much booty as he could. The authority of the remarkable Pope Leo, whose personal intervention had already saved Rome three years earlier from being attacked by Attila the Hun, was such that he extracted a promise from Gaiseric not to massacre the inhabitants or set the city on fire; though not enough to prevent him carrying off the Empress and her two daughters – one of them, now of age, the fiancée of Huneric. The Vandal booty included the famous seven-branched candlestick of the Jews, brought to Rome by Titus four centuries earlier (it was later retrieved by Belisarius and restored to Jerusalem, from where, ironically, it vanished for ever in the Persian sack of A.D. 614). Half the magnificent roof of gilded bronze tiles was taken from the temple of Jupiter on the Capitol.

Gaiseric's fleet returned to Carthage loaded with treasure and slaves, except for one ship which, weighted down with statues, sank. The spoils were divided between the Vandals and the Moors. Gaiseric had discovered an admirable method of keeping the latter quiet, although by enriching them and giving them a taste for gold he laid up trouble for the future.

The Empire was too weak, or too incompetent, to avenge this humiliation. Gaiseric adroitly destroyed two vast fleets which were sent against him in the 460s by the use of the new invention of 'Greek fire'. Even when he was succeeded by incompetent relatives, his kingdom seemed impregnable.

*   *   *

In September A.D. 493, some sixty years after the Vandal conquest, a young woman called Geminia Januarilla became engaged to a man called Julianus. She lived on the *fundus Tuletianos*, an estate which was part of a larger domain in an obscure corner of the province, somewhere on the modern border of Algeria and Tunisia between Negrine and Gafsa; its exact location is unknown. She was a daughter of the Geminius family, whose forebear Flavius Geminius Catullinus had once owned the domain; they were the most considerable people on the *fundus*, and at the time of Geminia Januarilla's engagement were busy buying up a quantity of modest leaseholds and freeholds in the area. They were rich enough to give her a trousseau worth several hundred olive trees. It included linen and woollen clothing, sheepskin slippers and jewellery. They were also provincial enough, in spite of great-grandfather Flavius's thoroughly Roman *trinomina* (three names), for Geminia Januarilla to have a wholly Berber taste in clothing.

Her *tabella dotis*, or dowry list, from which these last details are known, is written on one of fifty-six tablets dating from the 490s known as the *tablettes Albertini*, after the distinguished historian who devoted the last decade of his life to deciphering and interpreting them. They are written with a reed quill in ink, possibly of burnt wool or dried carob, direct

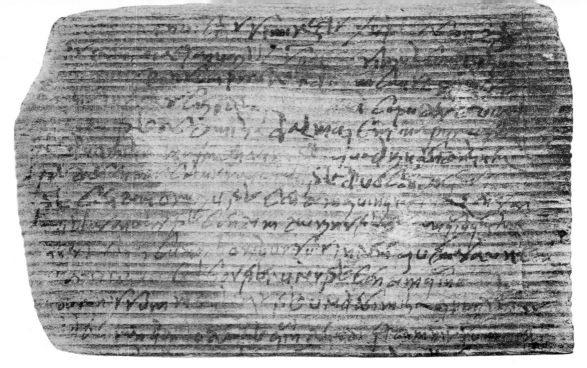

Dowry list of Geminia Januarilla—one of the tablettes Albertini dating from the Vandal period, now in the Stéphane Gsell Musée, Algiers

on to unpolished wood. Most are cedarwood; some are almond, poplar, willow or maple.

The circumstances in which they were discovered in 1928 remain mysterious. They were found hidden in a wall or a bank probably sixty miles south of Tébessa by some peasants; they appear to have been in a sealed jar, which accounts for their remarkable state of preservation. By devious means and several hands, a few at a time, they reached a government official in Tébessa, and are now in the Musée Stéphane Gsell in Algiers.

Forty-five have proved more or less legible, with the aid of photography, and together they form some thirty-four separate documents or fragments of documents. Most, but not all, relate to affairs on the *fundus Tuletianos*; most, but not all, are legal documents; a large number relate to the Geminius family. Apart from Januarilla's dowry list, a table of calculation and a financial account, and the bill of sale for a young slave, they are concerned with the sales of very small parcels of land or numbers of trees. The largest sale is of thirty-seven trees only. (Yet Geminia Januarilla's trousseau was worth several hundred.) They are, in fact, concerned with matters which could be of no interest except to the participants, and they were written on perishable material; yet for some reason, though there is no obvious common subject linking them, such as one family or one *fundus*, they were gathered together and put, not merely into safe keeping, but apparently into hiding. On several counts they are among the most important documents ever found in North Africa.

On these forty-five tablets writing from some thirty different hands appears. Half of them contribute only an X in place of a signature; the other fifteen write either the text or their names. Some documents were written out by a priest or by *magistri* – leaders of the community; but others were written by the peasant vendors. There is no sign of the work of a professional scribe. It looks as if the *fundus Tuletianos* and its immediate surroundings had at least fifteen men, all of whom could write their letters and some of whom were fully literate. Since the documents are so few, and cover such a short space of time and such a modest amount of property, these fifteen may have been only a fraction of the literate population of the domain. The language of the document is, admittedly, a debased Latin; but if the writers' schooling was rusty, it was not absent.

All wrote in lower case, not capitals; and the writing is cursive. The development of lower case and a running hand is crucial in the history of writing – all Roman stone inscriptions were in capital letters – and the *tablettes Albertini* give unlooked-for support to a mediaeval reference to lower-case letters as *litterae Africanae*. There are other, and much earlier, inscriptions in Africa which show the beginnings of the development of lower case; but they are too few and too tentative to offer more than a hint. But here, in a remote *fundus* on the fringe of the desert in an Africa under Vandal occupation, were fifteen unimportant men who wrote lower-case cursive which can be read today. That points to something that was already a firm tradition. The parties to the documents may, of course, have been the sons of formerly prosperous people dispossessed by the Vandals, and making what shift they could on land the Vandals did not want; in which case their education is perhaps readily explained. But they may not have been; they may have learnt that writing at some small village school. Or had the priest learnt it at some city grammar school long ago in his youth, and taught his parishioners himself? There is, alas, no evidence to show whether he was a Donatist, or a Catholic, or an Arian; it was certainly a Donatist neighbourhood, but it is tempting to hope that here was someone trained as a novice in one of St Augustine's monasteries, keeping alive, in the spirit of learning that was to be the glory of mediaeval monasticism, the script that St Augustine had perhaps used himself, and which was to flower in Merovingian and Carolingian France.

The documents reveal a remarkably ready familiarity with the proper forms of legal transactions: signatures were witnessed, guarantees were provided. They are vital evidence for any study of how Roman law worked at grass roots level, for they are the

Prosperous Vandal leaving his villa: late fifth- or early sixth-century North African mosaic now in the British Museum

only conveyances of their kind to survive from antiquity. And in the sphere of economic history, they prove that the system of Roman land tenure survived well into Vandal times: many of the transactions were undertaken explicitly under the *lex Manciana*. Nothing could show more clearly how little difference a change of masters had made to the mass of the population, at least as long as they were left in peace; the Vandals had simply taken over the Roman province, kept it Roman, and would leave it Roman.

The *tablettes* also yield much incidental information, about comparative prices, about irrigation, about the existence of ruins in the neighbourhood, about local trade (the various woods of the tablets were not local trees: they must have come from the Aures mountains a hundred miles away), and about the position of women: widows were clearly regarded as heads of families, and wives were closely associated with their husbands in transactions of land. They also show that the wealth of this now-desolate region was still based on sedentary dry farming.

E. Albertini had already noted that the only sign of the Vandal occupation in these documents was the dating by the year of the reign; neither they nor the increasing danger from the nomads (though perhaps they had made those ruins on one of their sudden raids) had yet disturbed the economy. Apart from their debased Latin, the *tablettes* might have been inscribed two centuries earlier. Another interesting suggestion, made by the editors of the *tablettes* who took over after Albertini's death, was that the Geminius family had fled abroad during the Vandal invasion; but that the sons or grandsons now felt safe enough to return and buy up their ancestral property. Justinian's political re-conquest in A.D. 533 may have been the spectacular confirmation of a social re-conquest begun half a century earlier. The editors also see in the low prices of the trees the possibility of an agricultural slump and consequent forced sales – the mechanism of the expropriation of the poor by the rich in action.

Even more significant for the future is a reference to a *via de camellos*. It attests to the presence of camel-borne nomads, or at least to caravans from the desert to Numidia; and it was the camel above all which turned the nomads of the desert into a dangerous long-distance striking force, even before the incredible expansion of peoples in the Arabian peninsula overwhelmed Africa for ever. For the last century or so before the Muslim conquest frontier life was made miserable by barbarian raids: this was nothing new, but the equipment of so many of the nomads with camels was.

*   *   *

How this change came about, or why it happened when it did, remains something of a mystery. Though it was not indigenous, the camel had long been known in North Africa. It was being used as a pack animal from the end of the fourth century B.C. in the eastern Sahara, and Julius Caesar captured twenty-two of them when he defeated King Juba of Numidia. They are represented, occasionally, on mosaics (but then so are crocodiles and hippopotami); a fine second-century example was uncovered at Thysdrus (El Djem) in 1959. Yet they are scarcely mentioned in any literary texts until the fourth century, and then only rarely. Arnobius refers to them; the corpse of Firmus was carried from the battlefield on one; and in the 360s Count Romanus was demanding four thousand of them. (This may have been a misprint for four hundred.) They must have existed; third-century sculptors from the frontier farms of Tripolitania show camels being used for ploughing, which suggests that they were no longer expensive. It is fairly certain that the Romans themselves encouraged the breeding of them in Tripolitania – possibly for policing the caravan routes. And there must have been many more beyond the Roman frontier. They were much too useful, with their stamina, strength, and independence of daily watering; they were the only animals, since the desert had become too dry for horses in late Carthaginian times, which could manage the long haul across the Sahara.

Yet, in spite of the strong possibility that

Silenus on a camel's back: detail of a mosaic of a Dionysiac procession, found at El Djem and now in the Bardo Museum, Tunis

the revitalized prosperity of third-century Tripolitania under Septimius Severus was due at least in part to an increase in the camel population and a consequent increase in trade across the Sahara – and the further possibility that the frontier had had to be fortified against *camel*-borne nomads – the camels themselves remain curiously in-

substantial. Count Romanus in the fourth century was never actually given his four thousand camels. It is as if, in the province itself, they remained an exotic rarity, the prerogative of kings like Juba and Firmus. Even in the fifth century, St Augustine never mentions them.

Not until the beginning of the sixth century, a few years after the *tablettes Albertini* were written, do they appear, as it were, in the flesh. The Greek historian Procopius describes the battle fought between the Vandals under King Thrasamund and a desert tribe under Cabaon, probably in Byzacena: 'Cabaon . . . placed his camels turned sideways in a circle as a protection for the camp, making his line fronting the enemy about twelve camels deep. Then he placed the children and the women and all those who were unfit for fighting together with their possessions in the middle, while he commanded the host of fighting men to stand between the feet of those animals, covering themselves with their shields . . . The Vandals were at a loss . . . for they were all horsemen, and used spears and swords for the most part, so that they were unable to do the enemy any harm at a distance; and their horses, annoyed at the sight of the camels, refused absolutely to be driven against the enemy. And since the Moors, by hurling javelins in great numbers among them from their safe position, kept killing both their horses and men without difficulty, because they were a vast throng, they began to flee . . .'

Suddenly, there are camels in quantity. They are no longer royal beasts, or patient pack-animals of trans-Saharan trade, but instruments of war and family transport, carrying whole tribes. At the same period, we hear of them being used by barbarian armies in Gaul, exported, no doubt, by the Vandals. But why had they taken so long to reach the Maghreb, when they had not been unknown, and when they must have been common enough in Tripolitania for three hundred years or more? The reason may be connected with a movement of the human population in the Sahara during this period, about which very little is known. The tribe which attacked Leptis Magna, the Austuriani, is heard of for the first time in the fourth century, part of a white population which had begun, very slowly, to displace the black Ethiopians southwards from the eastern desert at about the time of the Roman conquest. It seems to have been these white people who adopted the camel. There is, too,

a suggestion that at the end of the third century another white desert tribe, the Louata, also newcomers, whose raids the Emperor Maximian had to repel, had been camel-borne.

They were the harbingers of the Arabs, a greater race of *grands nomades chameliers* who, with the indispensable help of their strong, undemanding mounts, were to travel inexorably across the thirsty waste of the Libyan desert.

*   *   *

Meanwhile the Vandals had not been without troubles much nearer home. The territory they ruled was smaller than the old Roman province, and the withdrawal had led to the gradual development of a number of semi-independent Berber kingdoms. By the end of the Vandal period the province was virtually ringed with them. It is true that to some extent they and the Vandals shared tastes and outlook: they were barbarian brothers under the skin. And King Gaiseric, by offering bribes and lucrative opportunities for plunder overseas, undoubtedly exercised considerable authority over them. But after Gaiseric's death the

Christian tomb discovered near the site of the church at Kherbet Bahrarous in southern Numidia. The Latin cross suggests a fifth-century date

Mosaic of chapel dating from the Vandal occupation found at Tabarka

Berbers grew bolder. Mauretania Caesariensis was lost to a *rex gentium Maurorum et Romanorum* (he, too, used the Latin language, but he called himself king of a people, not a place); we hear of a prince of Hodna (the mountain chain south of Sitifis), another kingdom in the Aurès *massif*, and the beginnings of the formation of a tribal principality perhaps centred on Thala and Mactar, right inside the Vandal province. The latter, under its prince Antalas, proved a dangerous enemy not only to the Vandals but to the Byzantines.

One of King Gaiseric's first actions on conquering the province had been to order the inhabitants of the cities to dismantle their protective walls. The Vandals had no liking for siege warfare, and little aptitude: Hippo had held out against them for fourteen months. He kept the ramparts of Carthage, his capital, but otherwise he wanted the Africans where he could get at them, in case of civil war. Unfortunately, leaving the cities unprotected against their masters left them a tempting prey for the barbarian tribes. By the end of the fifth century the formerly flourishing frontier cities to the north of the Aures, Theveste, Thamugadi, Lambaesis and Bagai, had all been deserted by their inhabitants. So it seems had Thugga (near Teboursouk), which was well to the north in Africa Proconsularis.

The vicious but fortunately fairly brief reign of Gaiseric's son Huneric was distinguished by the murder of half his family, and the inauguration of a period of persecution for the Catholic clergy who had been tricked into attending a conference at Carthage in A.D. 484 in order to 'debate' with the Arian ascendency. It was the Council of A.D. 411 all over again; once more the issue was never in doubt, but this time the Catholics lost. The edict of persecution was couched in exactly the same words as Honorius's edict against the Donatists. It was carried out with considerably more force. Bishops were flung naked out of their cities, priests were flogged: nearly five thousand clergy were exiled to the prince of Hodna's territory. Hundreds more Catholic Christians fled to Spain. Their martyrdom was written up with edifying improvements (such as the story of the faithful of Tipasa who miraculously continued to enjoy the gift of speech after their tongues were cut out) by bishop Victor of Vita in exile. The many apostasies, which the bishop did not think to mention, were to create the usual problem when persecution was relaxed in the following reign. In A.D. 485 there was a serious famine, which the Catholics took to be the appropriate judgement of God, though it seems possible that general unrest aggravated it. Everywhere, wrote Victor of Vita, could be seen, 'like funeral processions, troops of young and old, youths and girls, children of both sexes: these unhappy creatures trailed round fortresses, villages and towns, scattered into the fields and the forests, fighting over dried-up tufts of grass and dead leaves . . . Mountains and hills, squares, streets and public highways were no more than an enormous charnel house of the victims of famine.'

Another judgement of God was the death of Huneric, *putrefactus et ebulliens vermibus*. He was succeeded by his nephews Gunthamund and Thrasamund, both of whose reigns were plagued by Moorish invasions (of which the inhabitants of the *fundus Tuletianos* may have been victims). Thrasamund was the dandy of the Vandal dynasty. He was handsome and cultivated, and his court became something of an intellectual centre. He was an Arian, but enjoyed indulging in theological debate with leading Catholics, although the price of too much persuasiveness, in Fulgentius of Ruspae for example, was exile in Sardinia; and from time to time the king persecuted them more actively. As an *homme du monde* he felt the allure of the sophisticated east and was on good terms with the Emperor so long as the independence of Africa was not threatened. Unfortunately a change of Emperor renewed intrigues between Byzantium and the Catholic Church in Carthage; Thrasamund, who was at this time trying to ward off both the horse-borne barbarians of Numidia and Mauretania, and the camel-borne nomads of Tripolitania who were menacing Byzacena, sought the support of his fellow Arian Theodoric of the Ostrogoths, and cemented the alliance by marrying Theodoric's sister, Amalafrida.

Shortly afterwards, however, he died, and was succeeded by his cousin Hilderic. Vandal policy was reversed, for Hilderic was half Roman himself, through his mother Eudoxia (she who had been part of the booty captured by his grandfather Gaiseric during the sack of Rome). He may have spent many years in Constantinople – he was now an old man – and known the Emperor Justin well and, more important, his nephew Justinian, who was shortly to become Emperor himself.

Coin portraits of Thrasamund (left) and Hilderic (right)

In any case, all his tastes were Roman rather than barbarian. He at once extended not only tolerance but approval to the Catholics. The exiled clergy returned: Fulgentius, whose eloquent sermons they remembered, received an ovation from the Carthaginian crowd. Barbarian instincts survived in Hilderic (though it must be admitted that few Roman rulers were free of them either), old as he was: when his late cousin's Arian brother-in-law Theodoric protested at this apparent treachery, at a time when persecution of the Arians had been renewed in the Empire, Hilderic retaliated by murdering Amalafrida, Thrasamund's widow, and the Gothic bodyguard she had brought as a dowry. The Vandal kingdom was only spared an Ostrogothic invasion to avenge his sister by Theodoric's death.

Hilderic was totally incompetent as a ruler. He had come to the throne by a law of succession laid down by Gaiseric, whereby the eldest of his descendants surviving at the death of the king should succeed, and not the eldest son. This was designed to spare the Vandal kingdom the hazards of long minorities; in practice, it was a law which 'tended to favour princes who were more remarkable for their longevity than for the soundness of their wits,' in Robert Graves's words. None of the Vandal kings illustrated this stricture better than Hilderic. He divided his kingdom against itself, Catholic against Arian, he turned his Arian subjects against himself, and his treatment of Amalafrida and his close ties with his old friend Justinian, with whom he would exchange expensive presents, gave his own family the excuse to call him traitor. This opportunity was seized by his cousin Gelimer, when an army commanded by Hilderic's nephew – Hilderic himself was quite uninterested in military affairs – was soundly beaten by the powerful barbarian tribe which, under Antalas, had formed a virtually independent kingdom in the mountainous plateau round Thala, within striking distance of Carthage.

Gelimer deposed Hilderic in May of A.D. 530 with the help of what remained of the army, and imprisoned him with his two nephews. He had assumed the throne of an embattled kingdom, but at least his policy was unambiguous: Africa for the Vandals. Unfortunately a century of luxury had softened this once-hard Baltic people. They were no longer the military élite they had been.

Worse, the usurper had given the Emperor Justinian just the excuse he was looking for. An irregularity of succession proved, in the event, as disastrous for the independence of the Vandal kingdom as the treasonable activities of Hilderic might have done. More so, perhaps: had the Vandals recognized the Emperor from the beginning, they might have survived to leave at least a faint imprint on the country, as the Goths and the Franks did elsewhere. As it was, they provoked a war of reconquest, and vanished almost at once.

Vandal jewellery found near Hippo and now in the British Museum

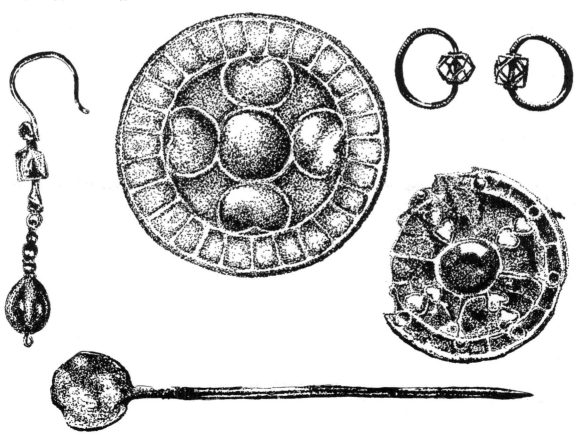

12   Africa returns to the east

The Capitol at Sbeïtla (ancient Sufetula) — incorporated into Byzantine ramparts. Sbeïtla bore the brunt of the first Arab attacks

'The Emperor never sleeps,' it was said of Justinian, who succeeded his uncle in the year that Gelimer usurped the throne of Africa. He ruled for fifty years, and took his duties as a Christian Emperor seriously. The final victory of the Catholic Church, still beset by heresy, and the recovery and glorification of the Roman Empire were his lifelong aims at home and abroad.

These two passions inspired two most remarkable achievements: the basilica of Saint Sophia at Constantinople, the greatest glory of Byzantine architecture, and the codification of Roman law in the *Corpus Juris Civilis*. (Justinian's greatest talent was for spotting talent in others, whether architects, lawyers, generals, theologians, a historian like Procopius – or his own wife Theodora, a reformed prostitute who was even more astute as a politician than he was.) They also inspired his recovery of the western Mediterranean lands from their Arian kings. Since Africa commanded the Straits of Sicily his first object was the conquest of the Vandals. His closest advisers, recalling the disasters that had befallen expeditions sent against the Vandals in the previous century, and unaware of the perilous weakness of their kingdom and of their once-powerful fleet under Gaiseric's successors, counselled against it; but a bishop from Egypt, prompted no doubt by his persecuted brothers in Africa or in exile, proclaimed to Justinian that Christ had appeared to him in a vision instructing the Emperor to reconquer Africa. Justinian accepted this as an omen of success, and in A.D. 533 five hundred ships, manned by thirty thousand sailors, set sail from Constantinople with an army of sixteen thousand men under the command of Count Belisarius. Six thousand horses also accompanied the expedition. For a generation, the armies of Constantinople had been fighting the Persians, whose mailed warriors mounted on 'cataphracts', or 'great horses', had given them a decisive advantage in the field. More than a third of Belisarius's army was similarly mailed and mounted, and armed with bows and arrows: they could not only strike from a distance, but also had an advantage in weight at close quarters.

The invaders (scandalously depleted on the voyage by five hundred deaths caused by cheap bread which had gone mouldy) landed on the flat coast of the Gulf of Syrte. The success of Belisarius's African campaign owed more to good fortune and his own common sense than to good generalship. The Vandals were caught unawares. Gelimer had sent his fleet on an expedition to Sardinia, and he himself was four days' journey inland. Belisarius moved north, unopposed, keeping a tight rein on his troops, in order not to antagonise the inhabitants. Soldiers caught stealing fruit were flogged, more for 'bringing their hostility' upon the Byzantine army than for the sin. The fleet kept them company along the coast. The local population, pleasantly surprised by an army prepared to pay for provisions, handed over their cities, and supplied food and horses. Only when his army reached the beautiful royal property on the coast at Grassa (probably Hammamet) did Belisarius allow them to plunder. The scene was described by Procopius, who had accompanied the Count to Africa to act as his secretary:

'In that place was a palace of the ruler of the Vandals and a park the most beautiful of all we know. For it is excellently watered by springs and has a great wealth of woods. And all the trees are full of fruit; so that each one of the soldiers pitched his tent among fruit-trees, and though all of them ate their fill of the fruit, which was then ripe, there was practically no diminution to be seen in the fruit.' The soldiers of Belisarius were as amazed and delighted by the fertility of this corner of Cape Bon as the soldiers of Regulus had been a thousand years before.

Gelimer, to whom news of the invasion had at last been brought at Bulla Regia, had no intention of yielding his kingdom. When Belisarius offered him surrender terms he promptly had the imprisoned Hilderic murdered and marched to meet the Byzantine army. In spite of their numerical superiority, however, the Vandals were routed ten miles from Carthage, and on St Cyprian's day, September 15, Belisarius sat down to eat in Gelimer's palace in the capital. 'It happened that the lunch made for Gelimer on the preceding day was in readiness. And we feasted on that very food and the domestics of Gelimer served it and poured the wine and waited upon us in every way.' Procopius points the moral: Fortune was making quite clear 'that all things are hers and that nothing is the private possession of any man'.

The Vandals had lost their kingdom after a hundred years. But the remnants of their army were gathering at Bulla Regia, and Gelimer was soon besieging Carthage, whose walls Belisarius had hastily had repaired. Gelimer cut the great aqueduct ('a structure well worth seeing,' notes Procopius), and tried to bribe Belisarius's Hun mercenaries; but when, in December, the Byzantines emerged to do battle the Vandals were routed once more. Gelimer himself, without a word to his officers, leapt on a horse and fled from his stockaded camp, followed by his relatives and servants. His army, not unnaturally, followed his example. When the Romans moved into the camp, there was not a man in it; only the womenfolk and children whom they had deserted and 'a quantity of wealth such as has never before been found, at least in one place. For the Vandals had plundered the Roman domain for a long time . . . and the revenue collected from the commodities produced there was not paid out to any other country in the purchase of a food supply, but those who possessed the land always kept for themselves the income from it . . . And from this it resulted that their wealth, amounting to an extraordinary sum, returned once more on that day into the hands of the Romans.' Belisarius, who was afraid the Vandals might return, had considerable difficulty in restraining his soldiers, 'becoming all of a sudden masters of very great wealth and of women both young and extremely comely'.

Perhaps it was the acquisition of such wealth which had sapped the fighting qualities of the Vandals. The fate of their king is instructive. Gelimer and his party found refuge in a Moorish fastness on a mountain overlooking Hippo. It was winter; accustomed to luxury, they were soon cold and hungry. Procopius gives a vivid account of the wretchedness of the deposed king and his followers in the 'stuffy huts' of the Moors. There was a touching exchange of letters between Gelimer and Pharas, the Hun soldier whom Belisarius had put in charge of the small company guarding the mountain, which Procopius quotes. 'What in the world has happened to you, my dear Gelimer, that you have cast, not yourself alone, but your whole family besides, into this pit?' wrote Pharas, delicately urging him to surrender, since 'they say that it is the wish of the Emperor Justinian to have you enrolled in the Senate . . . and to present you with lands both spacious and good and with great sums of money, and that Belisarius is willing to make himself responsible for your having all these things . . .' Was it that Gelimer dreaded becoming a slave? 'As though liberty were worth possessing at the price of all this misery!' Gelimer, weeping, could not but agree. He did not give himself up at once, but wrote back gratefully to Pharas, begging to be sent 'a lyre and one loaf of bread and a sponge'. Sick of the unleavened barley bread of his hosts, he longed for a taste of freshly-baked wheat bread; the sponge he needed for an inflamed eye, the lyre to accompany an ode he had composed on his misfortunes. Pharas, deeply moved, sent them to him – 'but kept watch more closely than before'.

What finally weakened Gelimer's resolution, even more than the worms the Vandal children were suffering from, was the sight of his small nephew and a Moorish child fighting over a tiny corn cake. The Moor struck the young Vandal over the temple 'and thus compelled him with great violence to cast out the cake which was already in his throat'. The king and other leading Vandals were taken to Constantinople, where they formed part of Belisarius's triumph; Gelimer, as promised, received large estates in Galatia. But the Vandal people simply disappeared, either fleeing to Spain or being absorbed into the population of North Africa, a tiny fraction of the whole: no 'Vandal type' survives there, and the Berber vocabulary contains no Vandal words.

They would hardly have been heard of by most people today had not their name been resurrected at the end of the 18th century by a bishop of Blois to form the word *vandalisme*. They had been execrated by churchmen of St Augustine's day and those who suffered under their persecution, and 'Vandal' was a pejorative term to Voltaire; but the bishop's inspired coinage gave it a wider currency, and saddled the Vandals with a reputation for wholesale destructiveness which they scarcely deserved. If they pulled down the outer fortifications of the cities of North Africa and exposed them to the depredations of the Berber tribes, it was left to the Byzantines to use many of the most splendid monuments of classical Rome as quarries for the building of defensive walls and fortresses. They were not vandals in the modern sense. Their principal desire had been to enter into and enjoy the Roman inheritance, not to destroy it.

* * *

In three months a kingdom had fallen to a few thousand cavalry: 'one would justly marvel at it,' said Procopius. Nothing could better illustrate the weakness of Vandal rule. The Berber tribes, waiting to see who would be the victors, had not come to their assistance. Once Belisarius was the master of Carthage, they hastened to declare their allegiance to him, asking only that they should receive recognition from the Emperor.

Yet, in spite of the welcome the former Roman population extended to the Byzantines, their rule was scarcely more secure. It was also virtually confined to the old Africa Proconsularis. The three Mauretanias remained outside their control, except for a handful of coastal cities.

Almost as soon as Belisarius had sailed for Constantinople, there were two serious barbarian uprisings in the south. Iabdas king of the Aures descended from the mountains to ravage Numidia, and Cutzinas invaded Byzacena. Belisarius's successor, the able Armenian general Solomon, with an army far better able to fight camel-borne nomads than that of the Vandals, marched south to deal with Cutzinas whom he defeated after two hard-fought battles (and who later

became a valuable ally). But Solomon had no time to deal properly with Iabdas before a dangerous insurrection broke out in the Byzantine army. Many of the soldiers had married the Vandal women they had acquired on the battlefield. These latter, having no wish to be worse off than before, considered that their new husbands should be allowed to enjoy their former husbands' properties, instead of seeing them confiscated by the State or returned to the families of their former owners, as Justinian had decreed. Their new husbands were equally eager to settle down to the enjoyment of the prizes of war, rather than embark on a disagreeable campaign in the hot south. In addition, the Hun mercenaries, who were Arians, deeply resented the proscription of their religion which had been a natural consequence of the Catholic Justinian's victory. There was a plot against Solomon, who barely escaped with his life in time to flee overseas to seek the assistance of Belisarius.

The rebels were under the command of Stotzas, a former member of the guard and a gifted demagogue, who soon attracted to his banner some two thirds of the Byzantine army and the remnants of the Vandals. The situation was grave, though fortunately the return of Belisarius prevented the capture of Carthage – more from fear inspired by his reputation than the reinforcements he brought. But the province was saved for Byzantium by Justinian's cousin, Germanos, whose lavish promises caused a sufficient number of defections from Stotzas, and by the providential failure of Iabdas and his Berber ally Ortaias, the prince of Hodna, to support the rebels. At Cellas Vatari in Numidia, Germanos defeated Stotzas, who fled to Mauretania; there he married a Moorish princess and waited for a chance of revenge.

Iabdas might have helped put an end to Byzantine domination before it had properly begun. Instead, he preferred to wait and see which way the battle went, and join in the subsequent looting. He was soon punished for his greed. Although Solomon had been a harsh and unpopular general, Justinian rightly recognized his quality, and sent him back to Africa in 539. He was given both the civilian position of praetorian prefect and the military rank of *magister militum Africae,* powers which Justinian normally divided between two men. Solomon was determined to take his revenge for the trouble Iabdas had caused him during his first term of office three years earlier. This time he took the precaution of severely disciplining and reforming his army (and exiling their Vandal wives); and when he invaded the Aurès he defeated Iabdas who, like Stotzas, fled to Mauretania. There followed five years of peace, which Solomon used to complete the remarkable defensive structure of the province he had undertaken on Justinian's orders immediately after the defeat of the Vandals, and whose ruins still survive in profusion.

Justinian had ordered the old Roman *limites* to be restored, and the frontier was soon marked by fortresses, walls, watch-towers and garrisons, repaired or new-built as necessary. But Solomon also constructed a second and a third line of forts and fortified towns within the province. The Vandals had pulled down the walls of all cities except Carthage and Hippo Regius; all were now rebuilt or, if the city had been too much devastated by the incursions of the nomads, one quarter of the town at least was fortified. Scarcely a village was without its look-out post or a secure place of refuge for the local inhabitants. Prodigious labour was involved. It has been calculated that the fortification of Tébessa alone, where the enormous walls still seal off the heart of the town from its suburbs, and where one gate still bears the name *porte de Solomon*, must have taken nearly three hundred and thirty-six thousand working days, or the employment of between eight hundred and eight hundred and fifty workmen for two years.

The work was urgent, since the province was all too plainly at the mercy of Berbers grown audacious during the Vandal occupation. For this reason it was quicker to use the masonry of neglected monuments in the new walls; the Byzantines were guilty of dismantling much of old Roman Africa. In some places Roman monuments formed part of the fortifications: a church at Haïdra, the great triumphal arch of Caracalla and perhaps a theatre at Tébessa, baths at Guelma, the Capitol at Sbeïtla, even a simple classical gateway, complete with columns, at Teboursouk. The new constructions showed every sign of improvisation: the blocks of stone varied greatly in size, dressed masonry was mixed up with roughly cut stone or even rubble and brick. Yet these huge crenellated walls, which were usually between eight and twelve feet thick, well over twenty-five feet in height and punctuated with towers, were properly provided with stables and large reservoirs for the collection of rainwater; and it is also clear that the Byzantine engineers, for all their lack of time, chose the most strategic positions for their fortresses.

Of Justinian's policy in Africa, Procopius wrote in his *Secret History*: 'Justinian, after the defeat of the Vandals, took no trouble to ensure the complete occupation of the country. He failed to realize that the best guarantee of authority resides in the goodwill of the subject . . . but administering the African provinces from a distance, pillaged and sucked them dry at his pleasure. He sent agents to estimate the value of the soil, instituted new and heavy taxes, himself claimed all the best lands, forbade the Arians to practise their religion, and ruled the army very harshly, continually putting off the despatch of reinforcements.' This was less than fair to the Emperor, who had received the news of Belisarius's success with joy, and had already, in the confident expectation of victory, prepared elaborate plans to expunge all Vandal influence and reorganize the administration. Thereafter, he took the closest personal interest in the province whose recovery enabled him eventually to win all the western provinces for Byzantium. Few details of defence or administration were too small for his concern; the hierarchy, both civilian and military, was reformed; the province was honoured (not always to its advantage) with a succession of governors who were either his favourites or members of his family; and he celebrated the conquest with a civic building programme which reflected, though it could not match, the military constructions undertaken by his lieutenants. Several new towns were expressly founded by Justinian; at Carthage, the port was developed, baths were erected in honour of his Empress, a great basilica was built, higher learning was encouraged; Leptis Magna, half ruined and virtually deserted, was re-built on his orders, and the exquisitely carved pillars in the great Byzantine church which had once been the secular basilica of Septimius Severus are among the most famous works of art which, directly or indirectly, Justinian inspired in Africa. Throughout the richer part of the province, learning and art, particularly the art of mosaic, enjoyed a minor renaissance, which was enthusiastically fostered in dozens of new monasteries and churches. Mundane concerns were not forgotten: everywhere, waterworks were repaired and improved, and the Emperor took pains to encourage agri-

Two of the magnificently carved Byzantine pillars in the apse of the Severan basilica at Leptis Magna

culture. A stream of instructions issued from Byzantium, and, if many were not obeyed, it was not for want of effort on the part of Justinian. His principal ambition was that Africa should be once more worthy of its inheritance.

Yet the cost was heavy, and the Africans paid the price. Many must have been worse off than they had been under the Vandals, when little was spent on the upkeep of buildings, let alone the construction of new ones; when any food exported was actually paid for, and Vandal revenues – lavishly augmented by the fruits of piracy – were spent within the country, on artefacts and entertainments and services of all kinds, so that money gradually percolated downwards; and when there was probably less pressure to raise large taxes in kind, since (as Procopius pointed out) there was no mother country to feed.

Byzantine Africa had to raise money for her own army and fortifications; she was also called on to raise money and men for Justinian's campaigns elsewhere in the Empire. His reign was long and in many ways glorious, but he bled the provinces white, even if it seemed to him to be for their own good. Shortage of money in the African public treasury was chronic throughout the sixth century A.D., and the army was frequently owed huge arrears of pay. Military discontent was compounded by civilian misery. The restoration of Catholic supremacy led to the proscription not only of Donatists and Arians but of Jews, pagans, and heretics of all kinds: many suffered forcible conversion, and hundreds more fled from the Byzantine province to swell the ranks of the tribes. Changes in the ownership of land also led to confusion and hatred. Even the heirs of the old Roman owners who were now reinstated were dissatisfied, since they felt that not enough was done for them. For Justinian refused to allow them to bring back into serfdom the descendants of the original tenants who had been tied to the land by the decrees of Diocletian and Constantine, if they or their fathers had escaped their bondage during the Vandal interregnum by fleeing to another estate or to the cities.

Matters were made worse by corrupt administration. Favours were bought and sold, the poor were sometimes taxed twice in a year, those converted to Catholicism continued, contrary to the law, to be taxed as pagans or heretics. Many of Justinian's rescripts were exhortations, or even pleas, that his subjects in Africa should be dealt with justly and gently. All too often his instructions fell on deaf ears, and the Emperor, ageing and preoccupied, was too far away to ensure obedience.

However, the reign of Solomon was a comparatively prosperous one; the African poet Corippus was to look back to it as a golden age. Count Belisarius had discovered that the ambitions of the Berber chieftains hardly went further than the recognition by the Emperor of their individual sovereignty; and Solomon made use of this to cement a number of alliances which safeguarded the peace. By paying the chieftains pensions, and flattering their dignity with titles and honours – such, still, was the Empire's magnetism – he ensured that at least they would not readily unite to attack the Byzantines. But it was a precarious peace, dependent almost entirely on the tact and diplomacy of the Byzantine commander towards the Berbers and his popularity with his own army, whose loyalty was constantly strained by delays in payment. In these circumstances, a bad appointment was an invitation to disaster.

It was not slow in coming. Anxious to reward his *magister militum*, Justinian agreed to the appointment of Solomon's nephew Sergius as duke of Tripolitania. Sergius appears to have allowed his troops to plunder the territory of the powerful Louata tribe, and then killed seventy-nine of the eighty deputies who came to Leptis Magna to complain. This massacre led to a general insurrection of the tribes of Tripolitania, and they were joined by Antalas, the powerful Berber chieftain in Byzacena, who had a private score to settle with Solomon. The alliance of Cutzinas was not enough to save Solomon. He won a battle near Theveste, but half his army refused to join in a second near Cillium because he had not let them plunder the battlefield. Solomon himself, fighting to the last with a few faithful guards, was killed.

Yet the insurrection would have died down – Antalas grandly declaring that he had no quarrel with the Emperor, and the Louata being eager to regain their nomad encampments in Tripolitania with their booty – had not Justinian decided to honour the memory of Solomon by appointing Sergius *magister militum*, with, as *co-magister*, his own nephew by marriage, Areobindus. Sergius alone had little hope of restoring peace, since he was hated by officers and men alike for his brutality and arrogance, and the tribes had sworn undying vengeance for the massacre of Leptis Magna. The divided command made matters worse, since the two men were jealous of each other and refused to go to each other's assistance. In the confused civil war which followed, Stotzas – Solomon's rebel officer – arrived from Mauretania to give his support to Antalas; the Byzantine army suffered a heavy defeat at the hands of the Louata tribe near Sicca Veneria (Le Kef, in northern Tunisia); Cutzinas and Iabdas joined the rebels, who at one point threatened Carthage itself; and Areobindus, at long last left in sole command by the recall of Sergius, was murdered by an ambitious duke of Numidia, Guntarith. The latter had been treating secretly with the barbarians and intended to make himself ruler of Africa and, at the same time, the husband of his victim's widow Prejecta. Africa seemed lost to Byzantium; Procopius wrote that the victories of Belisarius might never have been. Fortunately Africa found a temporary saviour – and Prejecta a protector – in the person of a brilliant and handsome regimental commander called Artabanes. Guntarith's hold on the army and on his barbarian allies was as precarious as Sergius's had been, and Artabanes became the leader of a conspiracy against him. In May of A.D. 546 Guntarith was murdered at a military banquet, and his reign of terror – there had been innumerable summary executions of possible enemies – was over. He had been in power for thirty-six days. But if control of Africa

had been technically restored to the Emperor, this was by no means true in fact. The barbarians were still unconquered, and the province soon lost the one man who might have achieved a stable peace.

Artabanes had fallen in love with Prejecta, and she, overjoyed to be spared a forced marriage with Guntarith, had agreed to marry him. He pursued her back to Byzantium. In vain: he already had a wife and, although Prejecta's grateful uncle Justinian loaded him with honours, he could not prevail against the implacable hostility of the Empress Theodora. Prejecta was married off to a member of the imperial court, and Artabanes' effective career was over.

Africa was left a prey to misery and uncertainty. For two years rival armies had marched back and forth between Carthage and Numidia, between Byzacena and Tripolitania: *fumans perit Africa flammis*, wrote Corippus, smouldering Africa perished in flames. The countryside was virtually uninhabited, for the people had sought refuge in the towns and cities fortified just in time by Solomon. The golden age was over. Yet the tribes did not take advantage of the weakness of their enemy to seize the empty farmlands once and for all. For their aims were always short term – an annual expedition from their mountain or desert fastnesses in search of booty, or a 'pension' from the Byzantines in return for a temporary truce. Their chieftains were inspired solely by the interests of their own tribe; they were as ready to take up arms against their fellow Berbers as against the Byzantines, whom, indeed, they regarded as useful allies in tribal warfare rather than as the common enemy. Nationalism was entirely foreign to them. This was the situation which the Byzantines were able to exploit, in the end successfully.

Artabanes' successor in Africa was John Troglita, the hero whom Corippus celebrated in his epic poem the *Johannides*. At long last Justinian had sent out one of his ablest generals, a man already experienced in African warfare, who had enough authority to restore discipline to the army, the diplomatic skill to win first Iabdas, king of the Aurès, and then Cutzinas, with his thirty thousand cavalry, to the imperial standard, and finally the decisiveness and confidence to carry the war into the desert. Even so, it took him two years of alternate fighting and negotiation, during which he himself suffered serious losses both in battle and from an epidemic (probably the plague). His enemies actually reached the walls of Carthage once more, before a great victory in the south broke the back of the Berbers' resistance for a generation. John Troglita was rewarded by fifteen years of peace. Within four years of the battle the province was sufficiently peaceful to send both troops and a fleet to help Justinian abroad.

The Church, too, was sufficiently free of the stresses of warfare to engage in what came to be known, erroneously, as the Three Chapters controversy. For eight years it was in combat with its benefactor Justinian, leading the resistance in the western Church against

Septimius Severus's basilica at Leptis. It became a Byzantine church

the Emperor's condemnation of three points of doctrine which the Church itself had not condemned. It was a period at once distinguished and desperate in the history of the African Church, distinguished because its leaders were men of intellectual authority and moral courage, and desperate because Justinian did not hesitate to use force in his determination to win: bishops were imprisoned, banished, sentenced to corporal punishment. Unfortunately the Papacy was on Justinian's side, and henceforth the African Church lost, this time for good, the theological ascendancy it had enjoyed in the days of St Cyprian and St Augustine. But during that time bishops from all parts of the province were constantly meeting in council at Carthage, and their leaders went on deputations to Constantinople; there appears to have been no trouble or threat of trouble in their dioceses to prevent them leaving home for weeks or months at a stretch.

Peace remained precarious, however. In A.D. 563, at the end of Justinian's reign, a disastrous new governor murdered Cutzinas, who had been a faithful ally for fifteen years, an army had to be sent from Constantinople to suppress the rising which the murder provoked, and the province was ravaged anew. In the years that followed, three Byzantine generals, two of them *magistri militum*, appear to have met their deaths in battle with the Moorish king Garmul, until Garmul was killed in A.D. 579 by the *magister militum* Gennadius. Many Africans fled abroad to Spain and elsewhere, and the inhabitants who were obliged to remain seem for the first time to have built fortifications on their own initiative. There are even rumours of Moorish raids on the coasts of Provence.

In the 580s the Emperor Maurice instituted administrative reforms whereby provincial governors were given more power, amounting virtually to that of vice-regency, and the provinces themselves were rearranged: Tripolitania was joined to the new exarchate (as a province was now called) of Egypt, and the modest territory round Septem (Ceuta), which was all that remained to

Byzantium immediately south of the Straits of Gibraltar, was joined to Spain and the Balearic Islands. Caesarea, for instance, had long since been lost to any semblance of imperial authority.

Maurice was an able Emperor, and Gennadius, whom he appointed his exarch in Africa, was at least militarily extremely successful. There were tribal uprisings in A.D. 587, and a barbarian attack on Carthage as late as A.D. 595–6, but thereafter the barbarian incursions that had been endemic since the Vandal period seem to have ceased. In A.D. 543 an outbreak of plague in the province had been a signal for tribal invasion, but in A.D. 599 a similar epidemic seems not to have been exploited at all. Sadly little is known of this period of North African history, from the death of Justinian to the Arab conquest; but whether by warfare or diplomacy Gennadius appears to have done his work well. Berber and Byzantine made their peace.

In the wake of secular victory came Christian conquest. From this time onwards populations hitherto untouched by Catholic or even Donatist influence were converted to Christianity – the tribes of the Aurès and the Mountains of Zab, of the Chott Djerid and the northern oases, even the Fezzan. Almost certainly, the great Byzantine fortresses to be seen at places like Zuila, in the desert more than four hundred miles south of Leptis Magna, also belong to the late sixth or early seventh century. This suggests a penetration of the Sahara greater than had existed even when the Empire had been ruled from Rome at her most powerful. But almost nothing is known of the cultural and commercial links which these developments perhaps reflect.

The Church enjoyed another kind of triumph in the exarchate itself, although the credit for it was to belong mostly to Pope Gregory the Great, and the papacy as an institution reaped the rewards. Peace, as usual, had its price, and the expenses of defence were, also as usual, paid for by those who could least afford it. In Sardinia, which was now part of the exarchate of Africa, men had to sell their children into slavery to meet their tax demands, though many of them were illegal. Maurice was no more successful than Justinian had been in stamping out corruption and oppression. In desperation, people turned to the Church to help them fight their secular oppressors (although the African Church was still almost as corrupt as the administration). In turn, the leaders of the African Church turned to Pope Gregory. He intervened with a will. His particular allies were Dominicus, the metropolitan of Carthage, and a bishop in Numidia, Columbus of Nicivibus. Through them, and through his notary Hilarus, who was commissioned to supervise discipline and finances, he established his authority over the African episcopate, and the Church in Africa clearly became, what had been unthinkable in St Cyprian's day, a daughter Church of Rome. Innumerable letters and instructions from Gregory reached Africa; they shed some light on an otherwise obscure period (we know, for instance, that the Pope was greatly exercised by the re-emergence of Donatism, and that he considered its suppression a prime duty of his correspondents).

But such was the impact of his personality that he also established his authority over civilian administration, and even the military. He mediated between the exarch Gennadius and the bishops; he did not hesitate to complain to the Emperor about the conduct of his officials; he made suggestions to the exarch about the defence of the province. Soon one prefect was confiding in him details of the shortcomings of the civil authorities; and Gennadius himself went out of his way to please the Pope and earn his approval, although to be sure – as Gregory pointed out – it was a way of pleasing not only the kings of the world but the King of Heaven.

Imperial authority grew weaker; the Pope and the exarch grew stronger.

The next exarch of Africa founded an imperial dynasty: Africa turned kingmaker again. At the turn of the century Heraclius, one of Maurice's most brilliant generals, was appointed to Carthage. From there he led the resistance after his patron was murdered and usurped by Phocas. Phocas was de-

Coin portrait of the Emperor Heraclius

tested; and when in A.D. 608 Heraclius withheld the corn supplies destined for Constantinople the rest of the Empire turned to him as to a saviour. Feeling himself to be too old, Heraclius sent his son, another Heraclius, and his nephew Nicetas in his place to avenge the murder of Maurice. An honourable and prudent man, he had hesitated to commit the Empire to what might have been a long and bloody civil war, at a time when the armies of the Persian Chosroes had reached Chalcedon. But once more an insult to womanhood provided the goad: his niece Eudocia, the fiancée of his son, and her mother were imprisoned as hostages by Phocas.

In the event the mere approach of the fleet commanded by the young Heraclius provoked a revolution in Constantinople. Phocas was killed; young Heraclius was acclaimed in his place and Eudocia survived to become the bride of an Emperor. He ruled for thirty years, and proved himself one of the noblest of Roman Emperors. He managed to save the eastern Empire from the Persians, a considerable achievement. Unfortunately an even more dangerous enemy was at hand. In A.D. 632, the prophet Muhammad died at Medina, and by the time Heraclius died in A.D. 640 the holy armies of his successors as leaders of Islam, the caliphs Abubeker and Omar, had made of Palestine and Syria a province of Arabia.

Meanwhile the links between Africa and Constantinople were closer than they had ever been. The elder Heraclius had died in office a year or so after his son had assumed the purple; and the province was shortly entrusted to the Emperor's friend and cousin Nicetas (and Nicetas's daughter Gregoria was married to the younger Heraclius's son and heir). Africa regularly supplied Byzantium with corn and olive oil; even the Berbers were devoted to the Heraclian dynasty, lending them troops for military expeditions and perhaps also paying them

taxes instead of, as for so long, receiving pensions; agriculture flourished, and the villages on the northern flanks of the Aurès *massif* were once more repopulated. So peaceful and prosperous does the province seem to have been that in A.D. 620, at a time when the east was particularly hard-pressed by the Persians, Heraclius seriously considered moving the seat of imperial government to Carthage. That he was dissuaded, and that he and his successors remained to stave off the Persians and later the Arabs, saved Constantinople for a future even more glorious than its past.

But the temptation for Africa to secede from the Empire remained. The temptation

Byzantine fortress at Aïn Tounga (ancient Tignica), in the valley of the oued Siliana near Dougga

was strengthened towards the end of Heraclius's life by the passionate opposition of the African Church (now restored to its role as the most energetic champion of orthodoxy) to the monothelite heresy, which the Emperor had embraced.

The Arab invasion of Egypt had meanwhile brought a flood of refugees to Africa, among whom were a large number of priests, monks and nuns. They were welcomed indiscriminately by the praetorian prefect of Africa, the devout and hospitable George, who arranged for them to be given monasteries and convents. Many of them, however, turned out to be ardent monophysites, eager to make converts of the orthodox Catholics. The Catholics were naturally deeply distressed.

At this point Heraclius died, and was succeeded by an orthodox Emperor; orders came from Byzantium that heresy was to be suppressed. George, who had been caught unawares, tried to confiscate the monasteries and convents he had given in good faith to the refugees, only to be faced with another change of policy and another set of instructions: the heresy was to be permitted once more. Tempers were now so high, however, and religious clashes so likely, that George was obliged to pretend that the new imperial instructions were a forgery. He even produced 'witnesses' that the Empress Dowager, who was responsible for this latest switch, was free of the taint of heresy. When, inevitably, he was summoned to the imperial court to explain himself, the Africans mourned his going with a fervour which boded ill for their continuing loyalty to the Empire.

The refugees were not all heretics, however. The African Church found its most effective defendant, and the house of Heraclius its most formidable critic, in the celebrated abbot Maximus, of whom after his death his biographer wrote: 'Not only clerics and bishops but also magistrates and people alike hung on his words, and clung to the saint like iron filings to the magnet, or sailors to the songs of the sirens.' As long as the race of Heraclius ruled, so long would God be hostile to the Roman Empire, was

Maximus's inflammatory theme. In A.D. 645 he scored a notable triumph in a public debate over the monothelite leader Pyrrhus, who confessed the error of his beliefs and did penance. The African bishops, while giving lip service to their loyalty to the Emperor, castigated the heresies which emanated from Constantinople with renewed confidence.

The lip service did not last long. The debate between Maximus and Pyrrhus had taken place in the presence of the exarch Gregory, who had ambitions of another kind, and in A.D. 646 proclaimed himself Emperor. The abbot Maximus had a useful dream, of choirs of angels chanting 'Victory to Gregory Augustus' sufficiently loudly to drown rival choirs of angels chanting 'Victory to Constantine Augustus'. There were rumours, too, that the Pope was a party to the usurpation, even giving Gregory his blessing, and although the African Church welcomed it with some caution, in view of their recent protestations, Gregory's move was accepted in the province without open demur. He made, however, no attempt to try conclusions with the Emperor in Constantinople; he remained in Africa. His action was a declaration of independence, the better to be able to face a new and deadly enemy.

*　　*　　*

The countries bordering the Mediterranean basin had been brought under the Roman standard in the first century B.C., and welded into an Empire. That unity had been broken by the northern barbarians in the fifth century A.D., but patched up by the armies of Justinian in the sixth. Under his successors the Empire began to disintegrate once more; but the Mediterranean basin was still unified in one important respect: in spite of heresy, schism and other disputes, it remained a Christian lake.

Islam exploded out of the Arabian peninsula in the 630s, and within a couple of generations of Muhammad's death the Mediterranean was a Christian lake no longer. North Africa, Egypt and the Middle East were lost to Christendom for good, and most of Spain for seven hundred years. At the beginning of the seventh century Islam was even threatening the heart of France.

The Arabs took half a century to swallow up North Africa, a half century for which there are almost no contemporary records. Arabs themselves are the main source of our information, but they are Arab historians of succeeding centuries: in the interval the stories of the conquest have been embellished, fantasized, and improved upon after countless re-tellings. As one French historian has put it, 'they obligingly supply the heroes of Islam with adventures worthy of *The Thousand and One Nights*.' But it is significant that, after Gregory, the Byzantines scarcely figure in the legends of the conquest of Africa. To the newcomers, the Berbers were their real opponents.

After seizing, in the space of a few years, Syria and Palestine and conquering the Persians who had been weakened by the long wars with Byzantium, the Arabs captured Egypt in A.D. 641. In A.D. 642 they occupied Cyrenaica, and the following year besieged Tripoli, laid Sabratha waste, and penetrated the eastern Fezzan. Their progress was only halted on the orders of the Caliph Omar, to leave 'the distant and treacherous far west' (Maghreb) alone. Byzantium, preoccupied with the Arab threat nearer Constantinople, had made no effort to prevent the losses in Africa.

These were the circumstances in which the exarch Gregory declared his independence from Byzantium. He appears to have had no difficulty in keeping the loyalty of the Berber chieftains, and in order to prepare the defence of the province he moved the capital from Carthage to Sufetula (Sbeïtla). The expected attack was not long in coming. The Caliph Omar had died in A.D. 644, and in A.D. 647 his successor, Othman, authorized the Governor of Egypt, Abdallah ibn Saad, to invade the Maghreb. The subsequent annihilation of the Byzantine army and its Berber reinforcements at the hands of an Arab force perhaps only twenty thousand strong sent a shudder of fear round the Empire; the defeat was reported even by obscure local chroniclers in Gaul and Spain.

Gregory died with all the courage of despair in the defence of Sufetula, and the warrior who killed him received the honour, it was said, of taking the good news back to Medina. Legend had it that Gregory's daughter fought at his side, and that her hand had been promised by her father to whoever killed Abdallah ibn Saad, and by the latter to whoever killed her father. But she did not live to be humiliated by her enemies. She committed suicide by throwing herself off the camel on which she was being carried away captive.

The remaining Byzantines retired to the fortified towns and fortresses of their second line of defence, leaving Sufetula and southern Byzacena to be pillaged by the Arabs. Like the Vandals, the Arabs had no inclination for siege warfare, and prepared to return to Egypt with their considerable booty. It had been an exceptionally profitable long-distance raid. It was made more so by an enormous bribe which the frightened Byzantines offered the Arabs in return for their departure. No one knows how much was paid, save that the amount astonished the invaders and gave them a very good idea of the possible wealth of the province as a whole. The tale was told of a significant exchange between the Arab general and a party of Africans: 'Seeing the coins put in front of him, Abdallah ibn Saad asked the Africans where their money came from. One of them looked about him, as if he were searching for something; then, having found an olive, he brought it to Abdallah. "The Greeks," he said, "have no olive trees in their country, and they come to us to buy oil with this money".' A country which commanded such an income would be worth making into a permanent conquest.

Meanwhile, the olive country had been devastated wherever the Arabs passed; and a huge exodus of the inhabitants began, inspired by the fear of the invaders' imminent return. But the internal troubles of the Arab Empire gave Africa fifteen years' respite, though the attempted invasion of Sicily and another, smaller raid on Byzacena in the 650s made it quite clear that the Arabs had not forgotten the west. During this period the Emperor in Byzantium re-established his authority over his African province, but it seems to have been a pitifully restricted authority: the southern part of the province was permanently abandoned, and the Berber chieftains became more independent than ever. As usual, money was lacking and taxation was cripplingly heavy; Arab historians record a revolt at Carthage. By the time the real struggle took place, the Byzantines had lost the initiative in the defence of north-west Africa, even though Constant II had moved the imperial court to Sicily.

A series of raids in the 660s, against which imperial reinforcements from Sicily were as helpless as the Africans themselves, was a prelude to the great campaign of Okba in A.D. 669. With a force, it was said, of only ten thousand cavalry, he subdued the desert south of Tripolitania, conquered the island of Djerba, and took possession of Byzacena. This time, conquest was intended to be permanent, and to this end he founded the city of Kairouan, both as an arsenal ('kairouan' means 'place of arms') and, equally important, as an outpost of Islam: 'When an *imam*,' wrote En Noveiri, 'invades Africa, the inhabitants save their lives and their property by professing Islam; but as soon as the *imam* leaves the country, they revert to their pagan beliefs.' (The Arabs later asserted that some of the inhabitants of Africa changed their religion thirteen times in all.) 'So it is essential to found a city which can serve both as a camp and as a foothold for Islam until the end of time.'

Kairouan took five years to build, yet the Byzantines, still entrenched in their line of mountain fortresses overlooking the site from the north, made no attempt to oust the invaders. To the south, the forces – and the religion – of Islam had a free run. The surviving Christian population faced massacre or enslavement; many, no doubt, suffered forcible conversion. But Okba's most notable triumphs appear to have been among the Berber tribesmen. Representing himself as a prophet and miracle-worker, he played on their natural superstitions, as the Donatists had once played on those of the settled African peasantry, and prepared the way for the mass conversion to Islam of almost the whole population of North Africa which was to follow in the wake of conquest.

But there was an unlooked-for setback. It was caused partly by a truce between the Arabs and Byzantium in the east which released Byzantine troops for the defence of Africa, and partly by the rise of a really powerful Berber kingdom in Mauretania under the chieftain Koseila; but mostly by Okba's own recklessness. In A.D. 683, confident of his strength – though not strong enough to attack the Byzantine fortresses to the north – Okba turned westward through southern Numidia and Mauretania. He intended to carry Islam to the Atlantic. In so doing, he was trespassing on the territories of the Berber chieftains, and he seriously miscalculated the strength of the opposition. There were hard-fought battles near Bagai and Lambaesis, and further west at Tiaret; Okba's army, though victorious, had been severely mauled. Yet without a thought for his lines of communication or the hazards of the return journey, Okba pursued his course to the Atlantic. It was, indeed, a notable expedition, much celebrated in the chronicles of the Arabs; but on his way back Koseila was waiting for him, and with substantial Byzantine forces at his side. Okba walked into an ambush near Thabudeos (just east of Biskra), and was killed with most of his army.

His death meant, for the moment, the end of the Arab occupation: Kairouan was abandoned. Yet the weaknesses of Islam's enemies were not cured by their victory. The Byzantines made no attempt to re-occupy Byzacena; the great Berber alliance shortly disintegrated, as was the usual fate of Berber alliances, when Koseila died. A large part of his prestige, however, accrued to the queen of the Aurès. This remarkable woman had already taken an important part in the defeat of Okba; now she was to lead the final, unavailing resistance to the Arabs. They called her 'the Kahena', 'the prophetess' – which suggests the kind of authority she wielded over her countrymen.

At the time of Hassan's invasion a decade later in A.D. 695 the strongest prince in North Africa, according to En Noveiri, was 'the commander of Karthadjinna': the Byzantines had recovered some of their lost supremacy, but not enough to impress the exarch's name on their enemies, or to keep them at bay. Hassan and his forty thousand men moved straight up the coast of Byzacena and captured Carthage. Then Hassan turned against the Kahena, only to be defeated by her enormous army which had been augmented by large numbers of Christians. The news of Carthage's fall had led to the sending of an

Byzantine fort of Ksar Lemsa, near Mactar

imperial army, which recaptured the city in A.D. 697. Defeated on two fronts, Hassan retreated to Cyrenaica; but in A.D. 698 he returned. This time Carthage was permanently taken. Only a few Byzantine garrisons in the old Africa Proconsularis survived; one by one they were invested and destroyed.

There remained the Kahena in the Aurès mountains. She summoned her fellow Africans to resistance, ready to fight to the death. Unfortunately she attempted to persuade her compatriots not only to die, but to destroy their livelihood – to burn their crops and their cities, and to cut down their trees, so that the enemy should no longer want their country. This intransigent scorched earth policy had little appeal for people who had already suffered enough; many defected to Hassan in despair. Somewhere between the Aurès and the sea – a dozen localities dispute the honour – the prophetess met her death after a long and bloody battle. Centuries later, the inhabitants of El Djem still firmly believed that their great Roman amphitheatre was her last citadel.

The Emperor, struggling to save face, continued to record the exarchate of Africa on the imperial lists: it consisted of Sardinia, Majorca and Minorca, a few places on the coast of Spain and, in Africa, Septem on the straits of Gibraltar. Septem, under Count Julian, survived the loss of Carthage by ten years. By then it had ceased to have even notional importance. Its occupation by the Arabs was mentioned only by western annalists. It was the last nail in the coffin of Roman Africa, but in truth Roman Africa had expired long since.

*   *   *

Justinian has been reproached with undertaking an impossibly heavy burden in attempting to resuscitate an imperial Africa well past its prime, which was dying a long slow death under the Vandals. In fact, the province revived remarkably under the Byzantines, so much so that, although much of its new administration was Greek, Africa itself remained resolutely Roman: its language and its literature were still Latin, and its Church attached itself more firmly than ever to the Roman half of Christendom. Both Latin and Christianity survived the Arab conquest, though in a necessarily tenuous form; but epitaphs were inscribed in recognizable Latin in the tenth and eleventh centuries, money was minted in Latin, the inhabitants of Gafsa still spoke it in the twelfth century (according to El Idrisi); and if most of the population adopted Islam, Christian communities survived, here and there, until the persecutions of the twelfth century – corresponding with Rome, disputing the primacy of Carthage, going into schism until the bitter end. Rome's ghost walked, and with a firm tread.

Yet it was doomed: in the last analysis the Byzantine revival postponed but did not avert the disappearance of Roman Africa. The achievement of Justinian and his successors was something more substantial. Under the Vandals or the Berber chieftains, the province would probably have soon relapsed into semi-nomadic barbarism: the desert would have defeated the sown. As it was, the Byzantines fortuitously provided the bridge which linked one civilization with another. The Arabs conquered, not barbarians, but a generation of Africans who were still accustomed to the usages of civilization, to reading and writing, to weaving and carving, to the upkeep of water supply and settled agriculture, to the breeding of animals and the keeping of books; who had not, in short, forgotten what the Romans had taught them.

The Arabs found much to admire in their new conquest: 'its continuous succession of villages, from Tripoli to Tangiers', the fertility of its fields, the magnificence of its olive groves, the splendid efficiency of its aqueducts. They, like the Vandals, were delighted to enter into the Roman inheritance. Unlike the Vandals, they brought gifts of their own. Under them, Africa was to flourish anew, but not in the Roman way.

Interior of the great amphitheatre at El Djem. The Arabs used it as a quarry

Selected Bibliography

The Stone Age of Northern Africa, by C. B. M. McBurney (Pelican, 1960)

The Ancient Explorers, by M. Cary and E. H. Warmington (Methuen, 1929, revised edition Pelican 1963)

Carthage, by B. H. Warmington (Robert Hale, 1960, and Pelican 1964)

Le Monde de Carthage, by Gilbert Charles-Picard (Paris, 1956), trans. as *Carthage*, by Gilbert Picard (Elek Books, 1964)

La Vie Quotidienne à Carthage au temps d'Hannibal, by Gilbert and Colette Charles-Picard (Librairie Hachette, Paris 1958), trans. as *Daily Life in Carthage at the Time of Hannibal* (Allen and Unwin, 1963)

The Buried City: Excavations of Leptis Magna, by G. Caputo and V. Caffarelli (Weidenfeld & Nicolson, 1966)

A History of the Ancient World, Volume II, Rome by M. Rostovtzeff (1927, reprinted with corrections 1928; revised edition published as *Rome* in paperback by O.U.P., New York, 1960)

Histoire de l'Afrique du Nord (Volume I, Des Origines à la Conquête Arabe), by Charles-André Julien (Paris, 1931, 2nd edition revised and edited by Christian Courtois, Paris 1951)

La Civilisation de L'Afrique Romaine, by Gilbert Charles-Picard (Paris, 1959)

L'Afrique Romaine, by Eugène Albertini (Algiers, 1932)

Some Authentic Acts of the Early Martyrs, by E. C. E. Owen (O.U.P., 1927)

Constantine and the Conversion of Europe, by A. H. M. Jones (Eng. U.P., 1948)

The Donatist Church, by W. H. C. Frend (O.U.P., 1952)

St Augustine, by Rebecca West (Macmillan, 1933)

Augustine of Hippo, by Peter Brown (Faber, 1967)

Les Vandales et L'Afrique, by Christian Courtois (Paris, 1955)

L'Afrique Byzantine, by Charles Diehl (Paris, 1896)

Le Passé de l'Afrique du Nord: Les Siècles Obscurs, by E. Gautier (Paris, 1937)

Other books referred to or quoted from in the text:

Very good translations of *The War with Hannibal* (Livy), *The Jugurthine War* (Sallust), and St Augustine's *Confessions* are published in the Penguin Classics series. They are also available in the Loeb translations, as are *The Vandalic War* (Procopius) and Polybius's *Histories*. *Fossatum Africae* by Jean Baradez was published in Paris in 1949, and the *Tablettes Albertini* (edited and commented on by C. Courtois, L. Leschi, Ch. Perrat and Ch. Saumagne) in 1952. *The Decline and Fall of the Roman Empire*, by Edward Gibbon, was published between 1776 and 1788. An abridged version was published by Penguin in 1963.

Index

Abdallah ibn Saad, Governor of Egypt – invaded the Maghreb A.D. 647, 177

Abitina, Saturninus of, 133

Abubeker, Caliph, 175

Acholla (Ras Botria), 55

Adherbal, son of Micipsa, King of Numidia, 36, 37

Ad Majores (Besseriani), 72

Adversus Nationes by Arnobius, 131

Aedemon, 45, 103

Aegates Islands, Battle of the, 23

Aemilianus of Zarath, Sicinius, 67

Aesculapius, Roman divinity, 113, 114

Africa Nova, 38, 39, 63

Africa Proconsularis, 42, 45, 47, 51, 126, 167

Africa Vetus, 38, 39

Agathocles of Syracuse (361–289 B.C.): invaded Africa, 17, 18, 20, 23, 29, 63

Algeria, French annexation of, 1830, 1

agriculture: under the Carthaginians, 13–16: under the Romans, 50–51, 61, 63–74, 80, 110

Agrigento (Sicily), 17

Ain El Djemala, 70

Alaric, king of the Goths, 148; sacked Rome, A.D. 410, 149, 153

Albinus, Clodius, military commander of Britain, 107, 108

Althiburos (Medeïna), marine mosaic at, 96

Amalafrida, sister of Theodoric, wife of Thrasmund, murdered by Hilderic, 162, 163

Ammaedara (Haïdra), garrison of the Third Augustan Legion, 42, 44; mausoleum at, 47, 85; 55, 85

amphitheatres: at Mactar, *80*; at Leptis Magna, *81*; at Thysdrus (El Djem), 86–87, *89*, 110, 111, *181*

animals of North Africa, 3

Annaba, see under Hippo Regius

annona (tribute), 63, 65, 66, 69, 70, 80, 104

Announa (Thibilis), 104

Antalas, Berber prince, 161; defeat of the Vandals, 163; joined insurrection against Solomon, 170–71

Antonine, Baths, 10, 32, *33*; itinerary, 52

Antonine Wall, built by Lollius Urbicus, conqueror of Scotland, 104

Antoninus Pius, Roman Emperor (A.D. 86–161), designated heir of Hadrian, 100

Apollinaris, Sulpicius, Carthaginian grammarian, 101, 105

Apologia by Apuleius, 103

Appian of Alexandria, Roman historian, 32

Apthungi, Bishop Felix of, 134, 136

Apuleius, Lucius (born *c.* A.D. 125 at Madauros), 1, 67, 85, 94, 99, 100, 102–03, 116, 120, 146

aqueducts – at Carthage, 10; at Germa, 46; of oued Miliana, 49, *50*, 55, 92

Arab penetration and occupation of Mediterranean countries, 176–80

Arcadius, son of Theodosius the Great, 148

arches, triumphal – at Leptis Magna, 84; at Tiddis, 84; of Caracalla at Volubilis, *41*, at Djemila, *93*, at Tébessa, *115*, 168; of Trajan at Timgad, 85; of Marcus Aurelius in Tripoli, *106*; of Septimius Severus, 139

Arae Philaenorum, 16

Areobindus, nephew of Justinian, co-*magister militum* of Byzantine Africa, 171

Arnobius, teacher of rhetoric, converted to Christianity, 131; author of *Adversus Nationes*, 158

Artabanes, Byzantine regimental commander, 171

Attic Night by Aulus Gellius, 101

Attila the Hun, 155

Augustus, Gaius Octavious (63 B.C. – A.D. 14), 38; defeated his rivals for control of the Roman Empire, 39; his campaign for the Romanisation of Africa, 40–1; 59, 109–10

Aumale (Auzea), 45, 52

Aurelius, Bishop of Carthage, primate of Africa, 147, 148

Austuriani, barbarian tribe, invaders

of Leptis Magna, 142, 160

Auzea (Aumale), 45, 52

Baal Hammon, *14*, 17, *18*, 113

Bagai, 161; scene of battle between Arabs and Berbers A.D. 683, 178

Bagradas, river, 15, 70, 79

Balbus, L. Cornelius, Roman proconsul of Africa, 44

Baradez, Colonel J., author of *Fossatum Africae*, 57, 59

baths – of Antonine, Carthage, 10, 32; at Capsa, *55*; at Leptis Magna, *83*, 89; at Guelma, 168

Belisarius, Count (*c.* 505–565), Roman general, 153, 155; commander of the Roman Invasion of Africa, A.D. 533, 165; final defeat of the Vandals, 166, 168, 170, 171

Berbers – gradual development of semi-independent Berber kingdoms, 160–61, 168; resistance to Byzantine empire broken by John Troglita, 172; opposition to Arab forces under Sidi Okba, 178

Besseriani (Ad Majores), 72

Biskra (Vescera), 52, 72, 178

Bizerta, see under Hippo Diarrhytus

Bocchus, King of Mauretania, 37, 38

Boniface, Count, Roman general, 146; defeated by the Vandals at Hippo, 151

Bou Grara (Gigthis), 54

Bou Taleb mountains, 58

Bougie (Saldae), 55

Bulla Regia, large statues found at, 84; underground houses, 94–*95*, 165, 166

Byrsa, citadel of Punic Carthage, 11, 12

Byzacena (central Africa Proconsularis), 126, 127; invaded by Cutzinas, 167, 170; occupied by Sidi Okba, A.D. 669, 178

Byzantines – Emperor Constantine I transferred his capital to Byzantium (Constantinople), 127; invasion of Africa in A.D. 533 under Count Belisarius, 165; who defeated Gelimer and captured Carthage, 166;

barbarian uprisings a threat to Byzantine domination, 167–68; restoration of fortifications by Justinian, 168–69; taxation and corrupt administration led to decline, 170; war with the Berbers and defeat of a Byzantine army by the Louata tribe, 171; order restored by John Troglita, 171–72; administrative reforms instituted by the Emperor Maurice, 173; weakening of imperial authority, 174; period of prosperity under Nicetas, 175; Arab invasion and a Byzantine army annihilated by Abdallah ibn Saad, Governor of Egypt, 177–78; Byzantine authority partially restored, 178; gradual defeat and destruction of forts by the Arab forces, 178–80; lasting effects of Byzantine civilisation, 180.

Cabaon, desert chieftain – his use of camels in battle, 160
Caecilian, deacon to Bishop Mensurius, 133–34; elected Bishop of Carthage, A.D. 312, 134; opposition to his election by the Donatists, 134–38; 140, 152
Caesar, Caius Julius (102–44 B.C.), defeated Pompey at Thapsus, 46 B.C., 37; extended Roman settlements in Africa, 38–39; assassination 44 B.C., 39, 40, 59, 158
Caesarea (Cherchel), 40, 45, 54, 55, 73, 79, 142, 150, 173
Calama (Guelma), 142, 148, 168
Caligula, Gaius Caesar (A.D. 12–41), Roman Emperor, 45, 103, 105
camels – their presence and uses in North Africa – camel caravans, 158, *159*, 160
Cannae, Roman defeat at, 216 B.C., 26, 27, 28, 30
Cape Bon peninsula, 13, 15, 17, 18, 39, 63, 165
Capellianus, governor of Numidia, killer of Gordian II in battle, 110
Capsa, 52; Roman bath at, *55*
Caracalla – Marcus Aurelius Severus Antoninus (A.D. 186–217), Roman Emperor, 52, 86, 108; arch of at Volubilis, *41*; at Tébessa, *115*, 168; at Djemila, *93*
caravan trade, 2, 16, 22, 37, 42, 47; *via de camellos*, 158, 159, 160
cardo maximus, 83
Carpi (Korbous), spa, 94
Cartennae (Ténès), region of Augustan colonies, 39
Carthage – founded by Dido in 814 B.C., 4; 6; struggle against Greece, 7; the rise and fall of, 9–33; 35, 36; refounded 29 B.C. by Augustus Caesar, 39, 52; major outlet for corn tribute, 54, 55, 69; road system, 83; amphitheatre, 87; public baths, 69; water supply, 92; tenement dwel-

lings, 97; an intellectual centre, 100–01; 110, 116; suffered pillage, 127, 128, 133; seized by Vandal king Gaiseric, A.D. 439, 151; remained an important Mediterranean port, 154; ecclesiastical conference, A.D. 484, 161; captured by Belisarius, 166; city developed by Justinian, 169; barbarian attack A.D. 595–96, 173; ceased to be capital city, 177; captured by the Arabs, 179; recaptured by imperial army, A.D. 697, 180; finally conquered by Hassan, A.D. 698, 180
Casae Nigrae, birthplace of Donatus, 135
Castellum Dimmidi, Roman garrison, 111
Cato, Marcus Portius (234–149 B.C.), Roman statesman, 13, 35
causeways, Roman, 55
Cellas Vatari, Numidia, scene of defeat of Stotzas by Germanos, 167
chariot racing, 87–8
Chemtou, see under Simitthu
Cherchel, see under Caesarea
Chosroes II (A.D. 590–628), King of Persia, 174
Chott Djerid oasis, 50, 72, 173
Chott El Hodna, 52, 58
Chott Melrhir, 3
Christianity, 11, 117, 118; St. Perpetua, first Christian martyr in Africa, 118–20; conversion of Tertullian, 120–122; adopted as the official religion of the Empire by Constantine, A.D. 313, 123; St. Cyprian, Bishop of Carthage, 122–26; Christian persecution by Decius, 124; by Valerian, 125–6; by Diocletian, 129, 133; spread of Christianity in North Africa, 131; schism and disunity, the Donatists, 132–143; St. Augustine's campaign against Donatism, 148–50; Donatism pronounced a heresy, by Edict of Unity, A.D. 405, 149; the Council of Carthage, A.D. 411, resulting in a victory for the Catholics, 150; Council at Carthage, A.D. 484, Donatist victory and Catholic persecution and exile, 161; return of Catholics from exile under Hilderic, 162; Catholic supremacy in reign of Solomon, 170; the Three Chapters controversy, 172; African Church loses its theological ascendancy, 173; spread of Christianity and fight against secular oppression led by Pope Gregory, 173–74; Church in Africa becomes a daughter church of Rome, 174; opposition of the Church to heretic movements, 176; invasion by the Arabs and gradual suppression of Christianity, 176–77; but survival after the Arab conquest, 180
Chullu, see under Collo

Cillium (Kasserine), Roman theatre at, 9, 52, 73; mausoleum at, 85, 170
circumcelliones, peasant bands of Donatists, 140–41, 148, 149, 150
Cirta (Constantine), capital of Numidia, 21; captured by Masinissa, 29, 31, 36; sacked by Jurgurtha, 112 B.C., 37; 38; Roman bridge at, 53; 67, 79; theatre at, 85–86; birthplace of Marcus Cornelius Fronto, 100; 101,125; pillaged,127; 133, 134,137
cisterns, Roman, 10, 61, 92
cities of Roman Africa, 79–97
The City of God by St. Augustine, 145, 146, 149, 150
Claudius, Tiberius, Roman Emperor, successor to Caligula, 45
Collo (Chullu), centre of Phoenician dyeing industry, 75
Columbus of Nicivibus, Bishop, 174
Constantine I – Flavius Valerian Constantinus (A.D. 288–337), Roman Emperor – adopted Christianity as official religion of the Empire, A.D. 313, 123; established his capital at Byzantium, 127; 128; promulgated the Edict of Milan, 132; 351 intervened in the dispute between the rival Bishops of Carthage, 136–39; 147, 148, 170
Commodus – Lucius Aelius Aurelius (A.D. 161–92), Roman Emperor, 67; succeeded his father Marcus Aurelius, A.D. 96, 104–05; weak and extravagant ruler, 107, 108, 110
Constantine, see under Cirta
Contra Cresconium by St. Augustine, 135
Contra Epistolam Parmeniani by St. Augustine, 135
Contra Litteras Petiliani by St. Augustine, 135
Corippus – Flavius Cresconius, African poet, 170; author of *Johannides*, 171
Cornutus, Lucius Annaeus, teacher of rhetoric and philosophy, 99
Corpus Juris Civilis – Justinian's codification of Roman law, 165
cothon (inland basin), 54, 55
Council of Nicaea, presided over by Constantine, 138
Cuicul (Djemila), veteran colony, 57, 83; cloth and food markets, 84; baths and latrines, 90; mosaics, 96
Curubis (Korba), statue of Demeter, *21*, 125
Cutzinas, barbarian king – invaded Byzacena, and defeated by Solomon, 167; in alliance with Solomon against Antalas, 170; becomes an ally of Antalas, 171; won over to support the Byzantines by John Troglita, 172; murdered A.D. 563, 173
Cydamae (Ghadames) oasis, 44
Cyrene, founded in 630 B.C., 5, 16

dar, Arab dwelling, 94
Decius – Gaius Messius Quintus

Trajanus (A.D. 201–51), Roman Emperor – his persecution of the Christians, A.D. 250, 124

De Baptismo contra Donatistas by St. Augustine, 135

decumanus maximus, 83

De Schismate Donatistorum by Bishop Optatus of Milevis, 135

Didius – Julianus Salvius, Roman Emperor in succession to Pertinax, 105; his murder, 107

Dido (Princess Elissa), reputed founder of Carthage in 814 B.C., 4, 5, 12, 21, 118

Divine Institutions by Lactantius, 131

Dio Chrysostom, Greek historian, 7, 16

Diocletian, Gaius Aurelius Valerius, Roman Emperor, succeeded in A.D. 284, 108, 126; redoubled size of frontier army and divided Africa into smaller provinces, 126–27; made his capital at Nicomedia (Turkey), 127; decreed that men should be 'tied' to their occupations, 128, 170; renewed the persecution of Christians, 129, 131, 133, 135

Diodorus Siculus, Greek historian, 13, 18, 31

Djebel Zaghouan, nymphaeum at, *49*

Djemila, see under Cuicul

Djerba, island of, 4; linked to mainland by Roman causeway, 55; 68, 75; conquered by Sidi Okba, A.D. 669, 178

Djidjelli (Igilgili), 39

Dolabella, Publius Cornelius, Roman general, 45

Dominicus of Carthage, 174

Domitian, Titus Flavius (A.D. 51–96), Roman Emperor, 99, 100, 103; assassinated A.D. 96, 104

Domna, Julia, wife of Septimius Severus, 108

The Donatist Church by W. H. C. Frend, 131

Donatist schismatics, 132–43; Petilian, Donatist Bishop of Constantine, St. Augustine's chief adversary, 147, 148; Donatism declared a heresy by the Edict of Unity, A.D. 405, 149; decision confirmed by the council at Carthage, A.D. 411, 150; Donatist victory at council of Carthage, A.D. 484, 161; Catholic supremacy restored by Hilderic, 162; re-emergence of Donatism causes concern to Pope Gregory, 174

Donatus, succeeded Majorinus as antibishop of Carthage, 135; his character and reputation, 135; 136, 137; in exile, 139; death in A.D. 355, 140

Dougga, see under Thugga

Edict of Milan, A.D. 312, 132, 135

Edict of Unity, A.D. 405, proclaiming Donatism a heresy, 149

education, 99–103

El Djem (Thysdrus), 38–39; became extensive olive growing area, 73, 79; amphitheatre at, 73, 87, *89*, 110, 111; camel mosaic at, 158, *159*; 180

El Haouaria, cliff quarry at, 75

El Juf depression, 3

El Kherba (Tigava), 133

Elissa, Princess (Dido), 4, 5, 12, 21, 118

Eshmoun, Punic god associated with Aesculapius, 114

Eudocia, Empress, wife of Heraclitus, 174

Evans, Sir Arthur, 4

exploration – by Minoans, Greeks and Phoenicians, 4; by Hanno, 16; inland by Romans, 45

Felix, Minucius, author of *Octavius*, 123

Felix of Apthungi, Bishop, 134, 136

Fezzan, the, territory of the Garamantes, 22, 45, 46, 173

Firmus, chief of the Jubaleni tribe – his revolt against Romanus, 142, 158

First Alpine Cohort, 104

Flaccus, Septimius, leader of exploratory campaign in the first century A.D., 45

Flaubert, Gustave, author of *Salammbô*, 24

Florus, P. Annius, Roman poet and rhetorician, 99, 100

fossa regia, 38

fossatum (ditch and dyke earthwork), 58, 59, 61, 151

Fossatum Africae by Colonel J. Baradez, 57

fountains – at Cuicul, *91*, *92*; *nymphaeum* at Leptis, 92; at Djebel Zaghouan, *49*

Frend, W. H. C., historian, author of *The Donatist Church*, 131, 147

Fronto, Marcus Cornelius (*c.* 100–70 B.C.), African born lawyer, 100–01, 102, 105

Gabès, port of, 44, 47

Gaetules, the, desert tribe in control of the west Saharan caravan route, 21–22

Gaiseric, Vandal king who invaded Africa A.D. 429, 151, 153; turned pirate and looted Rome A.D. 455, 154–55; faced growing power of Berber kingdoms, 160; succeeded by his son Huneric, 161; 162, 165

Galla Placidia, Empress Regent, 151

Garama (Germa) oasis, 2, 44, 46

Garamantes, the – a tribe of Tripolitania in control of the Saharan caravan trade, 16, 22; conquered by Balbus, 44; pillaged Leptis Magna, 45

Garmul, Moorish king killed by Gennadius A.D. 579, 173

Gauda, king of Numidia, brother of Jugurtha, 37

Gelimer, Vandal king, deposed Hil-

deric A.D. 530 and assumed the throne, 163; routed by Belisarius, A.D. 533, 165; further defeat and final surrender, 166

Gellius, Aulus (*c.* A.D. 130–80), Latin author of *Attic Nights*, 100–01

Gennadius, Byzantine *magister militum*, appointed exarch in Africa by the Emperor Maurice, 173, 174

George, praetorian prefect of Africa, 176

Germanos, cousin of Justinian I, 167

Gemellae, Roman army outpost at, 72

Germa, see under Garama

Ghadames (Cydamae) oasis, 2, 44

Gibbon, Edward (1737–1794), English historian, 35, 124, 153

Gigthis (Bou Grara), 54

Gildo, brother to Firmus, king of the Jubaleni, appointed *comes Africae*, 143, his support of the Donatists, 147; rebellion defeated by Stilicho, 148

gladiatorial combat, 86

The Golden Ass by Apuleius, 85, 99, 103

Gordian I – Marcus Antonious Gordianus (A.D. 159–238), Roman Emperor in association with his son Gordian II, 110, 111, 127

Gordian III – Roman Emperor, 126

gourbis (mud-walled huts), 65

Gracchi brothers, 36, 38, 39, 110

Great Persecutions – in A.D. 250 by Decius, 124; in A.D. 256 by Valerian, 125–26; in A.D. 303–05 by Diocletian, 129, 131, 133, 135

Greeks, the, 4; establish colonies in Cyrenaica, 5; struggle against the Carthaginians, 7; rise of Athens, 7; defeat of Carthage, 480 B.C., 12; Carthaginian attack on Greek cities in Sicily, 17; Agathocles of Syracuse invades Africa, 17; worship of Greek gods by Carthaginians, 18; Roman v. Carthaginian struggle for Sicily, 23

'Greek fire', 155

Gregory, exarch, proclaims himself Roman Emperor of the East, A.D. 646, 176; killed in defence of Sufetula, 177

Gregory the Great, Pope (*c.* A.D. 540–604) – his fight against secular oppression in Africa, 173–74

Guelma (Calama), 142, 148; 168

Gunthamund, successor to the Vandal king Huneric, 162

Guntarith, duke of Numidia, 171

Hadrian – Publius Aelius Hadrianus (A.D. 76–138), Roman Emperor, visited Africa A.D. 125 and moved Third Legion headquarters to Lambaesis, 52–53; 60; encouraged the cultivation of new land, 70–71; founded army outpost at Gemellae, 72; appointed Fronto as tutor to his son, 100; 101, 104

187

Hadrumetum (Sousse), port in Proconsular Africa, 6, 54, 55, 68, 72, 75, 79, 101, 116

Haïdra, see under Ammaedara

Hamilcar Barca (*c.* 270–228 B.C.) Carthaginian general, 19, 23, 24

Hammam Lif, Roman spa, 94

Hannibal Barca (*c.* 247–*c.* 183 B.C.) Carthaginian general, 13, 16, 19, 22, 24, 25; crossed the Alps into Italy: battles of Lake Trasimene and Cannae, 26–27; unable to follow up his victories, 28; landed in Africa, 29; his defeat by Scipio at Zama, 202 B.C., 30; fled into exile in 195 B.C., 31; 35, 113

Hanno, Carthaginian navigator, 16, 21

Hasdrubal, brother of Hannibal, 28

Hasdrubal, Carthaginian general, 28–9

Hasdrubal, son-in-law of Hamilcar, 24, 25, *26*

Hassan – Arab invader of north Africa A.D. 695: capture of Carthage, 178–79

heating systems – baths at Timgad, *88*, *89*; 90; underground house at Bulla Regia, *96*

Henchir El Kousset, remains of Christian basilica at, *141*

Henchir Mettich, altar inscription to Trajan, 66, 70

Heraclian, *comes Africae*, 150

Heraclius, Roman general, appointed exarch of Carthage, 174

Heraclius (*c.* A.D. 575–642), East Roman Emperor, 174–76

Herodotus (*c.* 484–425 B.C.), Greek historian, 1, 5, 22, 47

Hiempsal, son of Gauda, joint King of Numidia, 37

Hiempsal, son of Micipsa, King of Numidia, murdered by Jugurtha, 36

Hierbas, son of Gauda, joint King of Numidia, 37

Hilarus, notary to Pope Gregory, 174

Hilderic, Vandal king, succeeded his cousin Thrasamund, 162; deposed by Gelimer, A.D. 530, 163; murdered by Gelimer, 165

Himera (Sicily), 7, 13, 17

Himilco, Carthaginian explorer, 16

Hippo Diarrhytus (Bizerta), 6; captured by Agathocles of Syracuse, 17; 38, 55, 79

Hippo Regius, (Annaba, formerly Bône), 52, 79; St. Augustine became Bishop of, 147; became capital of the Vandal king Gaiseric, 151; 161, 168

Historia Augusta, 60

Hodna, 161, 167

Honorius, Flavius (A.D. 384–423), Emperor of the West – under the guardianship of Stilicho, 148; proclaimed an Edict of Unity, A.D. 405, 149–50; 153, 161

human sacrifice, 11, 27; of infants, 11, 115

Huneric, Vandal king, son of Gaiseric, 155; inaugurated period of Christian persecution, 161; his death, 162

Iabdas, king of the Aures – ravished Numidia, 167; defeated by Solomon, 168; 171; became an ally of the Byzantine empire, 171–2

Ibiza, first daughter colony of Carthage, 7

Igilgili (Djidjelli), 39

Januarilla, Geminia, her dowry list (*tablettes Albertini*), 155–56

Johannides by Corippus, 171

Juba I, son of Hiempsal, King of Numidia, 37, *38*, 40, 158

Juba II, King of Numidia, 38; became ruler of Mauretania, 25 B.C., 40

Jubaleni tribe, 142, 143

Julian – Flavius Claudius Julianus (A.D. 331–363), succeeded Constantius as Emperor A.D. 361; restored exiled Christian leaders, 140

Julianus, Salvius, African lawyer and consul, 101, 102, 105

Jugurtha, grandson of Manissa, seized throne of Numidia 111 B.C., 36; sacked Cirta, 37; 44

Jugurthine War by Sallust, 36

Justinian I, (A.D. 483–565), Emperor of the East, 139, 158, 162, 163; invaded Africa, A.D. 533, 165; 167; founded new towns, 169; appointed Solomon as *magister militum Africae*, 167–68; his policy in Africa described by Procopius, 168; imposed heavy taxation, 170; sent his general John Troglita to Africa to restore order, 171–72; in controversy with the African Church, 173; 176, the effect of his achievements on African civilisation, 180

Juvenal – Decimus Junius Juvenalis (*c.* A.D. 60–140), Roman poet and satirist, 14, 100

Kabylie mountains, 47, 57, 142

'Kahena, the' queen of the Aures: her resistance against Arab invaders, 178–80

Kairouan ('place of arms'), built by Sidi Okba, 178

Kasserine, see under Cillium

Kbor Klib, monumental altar at, *35*

Khémissa (Thubursicu Numidarum), 83

kohanim, Punic priesthood, 114, 115

Korbous (Carpi), spa, 94

Koseila, Berber Chieftain, 178

Kufra oasis, 2, 3

Lactantius Firmianus (*c.* A.D. 260–*c.* 340), Christian writer, author of *Divine Institutions*, 131

Laetus, Aemilius, prefect, 104–06, 107

Lake Trasimene, Roman defeat by Hannibal at, 26

Lambaesis, major garrison town of the Third Augustan Legion, 52, 54, 55, 56, 60, 72, 79, 83; deserted in fifth century owing to barbarian invasion, 161; scene of battle between Arabs and Berbers A.D. 683, 178

lapsi (Christian apostates), 124, 126, 133

latifundia (large estates), 36, 65, 140

latrines at baths, 90, *91*

Le Kef, see under Sicca Veneria

Leptis Magna, 1, 16, *42*; pillaged by the Garamantes, 45; *46*; Roman improvements to the harbour, 54; population, 79; 81; forums, 83; market place, 84; four-way arch of Septimius Severus, 84; baths, 89; latrines, 90; style of architecture, 91; *nymphaeum*, 92; 106, 108; devastated by the Austuriani, 142, 160; rebuilt by Justinian, 169; 170, 171, 173

Leptis Minor (Lemta), 29

Lex Manciana, 70

libelli (certificates issued by the Emperor to apostate Christians, 124)

Lucinius – Flavious Galerius Valerius Licinianus (A.D. *c.* 250–324), Roman Emperor of the East, with the Emperor Constantine promulgated the Edict of Milan, A.D. 312, 132

Limata, Bishop Purpurius of, 134, 138

limes (frontier zone), 57, 59, 61, 72, 127, 151, 168

Louata tribe, 160, 170, 171

Macrinus, prefect of the Praetorian guard, acclaimed Emperor, 108

Macrobius, Donatist bishop of Hippo Regius, 150

Mactar, 52, 67, 68, 74; amphitheatre, *80*; mausoleum, 85; excavations at, *130*; 161

Madauros, 69, 90, 102, 103, 146

Maghreb, the, 2, 3, 7, 69, 72, 113, 154, 160; invaded by Abdallah ibn Saad, Governor of Egypt, 177

Mago, Carthaginian agriculturalist, 13, 15

Mahdia (Tunisia), 37, 40

Majorinus, anti-bishop of Carthage, 135

mala punica (pomegranates), 14

Manilius, Roman poet, 99

mapalia (temporary huts), 69

Marcellinus, Ammianus, 142, 150

Marcellus, Roman centurion, Christian convert beheaded in A.D. 298, 133

Marcus Aurelius Antoninus (A.D. 121–180), Roman Emperor, 100, 101, 104–05, 107, 108

Masaesyli, the, 21, 28

Masinissa, King of the Massyli, (d. 148 B.C.) harassed by Syphax, 28–29; captured Cirta and became an ally of Rome, 30; supported Scipio at the battle of Zama, 31; his plans to develop North Africa, 31; his annexation of Carthaginian territory, 32; his plans to seize Carthage, 32; his death during the siege of Carthage, 36; 37, 43, 63

Massyli, the, Numidian tribe, 21, 24, 28

Maternus Julius, leader of Roman exploratory campaign, 45

Matmata, underground dwellings at, 47, 95

Mauretania Caesariensis, 47, 126

Mauretania Tingitana, 47, 126, 127

Mauretania Sitifensis, 126

Maurice – Mauricius Flavius Tiberius (c. A.D. 539–602), Emperor of the East instituted administrative reforms, 173, 174

Maximian – Marcus Aurelius Valerius, Roman Emperor (A.D. 286–305), repressed tribal revolts in Mauretania, 126, 127, 133, 160

Maximinus – Gaius Julius Verus, Roman Emperor (A.D. 235–238), acclaimed Emperor by the Rhine army on the death of Alexander Severus, 110

Mazippa, leader of the Mauretanians, supporter of Tacfarinas, 44

Medeina, see under Althiburos

Meninx, centre of Phoenician dyeing industry, 75

Mensurius, bishop of Carthage, 133; death in A.D. 312, 134

Mercenary War (the 'truceless war'), 24, 28

Micipsa, son of Masinissa, king of Numidia, 36

Milevis, Bishop Optatus of, 135

Miltiades, Pope, 135, 136

Montanism, 126

mosaics, 73, 75, 79, 86, 90, 92, 94, 96, 97; of African villa life, 128; of the Seigneur Julius, 128–29; Christian, 139; at Cherchel, 152; of camels, 158, 159; art of mosaic revived under Justinian, 169

Motya (Sicily), 6, 17

Muhammad, Prophet, died at Medina, A.D. 632, 174, 176

murex (purple dye), 5, 75

Musulamii – their revolt under Tacfarinas, A.D. 17, 44–45, 69

Musunii Regiani, 69

Nero, 66, 101, 105, 117

Nicetas, nephew of Heraclius, 174, 175

Nicomedia, capital city of Diocletian, 127, 131

Niger, Pescennius, military commander of Syria, defeated by Severus, A.D. 194, 107

Numidian cavalry, 16, 17, 69

nymphaeum – at Leptis, 92; at Djebel Zaghouan, 49

Octavius, adopted son of Julius Caesar, later Caesar Augustus, 39, 40

Octavius by Minucius Felix, 123

Oea (Tripoli), 42, 102

Okba ibn Nafi, Sidi, founder of the city of Kairouan – his campaigns and death, 178

olive cultivation, 14, 16, 61, 63, 68, 70, 71, 72–74

Omar, Caliph, 175, 177

Optatus, bishop of Milevis, author of De Schismate Donatistorum, 135

Optatus, Donatist bishop of Thamugadi (Timgad), 143

Ortaias, prince of Hodna, 167

Othman, Caliph, 177

Oudna (Uthina), 39, 71

Pannonia, 43

Parmenian, Donatist bishop of Carthage (A.D. 363–391), 135, 141, 143

Passion of St. Perpetua, 118, 119

Paulinus, C. Suetonius, 45

Paulas, Bishop of Cirta, 133, 134

pavimenta punica, 7

Pelagius, Welsh monk, 145

Pertinax – Publius Helvius (A.D. 126–193), Roman Emperor, 101; murdered by the Praetorian Guard, A.D. 193, 105; 107, 115

Petilian, Donatist bishop of Constantine, 135, 147, 148; exiled under the Edict of Unity, A.D. 405, 149; 150

Phoenicians – the first invaders of North Africa, 1; foundation of Carthage, 814 B.C., 4; first to open up trade routes to the far west, 5; trade in metals with Spain, 6; early settlements, 6; cultural influence, 7. For continuation see CARTHAGE

Phocas, East Roman Emperor (A.D. 602–10), usurper of the throne of Maurice, 174

plant life of North Africa, 3

Pliny the Elder – Gaius Plinius Secundus (c. A.D. 23–79), 1, 6, 52, 63, 68, 70

Pliny the Younger – Publius Caecilius Secundus (c. A.D. 61–c. 113), 116; became governor of Bithynia, 117

Polybius (c. 204–122 B.C.), Greek historian, 23, 24, 26, 31, 32, 33, 35

Pontius, biographer of St. Cyprian, 126

Possidius, Catholic Bishop of Calama (Guelma), biographer of St. Augustine, 148, 149, 150

Prejecta, wife of Sergius, 171

Primian, 135, 149

Procopius, Greek historian, 154, 155, 160, 165, 166, 167, 168, 171

provincial assemblies, 116

Psalmus Contra Partem Donati by St. Augustine, 135

Ptolemy, succeeded Juba II as the last king of Mauretania, A.D. 23, 45; murdered by Caligula, 103

Ptolemy's map of the world, 1, 52

Punic unit of measurement, 76

Punic Wars – in Sicily, 22–23; in Spain, 29–30; in Africa, 32–33

Punic wax, 14

Purpurius of Limata, Bishop, 134, 138

Pyrrhus, king of Epirus, 22

Pyrrhus, monothelite leader, 176

Qart Hadasht – Phoenician name for Carthage, 6, 25

Quietus, Lusius, awarded governorship of Mauretania, later governor of Palestine and consul, 103–04

Ravenna, 148, 149

Ras Botria (Acholla), 55

Regulus, 23, 29, 153, 165

Res Gestae, summary of the achievements of Caesar Augustus, 39

River Metaurus, battle of, 28

road system in North Africa, Roman, 51–54, 72

Rome, sack of by Alaric, king of the Goths, A.D. 410, 149; last Emperor deposed in A.D. 476, 153

Romanus, Count, 142, 158

Rusicade (Philippeville), 54

Sabratha, port in Tripolitania, 16, 42, 44, 78, 79; amphitheatre at, 85; 103

St. Augustine, (354 – 430 A.D.) 1, 60, 99, 100, 113, 123, 131, 132, 133; his written works against Donatism, 135; 140, 142, 143; born in Thagaste (Souk Ahras) in Numidia, 145; life as a young man, 145–46; attended school at Madauros, became a teacher of rhetoric and removed to Rome, 146; his conversion, leading to appointment as Bishop of Hippo Regius, A.D. 395, 147; struggle with the Donatists, 148–50; his death, A.D. 430, during the Siege of Hippo, 151; 159, 173

St. Blandina, martyrdom of, A.D. 177, 118

St. Cyprian, bishop of Carthage, 100, 122; his problem concerning church unity, 123; persecuted by Emperor Decius, 124; required the rebaptism of schismatics, 125; suffered martyrdom, A.D. 258, 125–26; 131, 134, 173

St. Felicity, 118–20

St. James, Numidian bishop, martyred at Cirta, A.D. 259, 126

St. Jerome, 122, 146

St. Marian, Numidian bishop, martyred at Cirta, A.D. 259, 126

St. Maximus, abbot of Chrysopolis, 176

St. Melania, 146

St. Monica, mother of St. Augustine, 145, 146

St. Perpetua, early Christian martyr, 118–20, 131

St. Salsa's basilica at Tipasa, 142, 143

St. Saturus, early Christian martyr, 118, 119

Saint Sophia, basilica of at Constantinople, 165

Salakhta (Sullectum), 55

Salammbô by Gustave Flaubert, 24

Salamis, Battle of, 450 B.C., 7
Saldae (Bougie), 55
Sallust – Gaius Sallustius Crispus (86–34 B.C.) Roman historian, author of *Jugurthine War*, 36; appointed first Governor of Africa Nova, 46 B.C., 38, 63
saltus (small estates), 65, 72; establishment of market days, 80
Saltus Beguenses, 68, 69
Saltus Blandianua, 71
Saltus Burunitanus, 67, 99
Saltus Neroianus, 70
Saltus Udensis, 71
Saturninus, priest of Abitina, 133
Satyricon by Petronius
Sbeïtla, see under Sufetula
Scilli martyrs, sentenced to death in Carthage, A.D. 180, 111, 117, 118
Scipio – Publius Cornelius, defeated by Hannibal (at the battle of the Ticinus), 26
Scipio – Cornelius Scipio Africanus, the Elder, 27; his successes in Spain, 28; his attack on Carthage, 28–30; defeated Hannibal at Zama, 30; 35, 38, 50, 99
Scipio Aemilianus Africanus, the Younger, his assault on Carthage, 146 B.C., 32–33
Secret History by Procopius, 168
Secundus of Thigisis, primate of Numidia, 134, 135, 138
Segovia aqueduct, 55
Selinunte (Sicily), 17
Septem (Ceuta), 173, 180
Sergius, nephew of Solomon, appointed by Justinian as duke of Tripolitania and co-*magister militum*, 170, 171; murdered by Guntarith, duke of Numidia, 171
Sétif (Sitifis), 53, 58, 126, 161
Severus, Lucius Septimius (A.D. 146–211), Roman Emperor, 81, 83, 91; appointed consul, A.D. 190, 106; proclaimed Emperor, A.D. 193, 107; reorganised frontier defences in Africa, A.D. 203–04, 108; death in York, A.D. 211, 108; 113, 114; decreed the persecution of Christians, 119; arch of, 139; 159; basilica of at Leptis Magna, 169
Sfax, 68, 104
Sicca Veneria (Le Kef), 23, 39, 70, 131, 171
Sicily, 6; loss of Carthaginian fleet at Himiera, 7; renewed attack on, 409 B.C., 17; yielded to Rome by Carthage, 23, 24; revolt by the Syracusians, 28
Silvanus, sub-deacon under Bishop Paulus, 133; appointed Donatist bishop of Cirta, A.D. 305, 134; 137; sent into exile, 138
Simitthu (Chemtou), marble quarries, 54, 75
Sitifis (Sétif), 53, 58, 126, 161
Sixth Ferrata Legion, 52; rock in-

scription in the Tighanimine gorge, A.D. 145, *53*
slave labour, 65, 66, 74, 75
Solomon, Armenian general – defeated the barbarian king Cutzinas, 167; appointed by Justinian as *magister militum Africae*, 168; his term of office comparatively prosperous, 170; killed at battle of Cillium, 170
Sophonisba, daughter of Hasdrubal, 28, 118
Souk-Ahras, see under Thagaste
Souk El Arba (Wednesday market), 80
Souk El Khémis (Thursday market), 32, 67, 80
Sousse, see under Hadrumetum
Spain, 4, 6, 16; conquest of southern Spain by Hamilcar, 24–25; Carthaginians driven out by Scipio, 28
Spalato (Split), Palace of Diocletian, 126
Stilicho, Flavius, guardian of Honorius; defeated rising under Gildo, 148; murdered A.D. 408, 149
Stotzas, rebel leader, defeated by Germanos at Cellas Vatari, 167; 168, 171
Sufetula (Sbeïtla), 52, 73; the Capitol at, 168; became capital of African Byzantine empire, 177
Sullectum (Salakhta), 55
Syphax, king of the Masaesyli, 28–29
Syracuse (Sicily), Greek city state, 17, 18, 22, 28

Tabarka (Thabraca), 30, 35, 54
Table of Peutinger, *50*, *51*, 52
tablettes Albertini, 155, *156*, 157, 158
Tacapae (Gabès), 44, 51
Tacfarinas, leader of the revolt of the Musulamii, 44–45, 52, 69, 142
Tacitus, Cornelius (*c.* A.D. 55–120), Roman historian, 44, 45, 116
Tanit, Punic goddess, 11, *13*, *19*; became identified with Juno-Caelestis, 113
Tapapius, Annobal Rufus, builder of the old forum in Leptis Magna, 1 B.C., 83
Tartessus (Spain), 4, 6, 16
Tébessa, see under Theveste
Teboursouk, 161, 168
Terence, playwright, 1, 99
Tertullian – Quintus Septimius Florens (*c.* A.D. 155–*c.* 222), 1, 72, 100, 116; converted to Christianity in middle age, 120–22; 123, 124, 126, 131, 135
Thabraca (Tabarka), 30, 35, 54
Thagaste (Souk-Ahras), Numidia, birthplace of St. Augustine, 145, 146
Thala, 161, 163
Thamugadi, see under Timgad
Thapsus, battle of, 46 B.C., 38, 42
Theodora, Empress, wife of Justinian I, 165, 171
Theodoric of the Ostrogoths, 162
Theodosius the Great, Roman Em-

peror (A.D. 378–95), 142, 148
Thelepte (Feriana), 69
Theveste (Tébessa), new headquarters of the Third Augustan Legion, 51, 52, 56, 61, 69, 79, 83, 133, 135, 138, 155, 161, 168, 170
Thibilis (Announa), 104
Thigisis, Secundus of, primate of Numidia, 134, 135, 138
Third Augustan Legion, 42–44; headquarters at Ammaedara, 47, *47*; construction of Tacapae-Ammaedara military road, 51; moved to Lambaesis, 52, 54, 55, 56; construction of *fossatum*, 59; 69, 76, 83, 110; disbanded by Gordian III, A.D. 238, 211; restored A.D. 253, 126; 127
Thrasamund, Vandal king (496–523), 160; succeeded his uncle Huneric, 162
Thuburbo Maius, 39, 104, 114
Thugga (Dougga), 52, 83, 104; deserted in fifth century owing to barbarian invasions, 161
Thubursicu Numidarum (Khémiissa), 83
Thysdrus, see under El Djem
Tiaret, scene of battle between Arabs and Berbers, A.D. 683, 178
Tiberius, Claudius Nero (42 B.C. – A.D. 37), Roman Emperor, 44–45
Tiddis, triumphal arch at, 84, 104
Timgad (Thamugadi), veteran colony, 56; geometric plan of city, *57*; 79, 81; market, 84; library, 84, *87*; public baths, 88, 92; Christian cemetery, *125*; churches built by Donatists, 139; 143, 150; deserted owing to barbarian invasion, 161
tin trade, 6, 7, 16, 20
Tipasa (Algeria), 6, 55, 76; sacked by the Donatists, 140; St. Salsa's basilica, 142, *143*, 161
Trajan Marcus Ulpius Trajanus (A.D. 53–117), Roman Emperor, 52; altar to at Henchir Mettich, 66; 70, 72; succeeded as Emperor, A.D. 98, 99; 103, 104, 108, 110; his policy for the suppression of Christianity, 117, 118; 127
transhumation, 43–44, 47
Tripoli (Oea), 42, 102
Troglita, John, Byzantine general, 171–3
Tyconius, Donatist theologian, 135; excommunicated by Parmenian, 143, 148

Urbicus, Lollius, conqueror of Scotland, builder of the Antonine Wall, 104
Uthina (Oudna), 39, 71
Utica, 5, 6; captured by Agathocles of Syracuse, 17; 29, 32, 33, 55, 79

Valens, joint Roman Emperor, son of Constantine, 148

Valentinian, joint Roman Emperor, son of Constantine, 148, 155

Valerian, Publius Licinus, Roman Emperor (A.D. 253–260) – his persecution of the Christians, 125–26

Vandals, 148; in Spain by A.D. 409, 149; invasion of Africa, A.D. 429, 151; effects of the Vandal conquests on Rome, 153–54; pirate raids and the looting of Rome, A.D. 455, 154–55; growing opposition from the Berbers, 160–63; defeat of Gelimer by Roman forces under Belisarius, 165–66

Villa Magna Variana estate, 70

Verus, Lucius, 100

Vescera (Biskra), 52, 72

Vespasian, Titus Flavius, Roman Emperor (A.D. 70–79), 101, 116

veterans' settlements, 38–39, 56, 59, 65, 72, 83

Victor, bishop of Vita, 161

Victor I, first African Pope, 118

Visigoths, 148; sack Rome, A.D. 410, 149; in Spain by A.D. 416, 151

Volubilis, 40, 47, 58, 79; water supply, 92; Roman withdrawal from, 126

water – distribution and conservation of: aqueducts, 10, 46, 47, 49, *50*, 55, 92; canals, 46, 92; cisterns, 10, 61, 92; fountains, *49*, 91, *92*; irrigation channels, 13, 61, *90*; terracing, 61; waterhouses, 92; wells, 60, 61, 92

Xanthippus of Sparta, 23

Zab, mountains of, 58, 173

Zaghouan, 71, 92

Zama, battle of, 202 B.C., 29–30, 35

Zeugitana (northern Africa Proconsularis), 126

Zliten, 86

Zuila, Byzantine fortress, 173

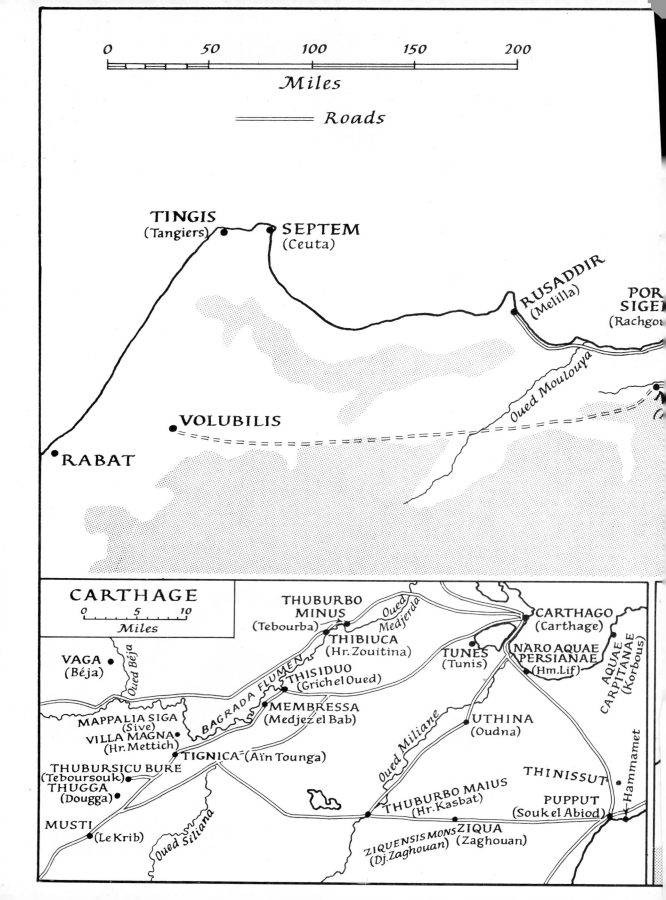

Miles

0   50   100   150   200

═══ Roads

TINGIS
(Tangiers)

SEPTEM
(Ceuta)

RUSADDIR
(Melilla)

**POR
SIGE**
(Rachgou

Oued Moulouya

VOLUBILIS

RABAT

CARTHAGE

0   5   10
Miles

**THUBURBO
MINUS**
(Tebourba)

*Oued
Medjerda*

CARTHAGO
(Carthage)

THIBIUCA
(Hr. Zouitina)

TUNES
(Tunis)

**NARO AQUAE
PERSIANAE**
(Hm. Lif)

**AQUAE
CARPITANAE**
(Korbous)

VAGA
(Béja)

Oued Béja

BAGRADA FLUMEN

THISIDUO
(Grich el Oued)

MAPPALIA SIGA
(Sive)

MEMBRESSA
(Medjez el Bab)

VILLA MAGNA
(Hr. Mettich)

Oued Miliane

UTHINA
(Oudna)

TIGNICA
(Aïn Tounga)

THUBURSICU BURE
(Teboursouk)

THINISSUT

THUGGA
(Dougga)

THUBURBO MAIUS
(Hr. Kasbat)

PUPPUT
(Souk el Abiod)

MUSTI
(Le Krib)

Oued Siliana

ZIQUENSIS MONS
(Dj. Zaghouan)

ZIQUA
(Zaghouan)

Hammamet

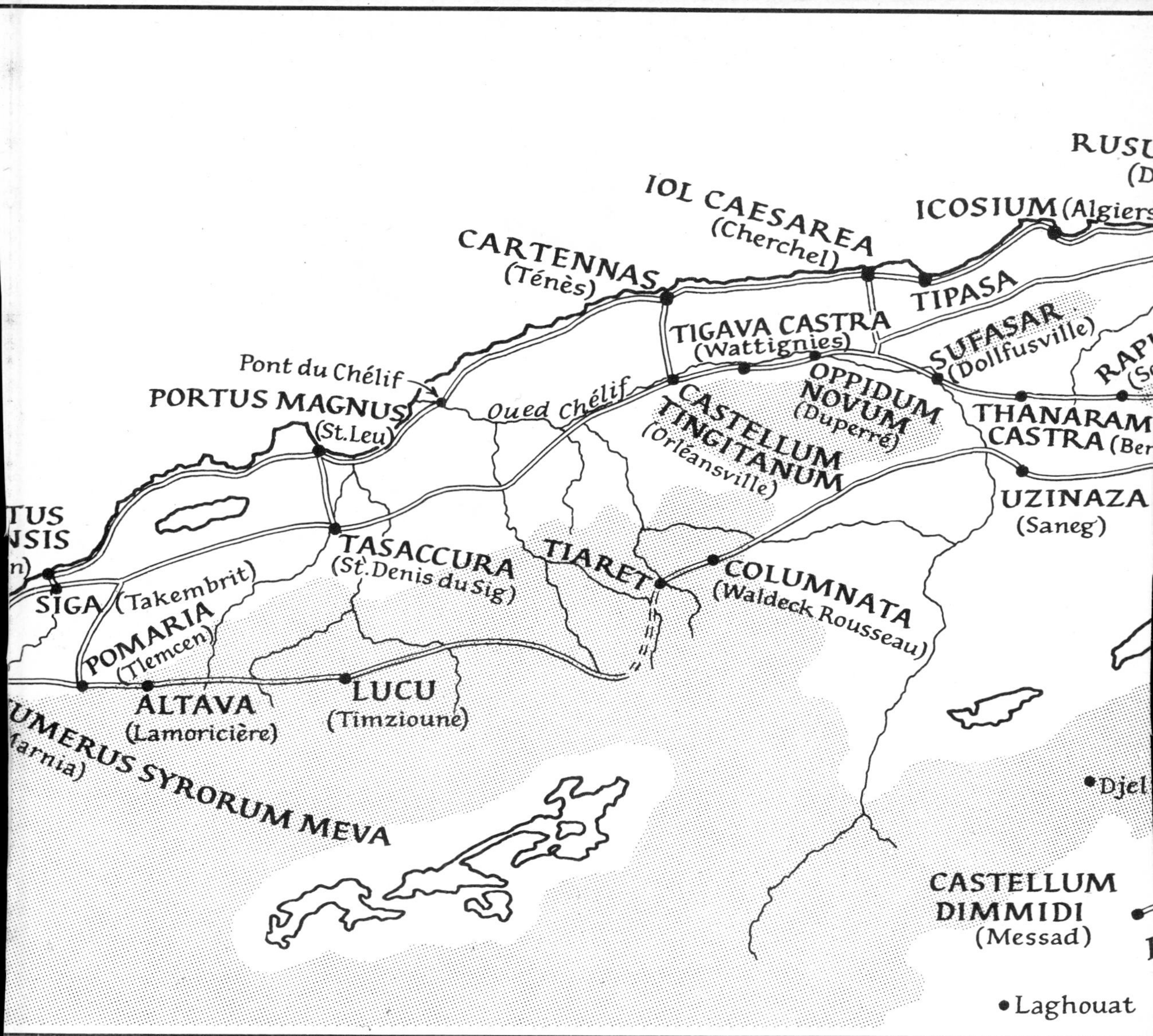

RUSU[...]
(D[...)

IOL CAESAREA
(Cherchel)

ICOSIUM (Algiers)

CARTENNAS
(Ténès)

TIPASA

TIGAVA CASTRA
(Wattignies)

SUFASAR
(Dollfusville)

RAP[...]
(S[...)

Pont du Chélif

OPPIDUM
NOVUM
(Duperré)

PORTUS MAGNUS
(St.Leu)

Oued Chélif

CASTELLUM
TINGITANUM
(Orléansville)

THANARAM[...]
CASTRA (Ber[...)

[...]TUS
[...]NSIS
(n)

UZINAZA
(Saneg)

SIGA (Takembrit)

TASACCURA
(St.Denis du Sig)

TIARET

COLUMNATA
(Waldeck Rousseau)

POMARIA
(Tlemcen)

ALTAVA
(Lamoricière)

LUCU
(Timzioune)

Djel[...]

[...]UMERUS SYRORUM MEVA
(...arnia)

CASTELLUM
DIMMIDI
(Messad)

Laghouat

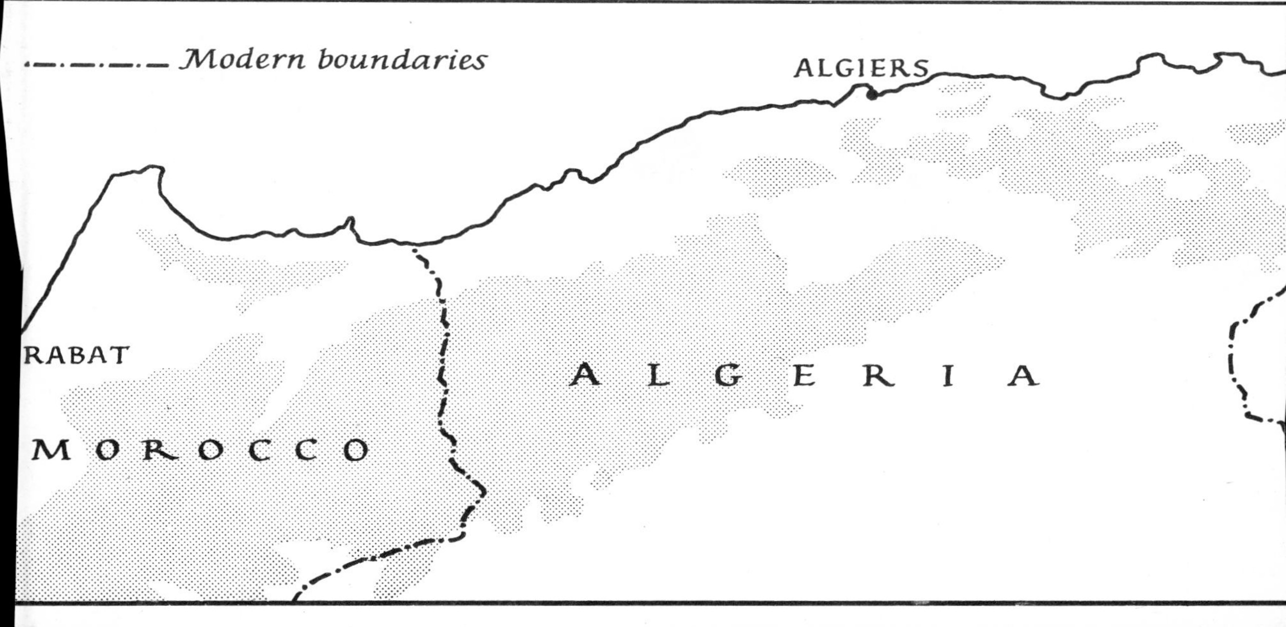

—·—·—·— Modern boundaries

ALGIERS

RABAT

A L G E R I A

M O R O C C O

RUCCURU IOMNIUM
(Tigzirt)

KABYLIE MTS.

CChul

IGILGILI
(Djidjelli)

Cape Bougaroun

CHULLU
(Collo)

RUSICADE
(Philippeville)

THABRACA
(Tabarka)

HIPPO REGIUS
(Bône)

KROUM

SALDAE
(Bougie)

TUBUSUPTU
(Tiklat)

TIDDIS

THIBILIS
(Announa)

CALAMA
(Guelma)

THAGASTE
(Souk-Ahras)

SIMI

MU
(Le Krib)

MILEV
(Mila)

CIRTA
(Constantine)

BAGRADAS

CUICUL
(Djemila)

AUZEA
(Aumale)

SITIFIS
(Sétif)

GENS SUBURBURUM

THUBURSICU
NUMIDARUM
(Khémissa)

MADAUROS
(Mdaourouch)

ZAMA

(Le Kef)

SICCA VENERIA
ALTHIBUROS
(Medeïna)

THA

USA
(ouaghia)

LAMBAESIS
(Lambèse)

HODNA MOUNTAINS

MACRI

TUBUNAE
(Tobna)

BAGAI

MASCULA
(Khenchela)

AMMAEDAR
(Haidra)

GENS MUSULAM10R

THAMUGADI
(Timgad)

THEVESTE
(Tébessa)

GENS
MUSUNIORUM
REGIORUM

C
(Ka

CHOTT EL HODNA

CALCEUS HERCULIS
(El Kantara)

AURASIUS MONS
(AURES)

THE

VESCERA
(Biskra)

Nementcha Mountains

BADIAS (Badis)

AD MEDIAS (Taddert)

GEMELLAE
(El Kasbat)

THABUDEOS
(Thouda)

AD MAIORES
(Besseriani)

Oued Djedi

CHOTT
MELRHIR

Tozeur

CHOTT
DJERID
(Lake Triton)

TUNIS

TUNISIA

TRIPOLI

LIBYA

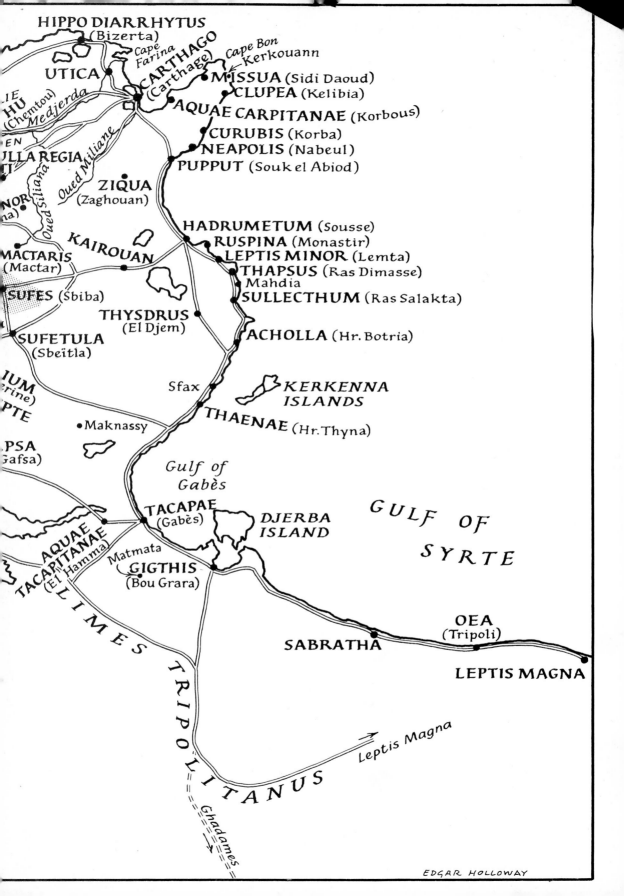